Remaking California

Reclaiming the Public Good

Remaking California

Reclaiming the Public Good

Edited by R. Jeffrey Lustig

Heyday, Berkeley, California

Library of Congress Cataloging-in-Publication Data

Remaking California : reclaiming the public good / edited by R. Jeffrey Lustig.
    p. cm.
   Includes bibliographical references and index.
   ISBN 978-1-59714-134-5 (pbk. : alk. paper)
1. California—Politics and government—1951– 2. Constitutional history—California.
I. Lustig, R. Jeffrey.
   JK8716.R46 2010
   320.9794—dc22   2010004607

Cover Design: The Book Designers
Interior Design/Typesetting: Leigh McLellan Design
Printed on demand by Lightning Source, USA

Published by Heyday
P. O. Box 9145, Berkeley, CA 94709
(510) 549-3564
www.heydaybooks.com

10 9 8 7 6 5 4

Contents

To Eli, Sonya, Ricky, and Andrew,
with apologies for the condition of the state we're leaving you,
and hopes that this book may help you improve it.

Editor's Preface

C ALIFORNIA'S CONSTITUTION guarantees its citizens the right
to "alter or reform" their government when "the public good may
require." This book urges that the public good requires that fundamental revision now. It is time to remake California politics.

The reference to the public good is significant. The U.S. Constitution
makes no mention of the term. But California's constitution commits the
state to the public good in the body of the document, shortly after invoking
"the common good" (Art. II, Sec. 1 and Art. I, Sec. 3). Both of these concepts
are old and rich, dating back to the origins of republicanism itself and the
basic idea of a *res-publica*, or government as a "public thing," itself.

The idea of the public or common good may be forgotten in the rush
and bustle of private affairs in modern society. But the quality of private
life, range of individual opportunities, and possibilities for private happiness are inseparable from and crucially dependent on the condition of
the public world. Californians have been rudely reminded of this in recent
years as their public facilities have deteriorated and their common wealth
has declined.

Keeping this central idea in mind in the welter of California's political
issues will help us remember the ultimate stakes in efforts to remake state
politics. It will remind us that the central task of a republic is not only to
protect private interests but to provide for the *common* good. It affirms that
this includes the provision of *public goods*—the schools, parks, libraries,
health clinics, and public transportation that are the marks of a democratic
society. It clarifies that the goal of reform is not only to repair operations in
Sacramento but also to fulfill the larger *public* good. And it alerts us to the

fact that the goal of this politics, beyond representing short-term interests, is to realize the long-term public *good*.

The chapters of this book analyze different aspects of the Pacific republic's politics and explain why they do not now provide for this good. They also explain why the political institutions established by the constitution of 1879 *cannot* provide for that good, nor even currently fulfill the normal functions of government. The book argues for structural reform of the state's politics and offers concrete proposals for that reform. And the epilogue ("If I Ran the Zoo") provides a compendium of ideas from distinguished California leaders, former officials, and citizens about how they would reform the state's government if they were in charge of a constitutional convention. Their ideas are but a small sample of the many original and creative proposals for improving state politics to be found throughout the state's communities today.

This is a sourcebook, then, of analyses, arguments, and proposals for understanding the state's current troubles and determining how to resolve them. As such it reflects some differences between the authors' views of constitutional reform. The state is in need not only of new ideas but also of intelligent debate about those ideas, and these disagreements help identify the topics for debate. Taken as a whole, this volume is intended as a contribution to the conversation now ensuing about California's political crisis and a way of expanding our ideas about how to resolve it.

Three further brief clarifications may be helpful at the beginning. First, the views presented in this book express the conclusions of their authors alone; they do not represent a group position or platform. Each author in this anthology is responsible only for the ideas in his or her chapter. As the book's editor, I will in my concluding chapter endorse some proposals from the book's various chapters, but that composite program is mine alone and the other authors bear no responsibility for it.

Second, as these ideas were put to paper in early 2010, a number of questions about constitutional reform remained unresolved. Whether a convention would be called soon and what kind of convention it would be, for example, had not been decided. Given the severity of the state's constitutional crisis, however, a new constitutional convention is only a matter of time. The following chapters have been written with that prospect in mind and offer reform proposals for the consideration of that convention. Whatever the short-term developments, we are confident that the central dilemmas of the Golden State will remain constant for some time to come, confounding leaders and testing the patience and ingenuity of citizens. We believe our analyses will also remain helpful in understanding those dilemmas and thinking about their solutions for some time to come.

Third, this volume does not assume that analyzing problems and proposing solutions are the end of the matter. To define a disease and prescribe a remedy is not to apply the remedy nor regain one's health. To achieve any of the goals for California suggested in the following chapters will require citizen mobilization and action, perhaps over a long period of time, as it has in the past. This book is written to encourage that mobilization and clarify its objectives in addition to achieving the goals mentioned above.

I want to thank a number of people whose support and intellectual contributions were necessary for the completion of this volume. In addition to writing chapters for it, John Syer and Ron Schmidt have been staunch members of the California Studies effort since we launched it twenty years ago. Richard Walker and Chuck Wollenberg have also been leaders and long-term participants in the California Studies Association and its conferences. I am indebted to them all for their scholarship, camaraderie, and admonishments, as I am to all those who have participated so eagerly and capably in the California Studies community over the years, including those who helped with an earlier stage of this book. I also thank the Mesa Refuge in Point Reyes for providing the special place for completing one part of this work, and a natural setting wonderfully conducive to that completion. And I thank the College of Social Science and Interdisciplinary Study, California State University Sacramento, for a Summer Research and Scholarly Activity Grant. Others too numerous to mention have helped me come to my understanding of this complex state, and I am deeply appreciative of them all.

For their keen eyes, indefatigable energy, and good cheer I am also much in debt to Lincoln Bergman and, at Heyday, Jeannine Gendar. Their editorial labors, skill, and felicitous use of the electronic blue pencil greatly helped to clarify the ideas in this volume. I thank them and others who read and offered comments on specific chapters: Frank Bardacke, Wes Hussey, Diana Penney, Tomas Summers-Sandoval, and again, John Syer, all of whose contributions were very helpful.

Malcolm Margolin played a special role in the gestation and development of *Remaking California*, as he has with so many books, not simply because he is the skillful chief at Heyday and captain of the University Avenue Irregulars, nor because of his many years of friendship. He also had the acuity to discern the germs of the present project in earlier ideas and an appreciation of the timeliness of the project. For his support and light touch I am grateful, as I am for his usual Giuoco Piano opening.

And the greatest appreciation goes to Nora. Her skill at cultivating, transplanting, and pruning has been a model for my own rougher labors here. These comments cannot convey my gratitude for her patience and support.

"*Let us not imagine ourselves in a fool's paradise, where the golden apples will drop into our mouths; let us not think that after the stormy seas and head gales of all the ages, our ship has at last struck the trade winds of time. The future of our State...looks fair and bright; perhaps the future looked so...to the unremembered men who raised the cities whose ruins lie south of us. Our modern civilization strikes broad and deep and looks high. So did the town which men once built almost unto heaven.*"

—HENRY GEORGE, "WHAT THE
RAILROADS WILL BRING US," 1868

PART I

California's Constitutional Crisis

California at the Edge

R. Jeffrey Lustig

FAILED. STALEMATED. BROKEN. That's how California politics are described today. Many people are calling for a new constitutional convention. But how is California's political system broken? Why is it broken? And who gets hurt by the breakage? These are the questions this book addresses in its explanation of the state's constitutional crisis and the prospects for reform. In this first chapter we take an overview of California politics, the state's distinctive characteristics as a society, and the economic changes that have also begun to transform California's social structure and politics.

Each June now finds California facing massive deficits and plunging its citizens and public programs into insecurity and hardship until its budget passes, months past the deadline. Its schools are deteriorating; its water plans crumbling; its prison, highway, and public health systems in disarray. The state's cities and counties cannot allay these hardships because they are hobbled in their own abilities to deliver on their normal range of services. What's gone wrong? This chapter proposes that three interconnected crises are at the root of the problem: a governance crisis, a crisis in representation, and a crisis in the relationship between the political system and its surrounding social context. These undermine not only California's effectiveness as a political system but also its prospects as a democracy. The call for a new constitutional convention reveals a growing awareness among citizens and leaders that these problems are systemic, not sectoral. They are structural, and not reparable by piecemeal remedies. In conclusion we survey the avenues for reform open to Californians, which will be explained more fully in chapter eleven.

"We are living in nearly twenty-first century California with early twentieth-century ideas, and nineteenth-century institutions."
— SENATE MAJORITY LEADER BARRY KEENE, 1991[1]

CALIFORNIA'S DECLINE has been precipitous. No one expected that in the course of a decade a state known for its attractive lifestyles, natural bounty, and high-tech skills would wind up first in the nation in job loss, adult illiteracy, and budget collapse, with the lowest bond ratings and near-lowest school scores in the nation. Looking back, it is clear, though, that the problems have been mounting for decades and Californians dealing with them sporadically and haphazardly, as is their custom.

The record of their patchwork repairs is a long one. In 1978 California homeowners passed Proposition 13 to cut property taxes and protect home values, and unexpectedly shifted local powers to the state and reduced rural towns' fire and police forces in the process. Voters then passed tough criminal sentencing laws in the 1980s, but they neglected to provide funding for the new prisoners the laws would produce. They toyed with government spending limits, tried to stop undocumented immigrants' use of state services, and imposed term limits in 1990, inadvertently reducing the legislature's power vis-à-vis private lobbyists. Their favorite tool for all this was the initiative—a blunt device limited to quick fixes on isolated parts of the political machinery. But legislators sometimes joined in too, deregulating energy in 1996, for example, and unexpectedly opening the door to the energy crisis and Enron's lootings of 2001. Each of these fixes only added to the state's gridlock and confusion.

Already in the early 1990s some observers saw the limits of this approach and proposed a more comprehensive remedy for the state's political problems. They suggested that even the federal constitutional model that California, like other states, had adopted was open to question. A design which had once seemed so elegant and effective was looking ramshackle on the West Coast, its checks and balances frozen by deadlock, short-circuited by the initiative, and cluttered by gimmicks like the Big Five who hammered out the annual budget behind closed doors. "Revolt Needed in California," declared Republican columnist Dan Walters in 1991; and later "Radical Change, Only Hope." From the conservative *Economist* came an atypical appeal for "radical reform" of California governance. Retiring Senate Majority Leader Barry Keene delivered a critique of state governance in 1992 and called for a new constitutional convention.[2]

Sensing the seriousness of the situation in the midst of a deep recession, the legislature appointed a California Constitution Revision Commission in 1993. And it duly reported back its findings in 1996, but to an empty house. With recovery, the legislature's attention had turned elsewhere. That recovery proved brief, and after the dot-com bubble burst in 2001 and the mortgage meltdown of 2007–08, all in the midst of continuing school and water problems, the sense reemerged that something was deeply wrong not just with separate parts of California government but with the system as a whole. Groups and leaders from Los Angeles to Eureka and Sacramento to San Francisco joined the appeal for structural reform.

Walters called again for an "overhaul of antiquated...governmental structures," and George Skelton of the *Los Angeles Times* added that a "mere tune-up and oil change" would not be enough.[3] Gloria Duffy of the Commonwealth Club advised during the gubernatorial recall of 2003 that people should "recall the system." Stanford Professor Jack Rakove called on fellow citizens to "rethink our entire constitutional system, not through the piecemeal process of the initiative, but systematically." And in summer 2008, Jim Wunderman, president and CEO of the Bay Area Council, reintroduced the idea of a constitutional convention as the place to do that rethinking. Declaring current California government "destructive to our future," he invoked the right and duty of the people to "alter or abolish" it. Lenny Mendonca, chair of the same council, announced that the effort was the beginning of "a revolution...though a peaceful one"—"the start of a people's movement to take back the state."[4]

The presence of a crisis and need for a convention are obvious in the communities of the state. Since its founding, most citizens of the Golden State have enjoyed something like a commons—a range of collective resources Peter Barnes describes as composed of "the gifts we inherit or create together, the set of assets that are shared as members of a community." It includes such resources as "air, water, ecosystems, languages, music, holidays, money, law, parks."[5] Since its founding the state has also been quite wealthy. Its $2 trillion annual product today makes it the eighth largest economy in the world.[6] But over the last two decades millions of its citizens have suffered from the enclosures of that commons and fallen into poverty. Public facilities and health clinics have been shuttered, care for the aged and poor reduced, library hours cut, college costs increased, and the public sphere depleted. The natural and cultural wealth that are the heritage of all have been put under lock and key or made dependent on the payment of high fees. Young people growing up in the state no longer have the sense of possibility and social support. They see fences raised around what Woody Guthrie called your land and my land, and signs warning of serious penalties for trespass. After two decades of cutbacks and economic hardship, what was once a spirit of openness and optimism on the West Coast has been replaced by a culture of suspicion and mistrust—towards students, the jobless, immigrants, and strangers. The shift is captured perfectly in the fact that California spends more now on prisons than on higher education—more on locking up human potential than on cultivating it.

It is indeed time for a new constitutional convention in California. The last one was held in 1879, when the entire state had 865,000 people. That is less than the size of one congressional district today.

But what should such a convention do, and how would it do it? What are the most important reforms it should consider? What *is* a constitutional crisis exactly, and what are California's specific crises? These are questions this book attempts to answer. To get to those answers, it examines how California's different political institutions work today, and how policies are made and carried out in some of the state's key problem areas. It looks not only at formal political operations in Sacramento but also at the way those operations affect the lives of citizens and local communities. That is because a constitutional crisis is primarily a crisis in the lives of the state's citizens. This book, then, does three things. First, it provides a basic primer or text on how California government works. Second, it seeks to identify the main constitutional crises caused by these workings and trace how those crises manifest themselves in the communities of the state. And third, it offers proposals for how these crises may be resolved and California may regain effective and responsive governance.

California's Constitutional Crises

California has many crises today. It has a budget crisis. It has a governing crisis because the legislature cannot solve its most basic problems. It has a leadership crisis because no one has the skill to break its deadlocks, even the Terminator failing in the task. The state has an electoral crisis because only a third of its voters vote, and 65 percent of those voters are white, while whites make up only 43 percent of the population. It has a water crisis, global warming crisis, energy crisis, health-care crisis, and a children's crisis in that a million of the state's youth lack health insurance and almost 20 percent live in poverty.

The list is daunting but the dilemmas are real. For a crisis is a time when regular procedures yield unexpected results, hopes are dashed and all courses of action, even the failure to act, become dangerous options. It is a time when problems multiply even as people rush to deal with them.

Some of the predicaments, however, are more fundamental than others. Three in particular stand out. We will note them briefly here and postpone a fuller discussion of them until we have acquainted ourselves with the broad features and contemporary developments of California life. The first and most obvious of these crises is the state's governing crisis. The legislature's continued inability to pass an annual budget by the constitutional deadline and the adoption of accounting gimmicks and fiscal fantasies to hide mounting deficits are the most glaring faces of this crisis. Each year's delay means insecurity and increased hardships for people dependent on state monies—teachers, nursing homes, contractors, and others. California government can't seem to solve any of the problems that matter. The governor may call special sessions of the state legislature, as he did in 2007 to deal with water and schools, or appoint blue-ribbon commissions, as he did in 2009 to deal with taxation, but the efforts predictably come a cropper. The problems intensify, and legislators sink deeper into mutual recriminations.

Second, California suffers a crisis of representation. As the low voting rate suggests, the state's peoples and communities are not all equally represented or served by its political system. State government is unable, in fact, to serve the needs of the majority of the population. This problem is more significant than is usually acknowledged. The U.S. Constitution guarantees to every state a republican form of government. At the heart of republicanism, historically and as reiterated in the California constitution, has been a commitment to the public good. That commitment is explicit in the etymology of the word, *res-publica*—"the public thing." That is what the term referred to in Rome. Even the Florentine Machiavelli (writing on republics, not in *The Prince*) observed that "the general good is regarded nowhere but in republics, because whatever they do is for the common benefit."[7]

A republic, then, represents not only private interests but also the long-term public good. To exclude some interests from representation is to create a situation in which there can only be a skewed and flawed formulation of that good, if any at all. This is a key failing of California governance today and it jeopardizes the state's status as a genuine republic.

Third, California suffers from an increasing mismatch between its constitution and that constitution's necessary social context. Constitutions do not hold all the keys to their own survival. In addition to the problems that can arise within their mandated institutions, other problems may strike them from the outside world. Different kinds of constitutions, for example, require different social bases or underpinnings. Republicanism could not have found a footing in the feudal era, with its hierarchical relations of lordship and dependence. The Iroquois Federation could not have found a footing in the Aztec empire. A constitutional crisis may therefore emerge when the social foundations of a particular political system change and pull different provisions of its organic law in different directions. This has been happening in recent years in California. And it has been facilitated, paradoxically, by a weakness in the state constitution carried over from the federal model it copied. Both lack adequate checks on what James Madison called "minority faction," as we shall see below.

But to understand all this and the significance of these crises, it is necessary first to know more about the state in which they have developed. We need to remember what's distinctive about California as a state, and to know something about recent changes in the state's political economy which have made the nineteenth-century institutions and twentieth-century ideas Keene noted in the epigraph to this chapter largely obsolete. Let us turn to these topics now.

Exercises in Balkanization

California is an eccentric among the states. It extends over 100 million acres and contains more regions than do most nations of the world. The experts have never agreed, though, on their exact number. The Public Policy Institute of California maps nine regions, poet Gary Snyder says six, and geographer Raymond Dasmann five, three of which lie in what others just call "wilderness." *Sunset* magazine locates seventeen growing zones. There are twelve media markets. And AT&T divides the state into twenty-six area codes, ten of which are in L.A. The novelist Gerald Haslam has located five geo-literary regions, the fifth of which, Fantasy California, may overlap a good deal of the other four (North Coast, Southland, Heartland Valleys, and Wilderness California.) All of these conflicting jurisdictions are split, finally, into fifty-eight counties, the last of whose lines (Imperial's) were drawn in 1907.[8] The state's population in 2008 was thirty-eight million, larger than Canada's.

These regions are economically differentiated, with Silicon Valley and finance capital in the Bay Area, trade, apparel, and entertainment in the south, agriculture in the Central Valley, and towns in the mountainous regions of Northern California still trying to recover from the decline in extractive industries that began in the 1980s. The communities were also ethnically differentiated long before the state's recent influx of peoples. There were Portuguese dairymen in the coastal cities, Slav longshoremen in San Pedro, Armenian farmers in Fresno, Jewish garment workers in L.A., Finnish lumberjacks in the north woods, and the Irish of San Francisco. Add to this profusion of regions and peoples the multiplicity of political associations formed by people in these groups and jurisdictions, the homeowners', neighborhood, and trade associations, the local precinct organizations of the two major parties, and protest groups outside the party system, and you have an extraordinarily balkanized political terrain.

The continuous arrival of immigrants adds a temporal dimension to the balkanization, different groups arriving at different times into different Californias. Immigration has been so strong that the state's population doubled in the mid-twentieth century every twenty years. By 2010 its 1970 population had doubled again, the newcomers arriving with little knowledge of the state they were entering and few political moorings.

Providing order and stability for such a crazy quilt of regions and peoples would be hard for any political system. But making order out of the different segments of West Coast society is hindered further by conflicts that have divided it since the state's founding. Two can be mentioned here which will be discussed further in the chapters that follow: the conflicts over race and over water.

Patterns of racism marked California from the first, some delegates at the 1849 constitutional convention in Monterey announcing that California should be a white man's republic.[9] Indians, blacks, and later, Chinese were denied the rights to vote, testify against whites, or serve on juries. That meant that whites could harass and oppress them with impunity. California did reject slavery and entered the Civil War on the side of the North. But it is often forgotten that California's U.S. senators at the time and many of its leaders favored the South. California refused to ratify the Fifteenth Amendment, which gave blacks the right to vote, until 1962. It is not accidental that California was the state where 110,000 Japanese Americans were interned during World War II without trial or appeal.

The structures by which the state legally sanctioned discrimination have slowly been dismantled over the years. And public expressions of white supremacist doctrine were never as widespread on the Pacific Coast as they were in the American South. But when a *Look* magazine writer announced in 1962 that California was the first place where "the twin ideals of equality and freedom have been successfully realized" and that its "needy minorities of the past are becoming the prosperous majorities of the future," he had gotten a good deal ahead of the story.[10] Two years after his article, in the midst of the civil rights movement, the state's voters revealed by a two-to-one majority on Proposition 14 that they still favored the right to racially discriminate in housing sales and rentals. Restrictions on what jobs minorities could hold, where they could live, what credit they could obtain, what schools they could attend, and what legal protections they could enjoy have been constants throughout the state's history. Most of the state's new suburbs retained racially restrictive covenanting well into the 1960s and 1970s.

Deep racial and ethnic disparities continue in California and can be expected to become more pronounced as high unemployment and the housing crisis continue and the public sector collapses further. California's individualistic culture may have a difficult time acknowledging this. Individualists, as Joan Didion noted in *Where I Was From,* have a hard time thinking of "life as defined or limited or controlled, or in any way affected, by the social and economic structures of the larger world."[11] But though it is invisible to some, California's institutional racism survives. And the patterns of disadvantage and advantage in the state's structures of opportunity can manifest themselves in quite palpable ways, like its pattern of nonvoting.

A second longstanding series of conflicts in California history involves water and water rights. Although some who arrived in the gold rush era, like Henry George, viewed California's vast resources as an enormous commons, most newcomers saw them as a treasure trove of raw materials free for the taking for their private advantage. The forty-niners never acknowledged that their wealth was extracted from the public domain. The men who Josiah Royce said had "left homes and families…and who [had] sought safety from their old vexatious duties in a golden paradise"—and who accordingly "had generally left their responsibilities elsewhere"—mined the land as they saw fit and left their tailings for others. They agreed about water rights among themselves (first come, first served while the appropriator worked the diggings) but ignored the farms and towns downstream that they parched, flooded, and buried by hydraulicking entire hillsides to find gold. They were followed by people who used the state's land and water as elements of raw power. The attitude of the "carelessly brutal American settler or miner" became elements of the state's political culture.[12]

Two-thirds of the newcomers to California would eventually settle in the arid half of the state which receives less than ten inches of rainfall a year. Megalopolises like the ten-million-person county of Los Angeles would not normally exist in a semi-desert terrain. Water therefore has to be imported.

But who gains the resources? Who loses them? And who pays for the water transfers? Water wars like the one triggered by the theft of water from the Owens Valley to fuel Los Angeles's growth in 1905 have erupted since the 1860s. They continue less violently if no less divisively today, as we will see in chapter nine, about the Sacramento–San Joaquin Delta.

During most of the state's history citizens and legislators sought to "tame" nature, with dams, aqueducts, drainage operations, and generators that could run water uphill over the Tehachapis. More recently, many people's attitudes have changed. That is clear from the public's 1982 defeat of plans for a peripheral canal and the state supreme court's 1983 protection of Mono Lake from Los Angeles's water diversions, under the rarely used public trust doctrine.[13] The massive water diversions need energy, and energy costs can no longer be left out of the equation. Many Californians are also coming to see that such unforeseen consequences as ruined riparian habitats, saline intrusion, and global warming cannot be left out either.

Many communities are therefore trying to shift from attempting to control nature to becoming stewards of it. They recognize that the current generation "holds the land in usufruct," as Thomas Jefferson put it, with obligations to the future.[14] This attempt to think about the long-term public good is important not just for ecological reasons. Societies suffering environmental catastrophe do not long remain democracies.

Viewed as a whole, in sum, California presents the picture of a large and dis-integrated society fractured further by a number of long-term conflicts. To complete this brief overview of the context of the state's constitutional crises, it is also necessary to get a sense of the forces that recently transformed the forty-niners' "golden paradise" into a more blighted terrain. Constitutions, we noted, require particular social grounds for their survival. In California those grounds have been shifting.

Trouble in Paradise

Since the 1980s California's political economy has been privatized, polarized, and structurally transformed. Proposition 13 struck the first of many blows that unsettled West Coast life and signaled the end of the prosperity and progress of the Pat Brown/Jesse Unruh era. Proposition 13 cut state revenues by 57 percent, or $7 million, in its first year (1979) and more in the years to follow, starving many state and local programs as well, as we will see in chapters two and three. The plant shutdowns of the 1980s and the broader deindustrialization they represented imposed hardships that communities and the state now had only limited abilities to allay. UC Davis demographers Louis Bouvier and Philip Martin saw a troubling trend developing in California society, the emergence of a two-tier economy—and one that was color-coded. Most whites and Asians were in the upper tier; most blacks and Latinos in the lower. Looking at contemporary poverty, Dan Walters noted that "Even if prosperity returns, California is likely to face increasing socioeconomic stratification...That's the new reality."[15]

Overlapping these developments, the new Republicanism originally shaped by both Nixon and William Knowland took hold and displaced the more broad-gauge orientation of midcentury figures like Governors Earl Warren and Goodwin Knight. Warren and Knight were heirs of the Progressive Era and admitted the need to regulate "predatory interests," make public investments, and at least partially recognize the rights of labor. Warren supported health care for the state in the 1940s. The new outlook rejected all this and embraced the first President Bush's program of privatization, the unfolding implications of which defined state developments for the next thirty years.

The privateers had a three-part program. They claimed that outsourcing government operations would make them more efficient, turning public programs over to the market would produce opportunities for everyone, and deregulating industries would expand people's liberties. The fact that it was the government's subsidies for highways, home loans, and mortgages that made the state's new suburbs possible in the first place—and, indeed, that federal largesse had buoyed the state ever since the building of the transcontinental railroad—did not figure in this formula. California commenced outsourcing not only administrative services, some schooling, and all public housing, but also functions that had previously been considered elements of sovereignty itself—policing, incarceration, and parts of the judicial process, at least for those wealthy enough to rent their judges directly.

Privatization and deregulation became popular in the state, even though it is not at all clear why workingmen with reduced unemployment benefits or single mothers who fell into poverty (which they began to do in record numbers[16]) were freer than they would have been with more benefits and support. Nor was it clear why, say, commercial fishermen who could no longer catch salmon had more liberty than if the state had restrained timber companies from destroying the watersheds and spawning beds. Nor did the deregulated market prove capable of preventing businesses from making their profits by adulterating products, arranging kickbacks, or assaulting citizens' liberties via their pocketbooks, as Enron would do successfully during the energy debacle of 2001.

The recession that hit in 1991 revealed the outlines of the new reality Walters predicted. 1991 was the first year of the huge budget shortfalls and missed budget deadlines that would punctuate the future. Pundits initially explained California's unprecedented $14.3 billion deficit as the product of national recession and cyclical economic conditions. And Governor Pete Wilson resolved the problem quickly with a combination of tax increases on one hand, and cuts to schools, dependent children, in-home care, and welfare on the other. But further deficits and missed deadlines followed, and once Republican opposition to new taxes hardened, the deficits mounted and delays lengthened.

Civil unrest and natural disaster added to the sense of crisis. The Los Angeles riots erupted in spring 1992, reminding people of the Watts riots of 1965 and raising doubts as to whether racial progress had really occurred in the intervening years. Then came the added insults of flood, drought, fire in the Oakland Hills, el Niño, and the eventual Northridge earthquake. Newspaper headlines announced, "Broken Government," "California Failing," "Golden Age Over?" and more petulantly, "Californians Tired of Hearing the Meaning of it All."[17]

Defense shutdowns added to the recession's toll. One hundred and fifty thousand aircraft jobs disappeared by the end of 1991, each loss taking two support occupations with it. By1992, nine hundred thousand jobs were gone from a base of 14.4 million workers, including those in the best-paid, most racially integrated plants, like tire, rubber, and auto assembly in the cities south of Los Angeles.[18]

The national recession ended by late 1991 but California's unexpectedly deepened. Unemployment remained high. Poverty increased. New investment lagged. Los Angeles County's unemployment rate doubled to 11.9 percent in 1993. At 9.8 percent the state's unemployment rate was the highest of any of the large states in the nation. By 1995, 465,000 jobs had hemorrhaged from just manufacturing alone, a quarter of that sector's previous number. For the first time in state history the standard of living for large sectors of the population consistently fell. Average income for the bottom tenth of California households dropped between 1976 and 1994 by 30 percent, compared to a national decline of only 8 percent.[19] The number of people living below the federal poverty line as a proportion of the population increased to 13 percent in 2004, with higher concentrations among Latinos and blacks (20% each), Southeast Asians (24%), and families with single mothers (37%).[20]

More than recession, it soon became clear that California's economy and society were undergoing a massive restructuring. From an economy dominated by manufacturing and assembly plants with a large public sector it was shifting to one led by communications, technology, and trade, with a smaller public sector. This simple idea of a "shift," however, hides the fact that Silicon Valley and its sister high-tech complexes across the state would never deliver the large job base, high wages, upward mobility, and avenues for immigrant inclusion that the mass production industries had provided the state since the 1920s.

This and the particular character of the restructuring became clear with what was called the recovery. A recovery, properly speaking, restores old jobs. But the old companies and their jobs were gone. And the new jobs created in their place after 1995 were low-paying—37 percent of them being in the bottom fifth of the income scale, compared to only 18 percent in the 1980s. (Forty-three percent of the new jobs created between 1999 and 2005 would also be in the bottom fifth.[21]) Nor were they career-long jobs, with health and pension benefits. Two-earner families became the norm to shore up family income. Rates of job turnover became higher, and chances for advancement rare. "The nature of employment in California has been altered in fundamental ways," Edward Yellin of UCSF's Institute for Health Policy Studies concluded in 1998. To columnist Peter Schrag the state's recovered conditions looked "less and less like the post-war California dream and more like the Darwinian world" of developing nations.[22]

In 1997 wages for most people still lagged behind what they had been in 1969—40 percent behind for those at the 10th and 25th percentiles—though those at the 90th percentile did better: their incomes were 60 percent higher. Founded originally with a promise of broad equality, California was becoming one of the most inegalitarian states in the most unequal nation in the industrialized world.[23] Bouvier's and Martin's prediction of a two-tier society was coming true. In the first decade of the new century, poverty in the state remained 13 percent higher than the national average, and still higher for African Americans, Latinos, and Southeast Asians. Large numbers of these new poor were working poor. They had jobs, but the jobs no longer provided for a decent standard of living.[24] With the mortgage crisis, bank crashes, and national recession of 2007–2010, job and income conditions worsened further. That was indeed the new reality, the new social structure. It was not something the state could simply grow itself out of.

Beyond the bare statistics on employment and income, this society was also marked, finally, by a new culture of insecurity. During the mid-twentieth century, state government and business had instituted programs to partly socialize the risks of the unexpected misfortunes which can strike individuals—illness, accident, the loss of work because of a boss's bankruptcy. But as government reduced programs and businesses cut benefits, these efforts were reduced. There was a re-individualization of risk, and with it an increasing prospect that a blow to one component of a family's stability could bring down the others like a house of cards. Studies documented an increased "volatility of family income" stretching up into the ranks of the upper middle class. The new working poor suffered "not so much from a dearth of possessions, as from…chaos," wrote analyst Peter Gosselin.[25] That chaos was the flip side of the heralded flexibility businesses sought in order to enter California into the race to the bottom which they saw forced by the new, global "turbo-capitalism."[26] Though they were contributing members of a wealthy, interdependent society, hundreds of thousands of citizens were put out on their own again. For most Californians this increasing insecurity was the human face of privatization.

Changes like this have political consequences. Democracy is not just a thing of formal structures and rights but also, as John Dewey was fond of emphasizing, of human association, including "the school, industry, religion," and more. It is a matter of social relations.[27] Urban workingmen and rural farmers have understood since the Jacksonian struggles of the 1830s that formal rights are useless without material supports in the world. A formal right to free speech means little if one lacks the material independence to protect his or her dissenting ideas from reprisals. A formal right to property does not count for much if others own all the acreage. A formal right against racial discrimination is hollow if one lacks a job and the economic security to make one's way in the world. Gosselin calls these material preconditions the foundation stones of citizenship. He sees them consisting today of "an education, a job and benefits, health, a house, provision for retirement, and—as [the fate of] New Orleans illustrates—a functioning community."[28] Without enjoying such things, Californians are finding that the rights granted by their written constitution count for little. The effect of the recent changes in the state's political economy has been to dislodge those foundation stones from under many Californians' feet and to destabilize its democracy.

Constitutional Disrepair

The one remaining point to add, to understand the context of California's current politics, is that it attempts to cope with these balkanized conditions, long-term conflicts, and changing economics with an aged political framework modeled on the federal framers' eighteenth-century constitutional design and adopted by California in 1849. That design, while venerated by some, has been criticized by others for many years. But even at its best, it was the product of a particular time, place, and set of problems and cannot be stretched to apply to radically different conditions without damage to its internal coherence and effectiveness.

According to that plan, as every schoolchild knows, the legislature is supposed to pass laws, the executive to implement them, and the courts to blow the whistle when someone steps out of bounds. That's better than the executive setting itself up as judge, jury, and executioner, as in some systems. But California does not work according to plan. Its legislature fails to pass many laws it should. Many initiatives pass that shouldn't. Executive agencies make policies that look like laws, and governors increasingly preempt legislative labors with their vetoes. The courts cannot call the fouls, finally, because the players keep changing the boundary lines. Californians have tried to alter the basic federal model twice but have not succeeded in improving it. With these things in mind, we are in a position to return to the three crises noted above and explain them in more detail.

California's governance crisis. Whatever else it possesses, a state must have governing capacity—the ability to enforce laws, provide security, and respond to immediate social problems. In California the effect of hobbling government with initiative-based constraints, radically reducing commercial and corporate taxes, and deregulating private industries has been to destroy its leaders' governing and authority: their ability to act quickly and authoritatively to solve problems, from schools to water to prisons. They have not even been able to fashion an industrial policy or public works programs after twenty years of deindustrialization and rising poverty for millions of the state's citizens.

And California's budget deadlocks are now recognized to be structural, not cyclical, deficits, hardwired into the mechanisms of state finance in the economic conditions described above. The state's budgets were late in all but four of the last twenty years—an astonishing ninety-three days late in 2008, until collapsing revenues blew the budget's accounting gimmicks and fictitious projections to bits a few months later and turned budget making into a year-round ordeal. Each of these deficits has also been resolved eventually by cuts to the poorest and neediest and to long-term infrastructure, like roads.

California suffers a crisis of basic governing capacity. The criminal courts might call it diminished capacity. Twenty years of privatization have delivered it into a situation reminiscent of feudalism, when central governments were exhausted by ceaseless conflict with private domains built up at their expense.

The federal checks-and-balances system possessed this potential for deadlock from the start, as many constitutional scholars have noted. That potential is fully realized when the system is adopted by a society as large and fragmented as California's.

That some people greet such weakened governance as a boon to their liberties is a sign of deep confusion about democratic governance. To preserve their liberties citizens need political authority strong enough to preserve the material preconditions for those liberties and to defend their rights against private encroachment. "The limiting of government" does not mean "the weakening of it," constitutional historian Charles H. McIlwain explained in the 1940s. Democracy requires government energetic enough to exercise "full political responsibility to the people, and to the *whole* people...." Without that, he predicted on the basis of his study of Western history, "there is sure to be government for private interests...instead of government for the whole people."[29]

The crisis of representation. Republicanism in America since the founding era has meant representation. The great experiment has been to see if the nation could achieve democratic ends by republican means. The second crisis arises from the fact that this experiment in California is failing.

The most obvious sign of that failure is that fewer than half of the state's citizens vote. Representation involves more than the vote, of course. It includes the process by which voting districts are designed, interests are defined, electoral options are shaped, campaigns run, and laws made and implemented. A system could not be called democratic in which some groups, though granted the vote, saw the policies addressed to their needs regularly thwarted because of lack of funds for implementation. Representation is a matter not only of inputs (the vote), but also outputs (effective policies).

Republicanism is also a matter, we saw, of implementing the public interest. Madison acknowledged this in the famous *Federalist Papers*. He defined one of his key terms, "faction," as a group whose policies were "adverse to the right of other citizens, or to the permanent and aggregate interests of the community."[30] The last phrase was clearly a reference to the public good. Yet Madison also explained the main purpose of the new constitution as being to protect people's abilities to acquire "different degrees and kinds of property." And it is hard to see how this protection translates into understanding and implementing "the permanent and aggregate interests of the community."[31]

The problem can be illustrated with reference to California's water conflicts, and natural resources more broadly. The state's multitude of small farmers, agribusiness corporations, power generators, and municipal utilities have short-term interests in appropriating millions of acre-feet of water. Their property interests are clear. But it is not clear in whose short-term property interest it is to halt groundwater overdrafting or to protect Delta water quality if that is necessary for the long-term public good. Aggravating the problem in California is that most people know little about the land on which they reside; having moved so often, they are largely ignorant of place. The periodic droughts and fall fires on the hillsides chronicled since Frank Norris and Robinson Jeffers strike them as betrayals and aggressions rather than as normal features of the land. Californians remain mostly dis-placed persons, as Gary Snyder has observed.[32]

In sum, it is difficult to see how a political system geared to short-term interests is to register or provide for the public good. The Progressives of the early twentieth century tried to remedy this problem. In a clear rejection of the Madisonian interest-based approach, Senator William Kent of Marin County declared, "I would not be a dredger Congressman, or a farm Congressman, or fresh egg Congressman. I would like to be an American Congressman, recognizing the union and the nation." His concern was with the whole people. Convinced that "altruism is a bigger force in the world than selfishness," he practiced what he preached and donated the land for Muir Woods and Mount Tamalpais State Park to the state. He and other Progressives like Hiram Johnson sought to implement their approach by strengthening the state's executive agencies and introducing the initiative as a means of controlling special interests.[33] But these are the very agencies that have been recently weakened by privatization. And the initiative, the second of their major constitutional reforms, has been taken over by the very interests it was meant to control.

American constitutions provide for voting. But voting, again, is only part of the picture. And it is difficult," Tocqueville observed, "to conceive how men who have entirely given up the habit of self-government should succeed in making a proper choice of those by whom they are to be governed." American constitutions, unfortunately, say little about where those habits and a concern for the larger public good—and a sense of the mutual obligations necessary to provide that good—are to be acquired.[34] California's crisis of representation calls for a reexamination of this whole approach and a reconsideration of how those habits of self-government can be extended in the population. It would be no remedy for the state's ills if Californians restored the government's capacity to act but it still failed to act in everyone's interests.

The crisis of social context. The third of California's current crises arises from the fact its politics do not maintain the social conditions necessary for a democratic republic. While neither republics nor democracies require absolute equality, they do need a rough parity of social condition so that some citizens cannot lord it over others, and the others are not forced into an inferior social status.

But modern California, we saw, is becoming a hierarchical society. Between 1993 and 2007, the top 1 percent of taxpayers in the state, less than 150,000 people, nearly doubled their take of the state's total income, from 13.8 percent to 25 percent, while others' shares correspondingly plummeted.[35] This 1 percent made 25.5 times the income of middle-income taxpayers in 1995. Just twelve years later, this had grown to 50.7 times what middle-income taxpayers made.[36] How is it possible, in a republic, that some can count for more than fifty times what others do? Those at the top were also able to grasp most of the fruits of recent productivity increases for themselves. After World War II the productivity gains of recoveries meant increased living standards for everyone, with working people making the largest gains. But by 2007, 58 percent of the productivity gains of the recent recoveries had gone to those in the top 20 percent of California's income distribution. Corporations alone more than tripled their incomes: they grew by 261 percent. Even during the budget collapse of 2008-09, when health clinics closed, schools cut courses, the state reduced benefits to poor families, and many aged lost in-home care, a handful of those corporations was able to secure tax reductions which will eventually take $2 billion to $2.5 billion annually out of state revenues.[37] Observers have talked about California's political system being broken; but it has clearly not been broken for everyone.

This increased inequality has augmented the number of poor in the state. If the state's income distribution had simply stayed the same in 2004 as it was in 1969 throughout the different income levels, the 2004 poverty rate would have been 7 percent instead of the 13.3 percent it was, and 2.25 million Californians would have escaped the hardships of hunger and the loss of homes and health care.[38] The increased inequality deprives millions of California families, to put it differently, of the foundation stones of democratic citizenship. This is part of the state's new reality. For the first time in California history, Peter Schrag notes, even a college education will not open the way to "health care, a reliable pension, a reliable lifetime job...much less decent public services," because those things are no longer offered by the society.[39] It is not a matter of individual willpower, again, but of institutional realities.

Shifts in income and wealth of this magnitude would not be possible without a final kind of privatization, which has not received much discussion in California. This was the unstated objective of the thirty-year program: the privatization of power. In his explanation of "turbo-capitalism," the business writer Edward Luttwak identified this "shift of power from public authorities to both private and institutional economic interests" as the political essence of the current economic period. Luttwak added that it "inevitably... reduces the sphere of democratic control."[40] Whatever the claims of market efficiency, it is the growth of private power that has enabled industries to make their immense profits with methods that include those that inefficiently produce salmonella on the field crops, deposit PCBs in the soil, and leave new housing vulnerable to faulty levees.

This reveals an additional weakness of the federal and state governmental model. It fails to provide means to control what Madison called "minority faction." Madison and the Federalists were mainly concerned with majority faction, but they acknowledged in passing that minorities could also act adversely to the rights of others or to "the permanent and aggregate interests of the community." A recognition of the threat of minorities goes far back in national history, to John Winthrop's lecture to his Puritan brethren before landfall in Massachusetts that "particuler estates canott subsist in the ruine of the publique."[41] But the Federalists spent little attention on this danger, remarking only that relief from minority faction "could be provided by the republican principle"—that is, by voting.[42]

That was an inadequate solution for what would become a serious problem. A minority faction need not be voted into office to exercise its influence, in which case it cannot be voted out. Californians were among the first to discover that point when, beginning in the 1860s, they had to contend with the Central (later Southern) Pacific Railroad, the advance agent of corporate power, monopolist of the state's railroad lines, and equal opportunity corrupter of both parties. (By 1900, writes a noted historian, the state still "had only the shadow of representative government, while the real substance of power resided largely in the Southern Pacific Railroad Company."[43])

Californians tried to remedy the oversight at their 1879 constitutional convention by creating a Railroad Commission to establish public controls over the railroad corporation, the basis for the later Public Utilities Commission (PUC). This effort was quashed by the Southern Pacific. Reformers had no answer for another possible means of exercising private power in the political process already evident in the 1860s: campaign contributions. That these issues remain live ones today is clear from continued battles over such contributions, and the fact that the PUC was the target of privatization efforts in 1996, when the legislature deregulated energy at the behest of California's private utility companies. In the meantime such factions play a major role in the reshaping of social conditions on the West Coast.

Prospects for Recovery

Problems of this magnitude with roots in the basic governmental design indicate it is time in California to undertake fundamental constitutional reform. There are different possible ways to go about this reform as we will see more fully in chapter eleven.

The most comprehensive of them would be to hold a new constitutional assembly, a new representation of "the sovereign will of the people of the State of California," as delegates to the second convention of 1879 put it.[44] Such a convention would permit the different communities of the state to come together, voice their concerns, and through their delegates decide how to remake state government to remedy its current crises. Beyond redesigning the state's institutional framework, such a convocation could also provide a broad public education and find ways to join together what the state now puts asunder by formulating shared purposes and unifying principles.

The current constitution provides that citizens prepare for a convention by electing delegates "from districts as nearly equal in population as may be practicable" (Art. XVIII, Sec. 2). That is the traditional and the democratic way of doing it. Some contemporary reformers have suggested that the state pick delegates instead in the manner we pick jurors, or even appoint them, in order to avoid special-interest influence. This would diminish the role of the state's communities and raise the question whether convention members would actually be delegates in any meaningful sense of the term. We will discuss the benefits and liabilities of these different methods of selection in the last chapter.

A convention is not the only possibility. California Forward and a few other organizations propose that preparing a small number of specific initiative amendments is a preferable approach. This would sacrifice opportunities for public involvement and a coherent redesign of the state's organic law in order to maximize the potential for a few practical changes. Different people will evaluate this trade-off differently, but it is an approach worth remembering in reading the chapters that follow. A constitutional revision commission is a third possibility, though an unlikely one given the disappointing results of the last commission in the 1990s.

The last chapters of this book will recommend reforms that could be considered by a convention, amendment process, or commission. The proposals follow from the book's structural approach to the state's problems. They are presented, that is, as the logical and necessary prerequisites for resolving the state's political crises. The authors' concern has not been to suggest ideas that would necessarily gain the immediate support of the currently stalemated legislators or respond to the most recent opinion poll. Polls are the last word only for candidates who need to trim their sails in the short term to gather votes. And that short-term outlook is one of the main problems of the state's current politics.

Our concern in *Remaking California: Reclaiming the Public Good* is rather for restoring the polity's capacity to provide public goods and for the public good.[45] It is to clarify the kinds of reforms necessary to restore capable and democratic governance to the state. And for that, polling data are not the end of the matter, but the beginning. They identify the position from which constitutional rebuilders have to take their bearings in their efforts. Considering that no reforms, no matter how expertly drawn, can enact themselves, the polls identify the points of view from which popular mobilization and organizing will have to begin, the political views that those who want to remake the system will have to prepare themselves to discuss and debate.

In practical politics, sails sometimes do have to be trimmed and compromises made. But without a set destination, all the trimming and compromising in the world will not take one in a dependable direction. "If you don't know where you're going," as Yogi Berra put the matter, "you may wind up somewhere else." California has relied on various accidental discoveries in the past to set its course—gold, oil, film, defense, the silicon chip. Now it has indeed wound up somewhere else. Maybe it's time to try a different approach. It is to contribute to the debates that are now ensuing about where California wants to go, and to help in the conscious setting of the state's political direction that we offer the analyses and proposals that follow.

Decline and Fall

Dan Walters

CALIFORNIA'S CURRENT CONDITION comes into sharper focus viewed against the more prosperous and constructive era of the 1950s and 1960s. These were the years when the state not only built highways, aqueducts, and universities but also created the professional legislature. In this chapter, Dan Walters, California's premier Capitol correspondent, discusses this era and introduces us to the major figures of the past half-century: Pat Brown, Jesse Unruh, Willie Brown, Pete Wilson, and Arnold Schwarzenegger. He recalls Unruh's poignant reflections on the personal dilemmas posed by a life in California politics, and the political and demographic changes that altered the state's politics by the 1990s and revealed unintended consequences of Unruh's "professional legislature."

Walters explains the major routes of the state's decline from these halcyon years to its current paralysis, including: the shift of major responsibilities from local governments to the state; the self-inflicted wound of term limits; and the governors' and legislators' erratic efforts to remedy the state's ills and restore effective governance. Walters' writings have always had the virtue of presenting the big picture, conveying a sense of the whole beyond the particular events and troubles of the day. That virtue is evident in this panoramic view of recent California politics, which provides the context for the chapters that follow.

> **Dan Walters** has been a columnist for the *Sacramento Bee*, writing five columns a week, since 1981, for a total of roughly seventy-five hundred columns. He is a frequent speaker on California politics and has written *The New California: Facing the Twenty-First Century* and *The Third House: Lobbyists, Money and Power in Sacramento* (with Jay Michael).

ALIFORNIA HAD JUST become the nation's most populous state and had just begun to taste the political upheaval of the civil rights and antiwar movements when it experienced what turned out to be an historic contest for governor in 1966.

Democratic Governor Pat Brown, best known for water development and other big-scale public works, was seeking an unusual third term but was being challenged by Republican Ronald Reagan, a former actor making his first bid for political office, having been recruited by a powerful cadre of Southern California Republican business executives to run after making a much-heralded television pitch for GOP presidential candidate Barry Goldwater in 1964.

Brown, a classic liberal of the era, and Reagan, the champion of an ambitious conservative movement, agreed on almost nothing. They battled over taxes, spending, unrest on state university campuses, and myriad other issues. But they agreed to jointly endorse a ballot measure that would reconstitute the California legislature as a full-time, professional body on the promise that it would better serve the needs of a fast-growing and fast-changing state.

Brown and Reagan joined virtually every other major California political figure in urging approval of Proposition 1A, which was largely the brainchild of the legendary speaker of the State Assembly, Jesse Unruh. There was scarcely a dissenting voice as voters were told that the legislature would become more responsive and efficient, that special-interest influence would be diminished as legislators were paid living salaries and tougher conflict-of-interest rules were imposed, and that longer legislative sessions would reduce last-minute legislative logjams.

"Just about everyone unites behind state constitution revision measure," read one newspaper headline. "One of the key arguments of a salary adjustment is that a well-paid legislator is an independent legislator," a newspaper commentator wrote admiringly of Proposition 1A. He echoed Unruh's contention that professionalization would blunt special-interest influence, saying that lobbyists "have influence in inverse ratio to legislative competence."

There's no reason to believe that any of Proposition 1A's advocates were consciously misleading voters. Nevertheless, as the succeeding four decades proved repeatedly, shifting California to a full-time legislature was no panacea, and in fact may have contributed much to its decline from a widely praised model to something of a civic laughingstock, chronically incapable of balancing the state budget or addressing the myriad issues that have emerged due to California's social and economic evolution.

A decades-long water crisis, the nation's worst traffic congestion, a public education system that scores near the bottom in nationwide achievement tests, a prison system so jammed that federal judges have intervened, embarrassingly low access to medical care by millions of the working poor, as well as an economy that faces an uncertain future, are among the issues that have festered year after year. California is a canary in the civic mine, telling the rest of the nation what can happen when its governmental structure loses relevance to its socioeconomic reality, and when single-purpose decisions made in the political climate of the moment interact with each other to create unintended consequences.

As that observation implies, there's more to the California story than simply political expediency and failure. Shifting the legislature to full-time status, term limits, gerrymandered legislative districts, and other systemic factors may have contributed to the deterioration of the policy-making apparatus, but the other side of the equation is the dramatic cultural, demographic, and economic change in California itself during the last several decades—an evolution that not only generated myriad political issues but changed the civic climate in which those issues were addressed, or perhaps ignored. Which came first, one might ask, the political chicken or the socioeconomic egg? The question is impossible to answer, because both emerged simultaneously, interacting with one another in ways that weakened the policy apparatus and led many Californians to conclude that their state had become ungovernable.

The shift to a full-time legislature was not the only systemic factor affecting the Capitol's performance during the 1960s. The U.S. Supreme Court had also decreed, almost simultaneously, that legislative districts that were unequal in population violated the "one-man, one-vote" principle, thereby compelling California to radically change the makeup of the State Senate. Prior to the decision, the forty senators represented geography, not people—one senator to each county except for some small counties that had to share senators. Thus, for instance, Los Angeles County, with a quarter of the state's population, had just one senator. The redistricting that followed the decision created huge rural senate districts, some of them three hundred miles long, and many more urban districts, thus cracking—but not entirely breaking—the senate's long-dominant bloc of Republicans and rural, conservative Democrats.

Another factor was Unruh, the chief champion of legislative professionalism, who was, in the minds of many Californians, the embodiment of the power-grabbing professional politician. Known to many as "Big Daddy" (Unruh loathed the title), he had come to California from what he described as a "dirt poor" upbringing in rural Texas. As a teenager, Unruh hitchhiked to California to get a job in a defense plant just before World War II, sleeping in a chicken coop at his brother's house in Hawthorne. He later found a Navy recruiter who would overlook his flat feet and spent the war in the remote Aleutian Islands. Returning to California after the war, he used the GI Bill to get a degree in economics from the University of Southern California and became active in student politics. After college, he lost two bids for the State Assembly but finally won a seat in 1954 and quickly made his genius for political machinations evident. His acumen caught the attention of savings and loan tycoon Howard Ahmanson, who shepherded his career, and within a few years he was a Capitol powerhouse, aspiring to the assembly speakership. In 1970 he ran for governor and he later served as state treasurer.

Unruh was also the embodiment of the tension that every professional politician feels between tending to his political career and tending to the public's business, as he explained in a 1960s *Reader's Digest* article in which he was described as "Assemblyman X." The article was supposedly a first-person account of Capitol politics as told to journalist Lester Velie, whose exposé about Artie Samish, the long-dominant Capitol lobbyist, had helped send Samish to prison in the 1950s. And its theme was that although Samish was gone, business in the Capitol was being conducted pretty much the same way, albeit with new players.

"This is my dilemma," Assemblyman X told Velie. "If I had stayed away from the lobbyists I would have been ineffective. If I take their money and give them nothing for it, I am a cheat. If I do their bidding, I would be cheating the public. I find myself rationalizing what I have done. The tragedy is that I may wind up serving the very elements I set out to beat—yet, not even know that I have changed."

If there was a moral dilemma, the young assemblyman, later identified as Unruh, resolved it in favor of taking the lobbyists' money. "In the end," he said, "we found there was only one place where it could be had readily—from the "third house" itself. So stilling our doubts and scruples, we began to play the dangerous game of taking our money from would-be corrupters—to elect men who would fight corruption." Ultimately, Assemblyman X wrote, the strategy was successful in electing enough independent legislators that "we had broken the backbone of control from the outside."

In other words, Unruh didn't so much want to reduce special-interest influence in the Capitol as to replace Samish and other lobbyists as the conduit of power. He would then be collecting money from the interests and parceling it out to favored politicians who would do his bidding, a goal captured by his famous remark that "money is the mother's milk of politics." And professionalization gave Unruh the structure in which he could practice the same "select and elect" politics that Samish had pursued so successfully for so many decades—a system that his protégé, Willie Brown, was to perfect in the 1980s.

With Unruh and later his handpicked successor, Bob Moretti, wielding power in the assembly, the Capitol produced a flow of significant, even transforming, legislation in the decade that followed the 1966 enactment of Proposition 1A, and Republican Reagan was a full participant. Civil rights, welfare reform, abortion liberalization, consumer protection, and environmental measures, including the landmark California Environmental Quality Act, were enacted and the observers and pundits proclaimed professionalization an unqualified success that other states should emulate. In 1971, for instance, the Citizens Conference on State Legislatures declared that California "leads the list in our overall rankings. It comes the closest to having all the characteristics that a legislature should have."

Alan Rosenthal was hired by the Eagleton Institute, based at Rutgers University in New Jersey, as a specialist on state government just as Proposition 1A was being enacted and recalls Unruh as a national figure in the legislative reform movement. Unruh's top aide, Larry Margolis, proselytized professionalism as executive director of the Center for Legislative Improvement, carrying the message to other states, several of which followed suit. "They all went into the tank together," recalled Rosenthal, who is still affiliated with Eagleton and is considered to be the nation's leading authority on state governance. "I was carrying the banner as well." Rosenthal later became something of a skeptic of the theory that professionalism would cure all ills, saying that part-time, semi-amateur legislatures can serve just as well in some circumstances. "It can be done well either way (but) the California legislature was a model legislature. At the time, professionalization of the legislature looked like a good thing, but California may have overdone it."

Rosenthal was not alone in singing California's praises in the late 1960s and early 1970s. One of the others, political scientist (and one-time gubernatorial speechwriter and legislative staffer) William K. Muir, rhapsodized that the legislature had come to resemble a college campus where high-minded experts on public policy, either as legislators or staffers, would debate and eventually agree on policies that would enhance the state. He wrote a book singing its praises entitled *Legislature: California's School for Politics,* in which he described state legislators of the era as high-minded scholars who set aside petty partisanship and other crass motives to study the state's problems and collegially solve them.

"The California Legislature was organized to provide a first-rate political education and to discipline legislators to work hard in exchange for it," Muir wrote. "That is to say, the legislators functioned in a system of internal, institutional incentives designed to make them smarter and better public officials."

"In a nutshell," he added in another chapter, "it was a gathering of political representatives, most of whom were energetic, attentive, and informed individuals, learning from the best of its membership within a fair and versatile system the skill of coalition-building and the competence to govern a free people under law."

The Capitol was never as idyllic as Muir described, even though the period he chose as exemplar, the mid-1970s, was one of the brighter in the legislature's history. By the time his book appeared a few years later, whatever promise the legislature had shown had already been buried in a wave of partisan and factional warfare, and Muir now agrees that the legislature's effectiveness declined sharply after the first decade following Proposition 1A's enactment. "I did like the legislature in that period of time," the now-retired educator said in an interview. "It was a golden period."

What the fawning commentators forgot was that when professionalism was enacted in 1966, it had the effect of liberating a legislature that was mostly composed of citizen-legislators and that had already amassed an enviable record of achievement in the post–World War II era, such as the state's massive water development plan, and was held in fairly high esteem, as were governments generally in those pre–Vietnam War, pre-Watergate years. A cultural symbol of that popular esteem was that in the 1964-65 season, one television network aired a dramatic series entitled *Slattery's People* starring actor Richard Crenna, about a hardworking California legislator.

It would take a decade and, in effect, a generational change for Proposition 1A to begin having the more permanent effect of creating an inward-looking professional political cadre. Reagan and the Democrat-controlled legislature deadlocked over redrawing legislative districts after the 1970 census and the state supreme court intervened, creating new districts for the 1974 elections. The radically new districts and a special retirement benefit for legislators who retired due to redistricting prompted dozens of veteran legislators to retire. Democrats swept into power in statewide offices (Pat

Brown's son, Jerry, won the governorship) and the legislature. It was a huge turnover of legislative membership with dozens of newly minted legislators, many of them political pros right off the legislative staff that Unruh and Moretti had built. They were, in the main, whip-smart, career-minded political technocrats who created a subtle, but very noticeable, change in the Capitol's culture. From politics as the means to policy, the atmosphere evolved into policy as a means to political advancement.

Spending on legislative campaigns soared from a few thousand dollars each, easily raised from local sources, to hundreds of thousands and then millions of dollars, and to obtain the money lawmakers began hitting the third house, lobbyists, for major campaign contributions—and were somewhat surprised that the lobbyists' clients responded. But respond they did, because of the dirty little secret of legislative politics—the financial stakes in legislative decision making far outweigh what the politicians directly or indirectly demand as campaign contributions, on the order of 1,000 to 1 or even more.

The tension between the newcomers and the remaining policy-oriented legislators reached a climax in 1980 when a band of Democratic technocrats led by Assemblyman (now Congressman) Howard Berman tried to oust Assembly Speaker Leo McCarthy, an old-fashioned policy liberal. The contending Democratic factions staged a year-long battle, spending millions of dollars extracted from special-interest groups in the June 1980 primaries, often on personal attacks, each attempting to gain the upper hand on the other. Three decades later, the internecine battle was still being recounted in political circles for its viciousness, but it wound up as a draw that propelled Willie Brown, a character even more colorful than Unruh, into the speakership, which he was to hold for a record fourteen years.

As the Capitol was undergoing a cultural revolution in the late 1970s, so was California and so were its macropolitics. In retrospect, it's astonishing how many political and social events occurred during that brief period that were to profoundly affect the state and its governance in the decades ahead.

It was a time, for instance, of major erosion in the industrial economy that had blossomed in post–World War II California after sprouting during the war. California became the arsenal of the Cold War in which the Pentagon spent 20 percent of its dollars, but also was home to hundreds of civilian industries, including auto assembly plants in Northern and Southern California, aircraft factories, petrochemical complexes, steel mills, tire factories, glass factories, and lumber mills. Millions of Californians and their families—many of them lured to the state from elsewhere—depended on the plants for high-paying blue-collar jobs, but industrial expansion hit a plateau in the 1960s, and by the late 1970s factories were beginning to shut down throughout the state. A decade later, the end of the Cold War battered defense plants, the last industrial sector to survive. At the same time, however, California was seeing the beginning of the high-tech industry, centered in Northern California's Silicon Valley, and as global markets opened, the state's ports became the funnel through which shipments to and from Asia flowed.

The late 1970s also saw a new surge of population growth after a decade or so of relatively slow growth, during which Jerry Brown had proclaimed an "era of limits" and decreed that the state no longer needed to continue the expansion of highways, colleges, and other infrastructure that his father had begun. The new surge of population was driven by a new wave of immigration, primarily from Asia and Latin America, and a new baby boom, especially among young immigrants. It not only added millions to the state's population (six million in the 1980s alone) but dramatically changed what had been, for the most part, a white-bread society—Kansas on the left coast, in the minds of many.

The burden of providing public services for this new and different population, meanwhile, was shifted from local governments and school districts to the state in 1978 when its overwhelmingly white, homeowning, middle-class voters—perhaps fearing the social change they saw taking place—enacted Proposition 13, which imposed strict limits on local property taxes. Suddenly, the state was saddled with billions of dollars in new costs for schools and social services that had previously been borne by property taxpayers. As a result, the relationship between the state and some five thousand units of local government—everything from immense Los Angeles County to the tiniest mosquito abatement district—changed dramatically. Financial decision making was now concentrated in the Capitol, with the governor and legislators having the power—which they did not hesitate to wield—over what had once been purely local matters.

During the 1980s, for instance, Democratic lawmakers used that power to counterbalance a conservative takeover of the five-member Los Angeles County Board of Supervisors, spurred by Governor Jerry Brown's politically inept decision to fill the vacancy in a swing supervisorial district with an unelectable liberal who proved unable to hold the seat in the subsequent election. A decade-long political war pitted the board's dominant conservatives against Assemblywoman (later Congresswoman) Maxine Waters, a Willie Brown confidante who tried to micromanage the county's operations through "control language" in the state budget and other political tools.

The biggest clash between the state and "locals," as they were known, came in the early 1990s when Governor Pete Wilson and legislators forced cities, counties, and special districts to shift billions of dollars in local property taxes to schools, thereby reducing the state's school aid. The requirement festered for years until the locals won voter approval of a constitutional amendment to protect their revenues from state raids—albeit with a loophole that the state exploited during another budget crisis in this decade.

The new relationship, and often rivalry, between locals and the state created a boomlet in the ranks of Sacramento lobbyists as local governments and school districts, along with unions and others with direct stakes in those decisions, muscled up in Sacramento. The California Teachers Association, the League of California Cities, and the California State Association of Counties even occupied their own office buildings near the Capitol and "government" became the biggest employer of professional influence peddlers, fighting over pieces of the state budget and seeking various special provisions for themselves, such as broader authority to use redevelopment laws or bigger shares of the now-frozen pot of property taxes.

The 1978 elections also produced a crop of self-proclaimed "Proposition 13 babies"—conservative Republicans who replaced GOP pragmatists and believed they had been sent to the Capitol to say no to anything that smacked of new taxes. But they enthusiastically prodded Democrats into enacting dozens of new lock-'em-up anticrime laws that pushed prison populations, and their costs, once a minor part of the state budget, sharply higher.

Proposition 13's success also gave rise to a new factor in California's political matrix—the threat of initiatives to enact laws if the legislature balked, as it had done on property tax relief. Within a few years, qualifying and passing ballot measures became a new industry, eventually supplanting, in large measure, the legislature as the state's primary policy tool. Even elected officials began to use ballot measures to pursue their causes and bolster their election prospects.

Finally—but certainly not least—Jerry Brown signed legislation granting collective bargaining rights to public employees, thereby giving previously impotent public worker unions immense new authority and, of course, immense new motivation to become politically influential, especially in the post–Proposition 13 Capitol.

In brief, political power, especially financial power, had been concentrated in a Capitol that had become more overtly political with the elevation of professional careerists into positions of authority, and more internalized at the precise moment when it was assuming more responsibility for statewide policy issues. This conflict would haunt the building for decades to come. It was the situation that Willie Brown inherited along with the assembly speakership in 1980, although it's highly doubtful that he understood how the convergence of political and nonpolitical factors was changing the Capitol. And probably no one else in the building did, although Jerry Brown, who fancied himself something of an intellectual, was given to abstract pronouncements about social currents. Only a few academics and journalists were viewing California and its politics holistically, and they were largely ignored in the Capitol's obsession with careers and other matters of the moment.

The governor who succeeded Brown in 1983, Republican George Deukmejian, was a decent and fair-minded conservative whose career had been based on fighting crime and opposing taxes, but who demonstrated no capacity for understanding the ramifications of the sociopolitical upheavals hitting California and was largely content to launch a major prison-building program during his eight-year governorship. With Brown operating as the self-proclaimed "Ayatollah of the Legislature," legislators, with few exceptions, were no more attuned to or willing to confront the conflicts that Proposition 13, collective bargaining, population growth, economic evolution, and social diversity had created. The 1980s were a lost decade when it came to legislative action—which, among other things, fostered growth of the initiative industry. The newly ascendant California Teachers Association and other education groups, for example, persuaded voters to pass Proposition 98 in 1988, placing what was to become an unsustainable floor under school finance into the state constitution. A statewide election typically had a dozen or more ballot measures, some of which were sweeping in their scope.

Willie Brown loved the spotlight and was given to making lengthy and flowery speeches that had little content, while fostering an anything-goes atmosphere in which campaign checks and "honoraria" flowed to legislators—a syndrome that eventually was to draw the attention of federal investigators and prosecutors and result in the biggest California political scandal of the late twentieth century.

Brown was, if anything, even more flamboyant that Unruh, his mentor. He took the speaker-centered political system that Unruh had created and refined it to a machine-like institution, all aimed at keeping himself in power. It was not uncommon for issues to be kept alive year after year to milk as much campaign money and lobbying fees as possible from their principals. A case in point was the years-long conflict over taxing multinational corporations, largely financed by Japanese corporations, one resolved only when the Japanese finally concluded that they were being played for suckers and demanded that the issue be decided one way or the other.

Brown—like Unruh, a refugee from rural Texas who made his way to San Francisco, into law school and then into city politics, and a natural-born political genius—often demonstrated that he was less interested in the content of a legislative deal than in being part of the deal, whatever its content. The most famous episode of the anything-goes era of the 1980s was the so-called "napkin deal" in which a few lawmakers and lobbyists for personal injury attorneys, insurance companies, medical providers, and corporations—with Brown hopping from table to table—worked out a truce in the years-long war over the rules governing lawsuits and wrote out the provisions on a tablecloth at Frank Fat's restaurant, later transferring them to a more portable napkin that was paraded around the Capitol by proud participants. The deal was quickly hustled into law without any public hearings on its multimillion-dollar provisions. Years later, when running for mayor of San Francisco, Brown shrugged off reminders that the napkin deal had protected cigarette makers from lawsuits.

Unbeknownst to those in the Capitol (except for Deukmejian), the young U.S. attorney in Sacramento, David Levi, and the FBI had taken notice of the building's flagrant trading of influence and had quietly launched a sting investigation in which agents posed as Southern businessmen seeking a special tax break for a shrimp processing plant, then videotaped legislators and legislative staffers as they solicited bribes to enact the legislation. Dubbed "Shrimpgate" by some, the investigation burst into the public arena when the FBI raided offices of legislators and lobbyists one day. Within a few years, a phalanx of legislators, staffers, and lobbyists found themselves convicted and slapped into federal prison. Shrimpgate contributed to the public's souring attitude toward the Capitol and when conservative groups placed a legislative term-limit measure on the ballot in 1990, voters embraced it eagerly on the promise that it would end the Capitol's domination by professional political operatives and restore a legislature of civic-minded nonpoliticians. But this change, like the professional legislature that had been touted as a reform in 1966, didn't turn out as promised.

Political scientists such as William Muir and political pros inside and outside the Capitol often blame term limits for all the institution's ills, but they forget that the decade prior to their imposition was remarkably nonproductive and semi-corrupt. Term limits—six years in the assembly and eight in the senate—certainly changed the culture of the Capitol, driving out Willie Brown and many other long-serving members and opening the doors to more women and nonwhite legislators, weakening legislative leadership, and making the job of lobbying more difficult because of constant turn-over of membership and staff. The term-limit measure, Proposition 140, had another subtle effect—reversing the tendency of legislative leaders to recruit their own staffers as legislative candidates because of their political savvy and presumed loyalty. By limiting legislative tenure and eliminating legislative pensions, Proposition 140 made serving in the legislature a less attractive career option for staffers and their ranks. Those ranks had grown markedly during the Willie Brown era but diminished sharply in the 1990s. A fair conclusion would be that while term limits didn't improve the legisla-ture's performance, they probably didn't diminish it much either. However, the combination of term limits and gerrymandered districts after the 2000 census would have an injurious impact, driving the legislature to its ideologi-cal extremes by rendering the November elections all but meaningless and allowing the most liberal and most conservative groups to dominate primary elections. Effectively, term limits brought back the "select and elect" era in which Artie Samish and other high-powered lobbyists had flourished, with unions and other interest groups wresting power over candidate selection away from a much-weakened legislative leadership.

The economic and social change that broke over California in the 1980s also culminated in 1990 in the worst recession since the Great Depression, a distinction it claimed until an even worse recession struck the state in the first decade of the new century. The defense contract cancellations and military base closures that came with the end of the Cold War created an exodus from California to other states of as many as two million people, mostly Southern California aerospace workers and their families, and huge changes in the communities they had occupied, such as Long Beach and Glendale. It had the corollary effect of changing Los Angeles County, which had been more or less neutral in statewide elections, into a Democratic center and because of the county's size, tilting the state to the left in the presidential and gubernatorial contests that followed.

The half-decade-long recession cut deeply into state sales, income, and corporate tax revenues, creating what came to be a semipermanent budget crisis that was intensified by the Capitol's increasing levels of partisan polar-ization. The centrist Republicans and Democrats of the pre-professional era had given way to Democrats beholden to unions and other liberal groups and Republicans dominated by anti-tax zealots. Fashioning a state budget each year became a war, regardless of who occupied the governor's office. The polarization became even more evident when the legislature did a bipartisan gerrymander of legislative districts after the 2000 census, designating the party ownership of every district, thereby rendering the November elections almost meaningless and, along with term limits, making party primaries dominated by ideological true believers the only elections that counted.

The sociopolitical shock of the 1990s recession was magnified by a coincidental spate of natural and man-made disasters, ranging from drought to flood and earthquakes to riots, that forced Governor Pete Wilson to become a full-time crisis manager and forgo his hopes of becoming a Republican reformer who would make state government more efficient and more responsive to the state's rapidly changing socioeconomic atmosphere. Wilson, a centrist former state legislator, U.S. senator, and mayor of San Diego who had made his mark as an apostle of "managed growth," found that California had no growth to manage during the dark years of his governorship. Eager to win reelection in 1994, Wilson embraced one of the most controversial ballot measures in the state's history, Proposition 187, which sought to deny public services to illegal immigrants. While it passed handily, and Wilson won a landslide reelection after trailing in early polls, it drove a wedge between the GOP and Latinos that would plague the party in subsequent elections.

Meanwhile, the state's voters also were undergoing a major change. There were steadily fewer of them, measured as a percentage of the potential electorate, and they remained a predominantly white and relatively affluent group even as whites dropped to less than half of the state's population, and hundreds of thousands of immigrants, many of them illegal, continued to flow into the state each year. Between 1978 and 2009, the Field Institute's polling found, whites dropped from nearly 70 percent to scarcely 40 percent of the state's overall population, but their voter ranks declined much more slowly, from 83 percent to 65 percent—thus widening the cultural gap and making politics more complicated. At the same time, the two major parties were both losing market share—Democrats more than Republicans—while the ranks of independents were tripling to some 20 percent, enough to be decisive in a close statewide election.

California was fragmenting, becoming a collection of tribelike interest groups more interested in protecting their cultural and economic turf than in formulating common public policies, and the checks and balances that California had adopted from the federal system and then expanded with provisions such as the initiative and two-thirds votes on budgets and taxes made it easy for stakeholders on any issue to block policies they opposed. The institutional barriers to policy making combined with the political polarization of the Capitol to render it almost impotent on major issues, leading to decades of political gridlock in such areas as water and transportation. Although there were occasional efforts to deal with those and other issues, they collided with an emerging tenet of Capitol politics: Unless you have all the stakeholders in agreement, lasting action is impossible. And it had a corollary: If you tweak the policy product sufficiently to satisfy all stakeholders, it's likely to be some kind of unworkable monstrosity.

The latter description could be applicable to many recent state budgets, but the most graphic example is a massive electric power "deregulation" bill that sailed through the legislature unanimously in 1996 after being drafted semi-clandestinely in a process known to Capitol insiders as the "Steve Peace death march," so named for the legislator who ran the process. Peace and a few legislators, along with lobbyists for utilities, power generators, power brokers, and consumer groups, agreed that electric power service would be partially deregulated, superseding a plan being pushed by the state Public Utilities Commission. Supposedly, deregulation would have benefited everyone, but it was based on assumptions about long-term power prices that proved wrong, and it allowed some brokers and generators to game the supposedly free market in power that was being created.

The monstrous nature of the deregulation scheme became apparent four years later, driving huge utilities to the brink—and in one case, over the brink—of bankruptcy as wholesale power prices skyrocketed but retail rates were frozen, the latter a sop to consumer groups in the 1996 deregulation bill. The utility meltdown happened during the early years of Democrat Gray Davis's ill-starred governorship and he, characteristically, was indecisive in dealing with both the threat of blackouts and a concurrent state budget crisis that had been caused by squandering a one-time, multibillion-dollar windfall of state revenues. The twin crises drove Davis's popularity sharply downward and although the one-time top aide to Jerry Brown won reelection very narrowly in 2002, he soon faced an unprecedented recall. In 2003, voters threw Davis out and, in the Reagan tradition, elected an actor, Arnold Schwarzenegger. He was the polar opposite of Davis in terms of articulating and demanding action on pithy issues, but he was scarcely any more successful in dealing with them—and when it came to the budget, even less so.

Schwarzenegger may have brought more personality and civic intention to the governor's office, but he confronted a legislature that had fallen to new lows of productivity, thanks to the ideological polarization and domination by outside interests born of term limits and gerrymandered districts, and the weakening of legislative leadership. Term limits had finally driven

Willie Brown out of the Capitol (he became a two-term mayor San Francisco) but his successors were pale shadows. Brown wielded great power but rarely used it to make significant public policy; his heirs were virtually powerless even when they wanted to make policy. The result was pretty much the same—nothing.

The Capitol's institutional impotence was demonstrated glaringly when Schwarzenegger, basking in the surge of a landslide reelection in 2006, tried to expand health insurance to virtually everyone in the state. California had one of the nation's highest proportions of medically uninsured residents—one of the aftereffects of the state's deindustrialization and economic reconfiguration to a service- and retail-based economy with a semipermanent underclass of low-skill, low-pay workers. Although the governor and the Democratic speaker of the assembly, Fabián Nuñez, pushed a bill through that house, it was almost immediately killed in the senate, due to opposition from anti-tax conservatives and liberals who wanted a more expansive, single-payer system. Schwarzenegger had tweaked the bill repeatedly to eliminate stakeholder opposition but every change—such as eliminating taxes on doctors and substituting a tax on cigarettes—merely created new opponents. By the end of the yearlong effort, critics were likening it, with some justification, to the energy deregulation bill that had become such an embarrassment to the Capitol—too big, too complicated, and too fraught with downside risks and disastrous scenarios.

Schwarzenegger was still licking his wounds on health care when another major recession clobbered the state, this one born of the collapse of the housing industry. The budget began running immense deficits, demonstrating both the rollercoaster nature of the state's postindustrial economy and the even more volatile nature of its tax revenue system. The state had been experiencing boom-and-bust economic cycles about once a decade—the defense boom of the 1980s followed by the recession of the 1990s as the Cold War ended, the high-tech boom of the late 1990s followed by another crash as the century turned, and the housing boom that went bust when its assumptions of ever-rising home values collided head-on with economic reality.

As these economic swings were occurring, the state's revenue system was evolving from one with several legs to utter dependence on personal income taxes, nearly all of which were paid by those in the upper income brackets. In fact, fewer than two hundred thousand high-income taxpayers (in a state of thirty-eight million) generated a quarter of all the state's general revenues. And while the progressive nature of the tax system might please those on the ideological left, it left the state very vulnerable to even mild economic swings because those high-income taxpayers largely derived their taxable incomes from volatile stocks and other capital markets. This trend first became visible in the late 1980s, and there were occasional warnings from journalists and tax experts about the revenue system's increasing volatility, but those warnings were ignored by a Capitol more interested in the issues and conflicts of the moment than long-term trends.

The impacts of revenue volatility were magnified by a series of decrees by voters and legislators that had the effect of fixing many expenditures, most notably Proposition 98, the 1988 ballot measure that specified how much money the state must spend on schools each year. It has meant that school finance, roughly 40 percent of the state budget, occupies center stage in each year's budget wrangles, which more often than not involve deficits of some proportions. As the housing boom collapsed, the state's economy went into a tailspin, and revenues plummeted, the Capitol once again was frozen by its partisan and structural impediments, such as the two-thirds votes on taxes and spending, and turned to bookkeeping gimmicks and various kinds of loans to keep the state afloat—and doomed the state to even worse deficits in future years. Schwarzenegger decried a plainly unworkable budget system from the earliest days of his governorship. He tried, and failed, to enact budget reforms, such as setting aside windfall revenues in reserves for future downturns. And as his governorship wound down, the ever-worsening fiscal crisis sent his popularity, and that of the legislature, to record low levels. By 2009, the legislature's approval rating in statewide polls was in the mid-teens. Sweeping reforms were proposed, and there were efforts to return the legislature to part-time status, undoing Proposition 1A. As Capitol old-timers would say, "What goes around comes around."

PART II

Causes of the Crisis:
How State Government Currently Works

THREE

Proposition 13
Tarnish on the Golden Dream

Lenny Goldberg

PROPOSITION 13 HOLDS a special place in the chronicle of recent California politics. Adopted in 1978, as Walters noted, it added to the Golden State's long list of "firsts," making it the first state in the nation to initiate a tax revolt. In doing so it shifted state politics sharply away from mid-century efforts to expand and support citizens' liberties by providing public services and amenities.

This and the next three chapters make up a primer about how the main institutions of California government work, or fail to work, today. Proposition 13 played a major role in restricting the capacities of California governance and produced many of the problems discussed in this book. Though it was adopted to protect homeowners in a time of high inflation and increasing property taxes, it also produced many unanticipated results, as Lenny Goldberg explains, transforming the relations between the state and local governments, providing a large tax break for businesses, and institutionalizing the anti-tax agenda for the long term. Though Proposition 13 has remained popular and largely immune to revision, there is no doubt that portions need to be reviewed by those who would remake California's politics.

Lenny Goldberg is executive director of the California Tax Reform Association and has been director of Lenny Goldberg and Associates, a public interest advocacy firm, since 1985. He is the author of *Taxation with Representation: A Citizen's Guide to Reforming Proposition 13* (available at www.caltaxreform.org) and an authority on California state finance.

THE PASSAGE OF A huge property tax cut by the voters in 1978 had far more significance than the billions of dollars in property tax relief provided to homeowners and businesses. When voters passed Proposition 13, they knew little about the constitutional constraints on future taxation and spending they were imposing on the state. But this measure which launched the national tax revolt turned out to restrict taxation in California so rigidly that the downward slide of the state's public sector was nearly inevitable.

Proposition 13 contained restrictive features—particularly supermajority vote requirements and constitutional limitations for most taxes—which converted the measure from a limit on property taxes, strictly speaking, into an institutional straitjacket over California's future fiscal policy formation. Combined with other changes, it can be seen thirty years later to have driven California into a permanent budget crisis.

Politically, Proposition 13 may have provided a boost to the tax revolt and the Reagan Revolution of that era, but it provided no ultimate triumph for the anti-tax view. Its institutional impact, however, was profound, virtually ending rational discussion of taxation among California's elected officials and enshrining a rigid anti-tax perspective in the California constitution.

Courtesy of Rex Babin, *The Sacramento Bee*

A Little Tax History

Neither California's business leaders nor its politicians were historically afraid of the issue of taxation. The 1930s had seen the passage of sales taxes, ostensibly to pay for schools but broadened to become part of the state's tax base. While the property tax system had weathered various assessment scandals, with preferences given to large business owners at the behest of the assessors, it had been reformed various times in the interest of fairness. The state's income tax, also established in the 1930s, historically set high rates on the wealthiest taxpayers, particularly during World War II.

In the "golden era" of Governors Earl Warren and Pat Brown, the 1950s and 1960s, business leaders sought massive expansion of infrastructure—freeways, water projects, transit, and other benefits to growth and development—most of which were paid for with taxes, including an effective corporation tax. Governor Ronald Reagan's failed effort in the late 1960s to end withholding of income taxes was considered a failure of the effort to impose conservative ideology on the state's tax policy.

By the end of that era, Governor Reagan had negotiated with a Democratic legislature for a major tax increase, setting the stage for the rapid revenue growth that occurred in the run-up to Proposition 13. Reagan increased the top income tax rate from 7 percent to 11 percent, nearly doubled the corporation tax rate, and provided some property tax relief. Ironically, these changes fed directly into the surpluses accumulated under the administration of Jerry Brown, contributing mightily to the passage of Proposition 13 and perhaps to the election of Reagan as president.

Why did Ronald Reagan, a true fiscal conservative, raise taxes rather than cut spending? The immediate reason was that he inherited a deficit, but the larger answer lies with a critical element in the perennial tax debate: people's implicit assumptions about the appropriate function of government. In California, that function has historically been seen as fostering and responding to economic growth and development. Even during eras with fiscally conservative governors there has been a general consensus that most of California's spending consisted of necessary *investments* in a healthy economy and society. Through the 1970s California was a high-tax, high-spending state on schools—higher education in particular—infrastructure, parks, libraries, and social welfare. A complex, fluid, and rapidly growing society required those investments in order to stay abreast of and encourage the state's rapid population growth, the kind of growth then unique to California.

That growth consensus started to break down in the 1970s, as inflation drove home prices up but real incomes of working Californians remained static. The result for homeowners was a mismatch between incomes and property taxes. Rising nominal incomes also fed an income tax system not indexed for inflation and accordingly pushed taxpayers into higher tax brackets, so they paid more in income taxes despite the fact that their real incomes remained the same. A rising tide of revenue emerged from the system put in place during the Reagan regime.

In retrospect, the passage of Proposition 13 is often presented as having been inevitable, an uprising of voters against excessive government. But in reality one blunder after another led to its passage, as the administration of Governor Jerry Brown mismanaged both the property tax issue and the state's finances. After the legislature and governor failed to provide fixes to these problems, petitions for property tax relief circulated by Howard Jarvis, who had failed in previous attempts to get his measures on the ballot, qualified the ballot measure designated as Proposition 13.

The property tax burden had already begun to shift away from commercial property to homeowners. Between 1974 and 1978, assessments on single-family homes rose by 120 percent, while business property assessments increased by only 26 percent. Property tax rates, cumulatively set by cities, counties, and school districts, were reduced partially to offset inflationary trends but not sufficiently (because assessments were rising) to keep property tax bills from also rising.

In the absence of tax reform and the presence of inflation, the state accumulated a $5 billion surplus. Although early polling did not show Proposition 13 in the lead, the announcement just before the June election of huge assessment increases in Los Angeles County, combined with that growing state surplus, assured the success of the measure, which passed by a large margin. The political failures were in the statehouse, but the real impacts would be felt in the schoolhouse and city hall.

The Response to the Tax Revolt

How would the state respond? With a $5 billion surplus and an immediate tax cut of $5.8 billion, the obvious answer was for the state to bail out local government and schools—the first of the many "bailouts" which became emblematic of the new regime and provided one of the universally agreed-upon hallmarks of Proposition 13: the blurred distinction between local and state finance.

The centralization of virtually all finance in Sacramento was one of the major unintended consequences of Proposition 13. Prior to Proposition 13, the property tax was local, with the state intervening to set uniform standards and to assess utility property. The average rate statewide was about 2.67 percent, set cumulatively by local taxing districts. Proposition 13 lowered it to 1 percent, and rolled back and then limited assessments to no more than 2 percent per year in growth. The rate as well as the assessment change in Proposition 13 meant an immediate loss to local governments of $5.8 billion.

With the rate lowered to 1 percent, the state was required, by the language of Proposition 13, to be the one to decide how to slice the smaller pie. Effectively, local control over the main local tax source—the property tax—was now eliminated, and the legislature would now decide how to allocate the revenues, just as it does with state revenues.

Cities, counties, schools, and other districts thus received a fraction of their previous revenues, and, as assessments were now fixed for all but recently purchased properties, property taxes would be stable but not necessarily sufficient for local governments. By May 1979, the public sector had laid off one hundred thousand employees, seventy-two thousand of them in schools, and many of those jobs were in support services. As a condition of getting aid, public contracts were declared null and void (a provision later thrown out by the courts) and priorities were required for maintaining levels of police and fire protection. Neither of these actions had previously been within the purview of Sacramento.

Some of the impacts were arguably salutary in terms of budget equity. Counties previously had borne much of the cost of child and family welfare programs, but the state now assumed all costs of welfare grants—cash assistance to poor people. Polling showed that voters objected to welfare costs but did not want cuts to most other services. Equalizing treatment of the poor from county to county was a reform that appropriately went to the legislature.

Similarly, solutions to the major school funding equalization case, *Serrano v. Priest,* became more resolvable. In *Serrano,* the state was ordered to revamp school funding because when school districts faced wide disparities in property tax revenue, children faced unequal access to quality schooling. Equalization meant transferring some property tax funds to poorer districts, which arguably fueled the fire of tax revolt for those who resented their taxes going to other school districts. In any case, the centralization of school finance now meant that the disparities in school districts could be more easily resolved, insofar as the state would provide additional local financing in proportion to a district's lack of property taxes. The problem was that equalization meant leveling down instead of up, as school spending began its slide from above the national average to among the lowest of the states.

One issue left festering was the treatment of commercial property. In the summer of 1978, Assembly Speaker Leo McCarthy proposed to split the tax roll and permit housing to stay under the protections of Proposition 13, but not commercial property. In particular, the requirement for reassessment based on "change of ownership" was very difficult to apply to commercial property, since much of that property is owned in complex and diffuse forms, including publicly traded corporations, partnerships, and real estate trusts. The proposal to split the rolls did not pass the legislature; instead, a commission was appointed and wrote a statute on change of ownership which has been a legal mess for the subsequent thirty years. In effect, it was easy for commercial property ownership to be changed without reassessment.

Ideologically, most Democrats of the era, including Governor Brown, accepted the notion that there was a broader revolt against government, extending well beyond their own failure to address a legitimate tax problem. Perhaps more telling, Democratic leadership embraced and endorsed a highly restrictive government spending limit that was placed on the ballot in a special election in 1979, Proposition 4.

Known as the Gann limit (after tax cutter Paul Gann), the measure limited the growth of government spending to inflation plus population growth, by formula. In effect, it meant that as real economic growth brought in revenues above inflation, they could not be spent. However, because the measure originally was benchmarked to the higher pre–Proposition 13 revenue levels, it took a number of years for state spending to catch up with even this very restrictive formula. Other states, particularly Colorado in recent years, have had similar restrictions in place, with the result that the state could not even spend the revenues which came in from growth on improving public services, but instead had to rebate them to taxpayers. In California in 1979, Democrats cleverly felt they could pass a restrictive spending limit that had little impact at the time. Within eight years, however, that limit began to pinch.

In broad terms, California shifted from being a high-tax state to a middle-tax state and has stayed there ever since. As a percentage of income spent on public services, California declined by 20 percent between 1978 and 1987, and by 7.5 percent from 1970–87, even though spending increased during the 1970s. In 1978, California's spending level was fourth in the country as a percentage of income, over three percentage points above the national average; by 1986, it was twenty-fifth, and equal to the national average. Since then, the rankings have varied as other states have gone up and down and as revenues changed, but California's variation from the national average has been very small. In the 2000s, state and local taxes as a percentage of personal income were very slightly above the national average, and in the range of or below other large industrial states. The problem, as former Republican Finance Director Cliff Allenby put it succinctly, is that "Californians want high levels of services for their middle levels of taxes." And, we would add, the higher level of services is required by the many demands of California's complex economy and society.

Muddling Through

The shift in the politics of taxation was profound. Before Proposition 13, local elected officials set tax rates and had to answer to the voters for the levels of taxation they set. Now, local officials had little or no taxing authority—everything pointed to Sacramento. Republican State Senator Marion Bergeson, chair of the Local Government Committee, called it "a real revolution...a fundamental shift in power. The loss of local autonomy is one of the most bitter results of Proposition 13."

These changes have sorted themselves out differently among the different types of jurisdictions. With limited property taxes, cities now charge significantly more and higher fees for a variety of services. Cities also expanded the use of redevelopment in order to capture a greater share of the property tax. Long-term trends include a decline in investment in public works (infrastructure) and cuts in such "amenities" as parks and libraries.

One of the immediate impacts on cities was the complete elimination of the municipal bond market, which had generally been used for public works. Municipal bonds depended on an increase in the property tax rate, which was now constitutionally fixed. In a 1984 ballot measure, the ability to override the 1 percent tax cap by two-thirds vote restored the bond market. At the same time, the state has taken substantially more responsibility for issuing bonds for capital projects, backed by the state's tax revenues—in part because bonds require a two-thirds vote at the local level and a majority for passage at the state level.

Unlike cities, counties have had few sources of fee revenues to fall back on. Counties are generally responsible for a variety of services, such as health, welfare, children's services, jails, and sheriffs, which are not amenable to fees.

As noted, the state took over some of these responsibilities, but major burdens continued to be laid on the counties: by 1990, counties were describing their situation as "a crisis of governance"—no fiscal authority, major burdens and responsibilities, threatened bankruptcies. In the 1990s attempts were cobbled together to maintain some integrity to county finance, including "realigning" revenues with responsibilities, but the burdens of indigent health care, foster care, and other human services continue to be disputed.

Dramatic changes also occurred for the schools, which have become a point of continual contention in every budget fight in California. In the 1960s and early 1970s, school spending was among the highest in the nation, and California saw its schools as a part of the growth engine which drove California. School spending as a percentage of personal income peaked at 5.8 percent in 1973 and then dropped to 3.8 percent after Proposition 13. Prior to Proposition 13, the property tax accounted for 65 percent of school finance. This percentage fell to 24 percent by 1988, so that a formerly local school system now became a statewide system, to rise or fall with state finances. As of 2009, about 70 percent of funding came from the state. As a percentage of personal income, California has generally been in the bottom group of states for school funding. The leveling up that was hoped for in response to the *Serrano* decision became generally flat funding for most schools throughout the state.

At the state level, the limitations of the tax revolt—Proposition 13 and the spending limit—began to be felt in the 1980s, though the full force of it would hit later. In particular, when Republican Governor George Deukmejian felt the pressure to maintain education funding, he sought a sales tax increase in 1984 to increase funding for schools. Faced with the need to get a two-thirds vote, he was able to negotiate an agreement for that vote in the legislature, including Republican legislators.

The Politics of the Spending Limit

The restrictive spending limit imposed by Proposition 4 began now, however, to pinch. In 1986, federal tax reform increased the tax rate on capital gains, so investors cashed out billions in capital gains in advance of the rate increase. California, which had no special rate for capital gains, received a substantial revenue windfall in the 1986–87 fiscal year. This pushed the state over the spending limit for the first time. The governor and legislature returned the revenue which exceeded the limit to taxpayers, who received an income tax rebate totaling about $1 billion. However, in the following year, the state fell into a $1 billion deficit, which necessitated cuts because the surplus of the previous year was gone. Clearly, the spending limit had worked in an unexpected way: forcing a tax rebate as the result of an unusual circumstance rather than letting high revenues smooth the revenue cycle.

In addition to this revenue anomaly, the spending limit began to be seen as irrational. It particularly came to the notice of transportation advocates, those most concerned with adjusting to continual growth. They sought to increase gas taxes, but any increase pushed the state up against the limit. They also sought to redefine gas taxes as "fees" outside the limit, but the legislature sought a more comprehensive solution, not just for transportation but for all spending issues. An initiative effort to change the limit was made in 1988 but failed by a small margin, in large part because of business opposition.

The result was an instructive effort, one of the rare ones in the post–Proposition 13 era in which a consensus came together around changing one of the weapons of the tax revolt. The business-oriented California Taxpayers' Association identified the spending limit as a limit on growth, because revenues from growth could not be spent on infrastructure, amenities, or improvements, particularly transportation. With their involvement and that of the California Chamber of Commerce, and in negotiations with the labor-oriented California Tax Reform Association, which represented many public employee groups, the spending limit was revamped to reflect growth. Reforms were also enacted to allow for a gas tax increase for transportation, to allow the limit to work on a two-year cycle, and for local and state infrastructure spending to not be subject to the spending limits, among other changes. That measure passed in 1990 as Proposition 111, with voters narrowly convinced to vote for a gas tax increase and sweeping changes in the spending limit. While discussions of reintroducing tight spending limits continue to the present, one precedent was established: necessity was the mother of consensus for all groups concerned about the future of the public sector. And the critical relationship between growth and spending—between growth and investment in California—was reaffirmed as it had been in previous eras. One of the major questions in present-day discussions is whether such a consensus can be built again.

Part of the impetus for that consensus was Proposition 98 in 1988, put on the ballot by education groups led by the California Teachers Association, which set minimum standards for educational finance in the state's constitution, and also required that all revenues over the spending limit be dedicated to education. It was written with the expectation that the spending limit would be changed in the 1988 June primary, but when that attempt failed and Proposition 98 passed anyway in the general election, the voters' desire for improved education spending effectively blew a hole in the state spending limit. Proposition 98, modified by Proposition 111, is intended to set a floor for education, although some have argued that it sets a ceiling. In any case, virtually the entire framework for discussion of education spending has been set by this ballot measure.

By themselves, Propositions 98 and 111 were important reforms which may have ameliorated, though not resolved, the problem of the state's deteriorating fiscal condition. But their passage also represented another pattern which had been set by Proposition 13: the requirement that virtually all major changes take place by initiative. Many have argued, as Peter Schrag has in *Paradise Lost: California's Experience, America's Future,* that the use of the initiative process has been the defining feature of the last thirty years in California, particularly with regard to fiscal policy.

The Institutional Straitjacket

For local taxation, the requirement to take measures to the voters and the subsequent vitiation of the power of elected representation is a significant part of the regime imposed by Proposition 13. Not only has local control over many aspects of government finance disappeared, as noted earlier, but even if local elected officials have the desire to enact new taxes, ballot measures are required, most of which require a two-thirds vote of the electorate. So the role of the local governing body, whether city council, school board, or county supervisors, has been reduced to recommending taxes for the ballot, rather than making decisions themselves for which they will be responsible.

As a result of court decisions which interpreted the originally unclear language of Proposition 13, any local tax dedicated to a specific purpose ("special tax") requires a two-thirds vote of the people. Any tax for general government purposes, or unspecified purposes, requires a majority vote of the people. Since virtually all new local taxes have been for what courts have ruled are specific purposes—e.g., schools, transportation, law enforcement— a two-thirds vote of the people has predominated.

As a matter of democratic decision making as well as practical implementation, this system is highly problematic. It means that every "no" vote on a tax is worth twice a "yes" vote in terms of getting final approval. Yet taxation is one of the most difficult decisions made by government. To vote for taxes people have to feel they are getting something for their money, and

Courtesy of Rex Babin, *The Sacramento Bee*

they have to be willing to depart with their money in exchange for assurance that it will be handled appropriately. So to require that this difficult decision attract two "yes" votes to counteract every "no" vote is likely to force a fiscal straitjacket on local government.

Practically, the two-thirds vote requirement has meant that any organized objection to a tax or to a program is highly likely to prevail. For even the most favorable ballot measures on taxation—say, a local hotel tax which only taxes outsiders and is put to a favored purpose—the maximum likely vote is 80 percent; 20 percent of voters are likely to object to any tax. As a result, organized opposition to any tax has to convince just 13 percent of the remainder of the electorate that the tax is bad or the program (schools, parks, law enforcement) will waste or improperly use taxpayers' money. Virtually any tax proposal which has organized opposition will fail to receive the two-thirds vote. When the two-thirds vote has been reached, there was either no organized opposition, or, particularly for transportation, the measure only continued a tax already in place which had originally been passed by a majority. Over the years hundreds of local tax proposals have been defeated, not because they received less than a majority, but because they received less than a supermajority.

The legislature, of course, faces a supermajority requirement for both new taxes and the budget, which ties up the budget process year after year. Only two other states require a two-thirds vote for a budget, and only a handful more require two-thirds for taxes. Bond rating agencies cite the gridlock caused by these requirements as the reason they consistently rate California among the lowest in the nation for the reliability of its bonds. It is an irony that one of the wealthiest places in the world cannot be trusted by investors to pay off its obligations, not because there is insufficient wealth to pay for infrastructure, nor because the state has ever defaulted on its obligations, but because straitjacketed government cannot make the decisions to place their creditors at a sufficient comfort level to receive a reasonable bond rating.

Prior to the fiscal crisis of 2009, the state's last major tax increase to be enacted by the legislature rather than the initiative occurred in 1991, an instructive example compared to the current era. New Republican Governor Pete Wilson faced an enormous budget deficit, in part because of the recession hitting California at the time and also because previous deficits had been glossed over in order to avoid the hostility that new taxes would engender. Governor Wilson decided the $14 billion deficit could not be resolved without a program combining $7 billion in new revenues and $7 billion in spending cuts. And he put through a program of mostly sales taxes, though it also closed a few tax loopholes for the wealthy, and added temporary top brackets on the wealthiest taxpayers when an initiative began to circulate to increase those taxes permanently.

Until the fiscal disaster of 2008-09, that was the last time any taxes were raised, for a number of reasons. First, the term limits imposed by the voters hit home in 1996, with the result that legislators had to run for office continually and had no time to build up enough credibility with their constituents to be able to support anything as unpopular as new taxes. Second, the nature of the Republican Party changed after the national election of 1994. The single common denominator of the Gingrich revolution and the national Republicans was opposition to taxes. Anti-tax organizations such as Americans for Tax Reform and the Club for Growth excoriated and ran candidates against any Republicans who voted for or suggested new taxes. While that may not matter in states with ordinary majority vote requirements, it became extremely significant in California, where the defining badge in a Republican primary became opposition to taxes.

In the era of term limits, politicians had to run in subsequent primaries for other offices, and those who had approved of any new taxes lost their elections in California. Elections were run in districts that had for the most part been drawn (i.e., gerrymandered) to be safe for one party or another, so that in Republican districts the most conservative anti-tax elements defined the agenda.

Under most governing regimes, decisions are reached when a majority party negotiates with an executive which holds veto power. In California, the combination of the two-thirds vote requirement, term limits, and safe partisan seats where anti-tax ideology holds sway in a primary has made it virtually impossible to develop consensus proposals on taxation.

The system is a one-way street, a "roach motel" where tax breaks that crawl in never can be gotten out. Tax cuts which can be enacted by majority vote (for example, for tax breaks or new loopholes) can only be reversed by a two-thirds vote. So even useless loopholes or glaring holes in the tax system such as California's failure to tax oil production are off the table. Thus, after Governor Wilson negotiated the tax increase in 1991 and the new top brackets expired in 1996 and in 1997, with revenues coming in from economic growth, a significant new round of irreversible tax cuts took place: a cut in the corporation tax rate and an increase in the credit for children.

As revenues continued to roll in during the dot-com bubble of the late 1990s, the legislature in response to continued anti-tax agitation cut the vehicle license fee (the "car tax"). To avoid the roach motel effect described above, the proposal included a trigger which would allow the cut to be rescinded if revenue fell short. When the bubble burst and the state's finances went from surplus to deficit, Governor Gray Davis revoked the tax cut. Though this was authorized by law, it helped provoke the recall which brought Republican Governor Arnold Schwarzenegger to power. Schwarzenegger's first act in office was to restore the cut in the vehicle license fee, at a cost which began at $4 billion in revenue and in a few years increased to an ongoing $6 billion annually.

If tax cuts are irreversible, as they appear to be in this system, the only direction for the fiscal health and integrity of the state is downward. A broad-based effort of unions and public interest groups, including the League of Women Voters, placed Proposition 56 on the ballot in 2004 to allow taxes related to the budget to pass by majority rather than supermajority. However, the governor and legislature confused the issue by putting their Proposition 57 on the ballot, permitting the state to sell "deficit reduction bonds" and borrow up to $15 billion to resolve the looming deficit. Such borrowing to pay for current expenditures was unprecedented, but the alternative—raising revenues back to the level that existed before two rounds of tax cutting— was unachievable. Voters were faced with one measure that, in the words of opponents, made it "easier to raise taxes," and one that mandated massive borrowing, and they naturally chose the approach that looked like the easier way out. The governor's and the legislature's hope was that the state would grow its way out of debt and pay off the bonds without the pain of raising taxes. Proposition 56 went down to substantial defeat while the deficit reduction bonds passed, and the state went deeper into debt.

By 2008, the costs of paying off the bonds, the $12 billion costs of the permanent tax cuts, and the slowdown caused by the collapse of the housing market had led to yet another round in the intractable budget problems facing the state. Despite his pledges, Schwarzenegger was not inalterably opposed to new taxes. But he proposed yet more borrowing against the future, in this case the selling off of the state's lottery in order to bring one-time revenues to the state. California borrowed the last of its deficit reduction bonds and still faced the potential of massive across-the-board cuts. And the bond ratings of California plummeted to the worst in the nation—an indicator, again, not of the wealth of the society, but of the gridlock of its tax system.

The events of 2008 and 2009 included disaster and abundant irony: increased temporary taxes on ordinary taxpayers in exchange for $2 billion in permanent loopholes for large corporations; cutting programs even though it meant losing federal stimulus money; and voters rejecting all 2009 ballot measures, in part because of newfound trust in legislators, though it was their previous mistrust of those legislators that led them to pass the initiatives that caused the current crisis in the first place.

It is the continuing saga of this disaster that has led to general agreement that there is a crisis of constitutional proportions in California, calling for either reforms or thorough revamping.

The two-thirds requirement for budget passage creates opportunities for the legislative minority to demand major concessions for their vote (called, appropriately, "hostage taking"). Making an attempt at compromise in the September 2008 budget agreement, the Democratic majority proposed no revenue increases. But in exchange for mere revenue accelerations, the minority demanded two permanent (though delayed) corporate loopholes. Simple tax-collection measures were also eliminated from the July 2009 budget because of a small group of ideologues in one house. The two-thirds budget rule makes it possible for special-interest provisions to take precedence over the general welfare.

In February 2009, the prospect of massive fiscal disaster meant taxes would be temporarily raised, but negotiations also produced a package of regressive taxes coupled with a new loophole. This was the "elective single sales apportionment," which permits multistate or multinational companies to be taxed solely on their sales (not property and payroll) in California and to themselves choose the formula by which they can allocate less income or more losses every year. So in exchange for two years of increased taxes on ordinary taxpayers—including a cut in the child dependent credit, a vehicle fee increase, and a sales tax increase—the 2008 and 2009 budget gave the corporations a combined cut of about 25 percent. All of this was enacted without any public hearings. And, in exchange for his vote for the taxes, one state senator got a constitutional amendment put on the ballot to favor his own chances in future elections.[1]

The voters' defeat of budget reform initiatives in May 2009 was said by some to be another vote against taxes, but there were many reasons to reject these poorly drawn measures. The full destructive potential of the two-thirds requirement became clear in July 2009 as the state lost federal dollars and had to issue IOU's, and even tax-collection improvements were knocked out of the budget agreement.

It is at this point that the calls for new solutions arise. Short of a constitutional convention, proposals are also under consideration to adopt a majority vote on the budget, lower supermajority requirements for new taxes, reduce vote requirements for local taxes including those for schools, adopt two-year budgets, and more.

The Property Tax

It was the property tax, of course, which set in motion the events which led to this fiscal tailspin. Beyond the deeper governance issues which threaten the ability of the state to resolve its normal problems, what has happened to the property tax itself?

For homeowners, the results of Proposition 13 have proven popular, even as substantial doubts are expressed by younger people and new homeowners. The system provides tight limits on rates and a strict limit on assessment growth, no matter how home prices change. Assessments are brought up to market value when property is sold and then limited in growth to 2 percent per year.

Such limitations on rates and assessments are not without precedent around the country, though California's are much tighter than most. Homeowners everywhere have demanded stability in their property taxes, particularly in states like California where housing values tend to explode at times. Housing values can be stable for fairly long periods, but when they increase rapidly—as in the mid-1970s, late 1980s, late 1990s, and mid-2000s—homeowners are very vocal about increased property tax bills. Thus, even if Proposition 13 had not passed, some form of property tax stabilization for homeowners would have likely been enacted.

That said, the disparities in assessed value, and therefore property taxes, can be vast. Homes that sold for twenty to thirty thousand dollars in the 1970s may sell for five hundred thousand or more now, and a new owner can easily pay ten times the amount of property tax that older homeowners pay for an identical house on the same street. But there is no rebellion from the new homeowner, because over time, someone who bought at a high price in, say, 1990 will have substantial savings compared to a neighbor who bought in 2005; in a relatively short time the new homebuyer becomes the older one. Hence the political popularity of a predictable property tax payment, and the absorption of those who might at one time complain. Because of turnover and subsequent reassessment at the new value, property tax revenues, after falling precipitously, have recovered at a reasonable pace.

Still, the public services that owners of side-by-side homes receive are identical, and their taxes are not. That disparity led to a lawsuit brought by a homeowner in the 1990s, *Nordlinger vs. County of Los Angeles*, which was decided by the U.S. Supreme Court. The test in tax law, at least in this case, was whether there was a "rational basis" for unequal results. The Court decided that there was; despite the disparities the law would stand. To rule otherwise would have opened up to question the property tax systems of many other states which protect homeowners in one way or another.

On the commercial property side, however, there is no "rational basis" for the system. The assessment of commercial property is the most glaring deficiency in California's property tax system.[2] The rationale for protecting homeowners—incomes may not be related to rising assessments—does not hold for investment property, since its value is directly related to the amount of income which can be made from its utilization.

As a matter of law, the concept of "change of ownership" makes little sense in this context. The stock of publicly traded corporations changes hands daily, but the property may never be reassessed because it stays with the same company, despite different shareholders. Shopping centers, hotels, and office buildings are held by a wide variety of ownership forms—partnerships, Subchapter S corporations, limited liability corporations, real estate investment trusts—none of which change hands according to the usual homeowner model. As a result, corporations may avoid assessment on the market value of their property in a number of ways, even when 100 percent of the property changes hands. An important result of this system is that the burden of taxation has been steadily shifting away from corporations and toward homeowners, particularly in large counties such as Los Angeles, San Francisco, and Santa Clara.

The failure to assess commercial property stands good economics on its head. The best approach, according to economic theory, is to limit taxation of new investment but to tax windfalls, known also as economic rents. In California's case, all of the windfalls which accrue to commercial property owners, whether from new investment by others or from added infrastructure, are untaxed. Meanwhile, the investor who buys land and builds is taxed at full market value, usually with many fees and exactions by the local land-use authority, to pay for costs which should be shared with those who received the windfalls.

The failure to tax commercial property properly is anticompetitive. Companies which compete against each other have wildly different property taxes, not because of their location or value, but because of their ability to avoid reassessment. IBM in Silicon Valley in 2004 was taxed four-tenths of a cent per square foot of land while competitor companies were paying hundreds of times more. Interestingly, the major differences in assessments are on land, not buildings, because buildings are reassessed when they are improved. Business property, such as manufacturing equipment, is also taxed at market value: another tax on new investment instead of on the unearned and vastly undertaxed windfall on the land, a public good.

As a matter of fiscal policy, the system fails badly, particularly with regard to California's pressing need for capital investments in infrastructure. Investments in infrastructure are effectively investments in land values—e.g., a new freeway interchange will raise the value of undeveloped land—but none of that windfall comes back to the investor, that is, the public sector. There should be what economists call a virtuous circle: improving land values and then getting revenue back to invest some more. But that circle is broken in the once Golden State. Similarly, local governments do not get sufficient revenues to approve new nonretail development, so localities become antigrowth and exact many costs for new development, the opposite of the growth nexus which has been so important to California business in the past.

Finally, the system results in bad land-use policy. Without rising commercial property tax revenues, localities have strong incentives to seek sales-tax-generating retail outlets. Monrovia, offered the possibility of having an Eastman Kodak research facility or a Costco, chose the Costco because of all the revenue it generated, not the economic development and job opportunities a high-tech research facility might have provided. A retail warehouse sur-rounded by a parking lot may be a good fiscal choice, but it is bad land use. Similarly, many infill properties are underutilized because their owners have no tax costs and can hold them off the market forever. The system promotes sprawl and land speculation to the detriment of urban development.

Which Way, Reform?

Reforming Proposition 13 is a daunting prospect. The most obvious and rational reform simply involves reassessing nonresidential property at mar-ket value, which, in 2008, would have raised six to eight billion dollars for cities, counties, and schools. Not only would it have relieved major financial burdens of local government, but it would have improved infrastructure, land use, and likely local permitting and siting processes, which have been a barrier to new development. Rational though it may be, no one has yet taken such a proposal to the ballot, because it would face many millions of dollars in opposition from current property holders who avoid billions in taxes with the present dysfunctional system.

For homeowners, the likelihood of change is more remote, in part because equitable change will mean that a substantial number of homeowners with very low assessments will have to pay more. There have been many proposals for reform. A simple one is to increase maximum assessment growth from 2 percent to 4 percent, to keep up with increasing local costs. Another is to use a form of capital gains tax to recapture some portion of excessively low property taxes when a property is sold. These gains are currently exempted by state and federal law. The fact is, the combination of mortgage interest deductions, low property taxes, and large capital gains exemptions upon sale give the homeowner a favored position in the current tax system. That said, homeowners may be the most politically powerful single constituency should their position in the tax system be challenged.

Changing the two-thirds vote requirements which have straitjacketed both state and local governments may be the single most plausible reform, insofar as most voters did not know about them, or the damage they would cause to tax and fiscal systems, in the original measure. A coalition of busi-ness and education leaders succeeded in lowering the voting requirement for local school bonds to 55 percent, with business leaders leading the campaign because of their concern for investment in schools. Unfortunately, Proposi-tion 56, which would have lowered the threshold for the budget and taxes to 55 percent, was defeated in 2004, as noted above, because of business fears that Democrats might eliminate their tax breaks.

Are there other options to break the stalemate? Some hold out hope for the recent change in the reapportionment system: if districts are more competitive, anti-tax partisanship will be diminished and, proponents argue, centrist solutions to budget problems could be enacted. An open primary system could have that effect as well.

Another option would be to make it easier for the legislature, by majority vote, to put tax measures on the ballot which would be voted on as an alternative to cuts in services. Voters have in recent years passed tobacco taxes, for children's programs, and a tax on millionaires, for mental health. Despite criticisms of "ballot-box budgeting," a measure which breaks the legislative stalemate and provides the right to vote on taxes may at least shift the current dynamic. What we do know is that it is unlikely that anyone designing a system anew—as a constitutional convention might—would conceive of a two-thirds majority as anything but a drastic infringement on the democratic process.

In sum, voters got much more than they expected with Proposition 13. They expected property tax relief in a time of budget surplus. Instead, what they got was a stalemated government centralized in Sacramento at the expense of local governance and run more heavily than ever by the initiative process, and a steadily degraded public sector. The prospect with government is never "doom and disaster" all at once, as some opponents of Proposition 13 predicted. Rather, it is the long-term deterioration of the public sector such that expectations are lowered, the possibilities for improvements are stifled, and the opportunities for an aroused polity are few.

The California Legislature
and the Decline of Majority Rule

Christopher Witko

THE LEGISLATURE IS at the center of democratic governance and the crux of California's current problems, as Christopher Witko explains in this chapter. In recent years the legislature has been crippled by initiative-based measures and increasingly partisan conflicts that preclude the cooperation necessary for any recurrence of its previous success.

Where the California legislature once determined the state's political agenda, it now largely reacts to outside forces. The legislature's current paralysis results, in Witko's fascinating formulation, from the conflict of two contradictory "moments" of reform—the Unruh reforms of the late 1960s, which expanded legislative capabilities, and the ballot measures of the late 1970s and 1980s which restricted them. The state's legislature has had some successes in recent years with environmental, consumer protection, and civil rights measures. But the conflict released by those two reform eras has compromised the traditional principle of majority rule and the legislature's "power of the purse," or ability to make the decisions on state financial policy. An apparent contradiction has surfaced between the fulfillment of majority rule (as revealed by initiative votes) and the realization of the public interest.

Witko concludes by offering thought-provoking suggestions on how a constitutional convention can restore real majority rule and control over state financial policy with a new, unicameral legislature.

Christopher Witko is a professor of political science at St. Louis University and a scholar of legislative politics. His articles have appeared in *State Politics and Policy Quarterly*, *The American Journal of Political Science*, and *Political Research Quarterly*.

THE LEGISLATURE IS the heart of the American system of representative government. Thus, it is troubling that the California legislature is nearly universally appraised as incapable of coping with California's most pressing problems. In this chapter, we will see what the flaws of the legislature are and how its malfunctions have contributed to the state's constitutional crisis.

There is no shortage of possible explanations for the legislature's current ineptness. Some blame partisanship, while others say that the size and diversity of California make the state ungovernable, and still others point to the state's primary system. There is no question that governing California is difficult and that partisan polarization hobbles the legislature. But California faces problems that are similar to those of other states, even if larger in scope. And extreme partisanship in state legislatures is more the norm these days than the exception. Yet the California legislature seems virtually powerless to do much to address many of the major problems facing the state, like the perpetual budget crisis and the poor quality of its K-12 educational system. Some critics have claimed, and I argue in this chapter, that the main problem with the California legislature is that its ability to act on important matters of policy has been severely limited by initiatives passed by angry, mistrustful voters whose passions were stoked by politicians and organized political interests. Specifically, the legislature is almost completely unable to enact policy that requires the government to tax or spend, and this produces deadlock on important issues and prevents it from crafting workable policies for those issues that it does tackle. California's extreme term limits and partisan polarization make these difficult institutional obstacles nearly impossible to overcome.

To understand the current functioning of the legislature it is important to understand the institution's past. In the first part of this chapter, I will discuss how, not very long ago, the California legislature was the envy of the nation and a model for political scientists, following reforms of the 1960s. This transformation of the California legislature from an essentially nineteenth-century institution to a thoroughly modern, competent legislature was largely successful but was then assaulted by those unhappy with the status quo during the 1970s. This assault manifested itself in a series of reform initiatives that have stripped the legislature of many of its basic powers and weakened the legislative majority to such an extent that the institution has become ineffective.

California's different reform eras have produced a body rife with contradictions, a legislature with the desire to enact path-breaking legislation on

Monday but unable to fulfill even the most basic tasks of state government on Tuesday. We will examine these contradictions and I will end this chapter by proposing reforms that could improve the operations of the California legislature.

The California Legislature Reformed and Deformed

Article IV of the California constitution defines the basic structure and function of the California legislature. Since the state's legislature was not designed until 1849, its structure was influenced by the United States Constitution and by other state and colonial constitutions. Like all other state legislatures (except Nebraska's) and the United States Congress, the California legislature is bicameral. The upper house (the senate) now has forty members and the lower chamber (the assembly) has eighty.

California has the largest population of any state in the union but is among the states with the fewest members in its two legislative chambers. Therefore each legislator represents a large number of constituents compared to other states. As of 2008, California's estimated population was nearly 38 million people, meaning that each of the assembly members represents over 450,000 individuals and each of the senators represents over 900,000 people. Such large numbers would make it very difficult under even the best of circumstances for California legislators to interact on an individual level with their constituents and represent them properly.

Legislatures are *the* critical institution for representative government. By their nature they allow for the inclusion of a greater number of voices and a discussion of a larger number of perspectives than the other main institutions of government. But American legislatures have always fallen short of adequately representing the public, and California's is no different. For more than thirty years prior to U.S. Supreme Court and California State Court cases of the 1960s, senate seats were divided within the state on the basis of geography, with one per county for most counties, giving conservative, rural voters disproportionate influence in the legislature. Since this system has been ruled unconstitutional, assembly and senate seats are both now apportioned on the basis of population, with more heavily populated urban areas gaining greater representation in both houses of the legislature.

Political reform is like sunshine and traffic in California, and the current legislature is a product of different reform eras. To understand the current functioning of the legislature it is necessary to understand two contradictory moments of governmental "reform" in California. The first is the era of legislative modernization and professionalization which occurred under the leadership of Assembly Speaker Jesse Unruh in the 1960s. The second entailed the destruction of legislative capabilities and the partial undoing of the Unruh reforms and began in the late 1970s.

The Unruh Era and the Rise of the Legislature

In the late 1950s the California legislature was much as it had been in the late 1850s, despite the massive societal and governmental changes that had taken place. Like other states at the time, California had a "citizen's legislature" characterized by the fact that most members served in the legislature for a very short period of time and the legislature rarely met. Pay was low and service in the legislature was not very desirable, and consequently turnover between sessions was high and few legislators stayed more than a few terms.[1] The members that served had limited time and resources with which to address the problems confronting the state. For example, there was very little legislative staff with policy expertise and legislative sessions were limited to a total of 120 days in odd-numbered years and 30 days in even-numbered years.[2] Political parties were weak and nonprogrammatic, partly as a result of Progressive Era reforms which weakened these organizations, as will be noted in chapter six. Furthermore, though California was already a very diverse state, the legislature was comprised almost entirely of white males. In short, the legislature functioned as an eighteenth-century institution in a state that was rapidly urbanizing and modernizing.

The legislature was also weak relative to other centers of power in Sacramento, especially the state's powerful governors, like Hiram Johnson, Earl Warren, and Pat Brown. Given the lowly status and limited capabilities of the legislature these governors were able to wield great influence. The legislature was also well suited to allow for the influence of organized interests. The virtual control of the legislature by the railroad in the late 1800s is well known, but this type of influence extended into the mid-1940s when legendary lobbyist Artie Samish was able to control the legislature through his dispensing of money and favors to legislators.[3] The legislature as an institution was subordinate to the executive branch and to the interest group community (the "third house"). But neither the governor nor interest groups are able to represent the public in a way that a legislature is supposed to do.

Jesse Unruh, speaker of the California State Assembly from 1961 to 1969, sought to transform the legislature to address these problems. He wanted to strengthen the legislature to craft better policy, be more responsive to the public, and withstand the pressure of interest groups and the executive branch. In order to accomplish these goals he advocated more time in session with increased resources for staff, and especially nonpartisan policy experts, which he thought would lead to better public policy. He also advocated higher pay to attract a higher caliber and more diverse legislature, with members who would be willing to make a career out of legislative service.[4] These reforms creating the professional legislature were passed as constitutional amendments by the voters in the fall of 1966 as Proposition 1A.

At the same time and just as importantly, and encouraged by external reformers, Unruh helped to revitalize California's political parties. In the early 1900s California Progressives had enacted several laws that stripped the political parties of their power because the organizations had become controlled by big money interests, like the railroad. These laws led to a nonpartisan politics in the California legislature, where legislation was usually passed by bipartisan coalitions.[5] The party-weakening reforms were successful at limiting the power of parties but also had some unintended consequences. Americans are suspicious of partisanship, but many argue that weak parties reduce responsiveness to voters and increase the influence of special interests.[6] During the 1950s and 1960s with the abolition of some Progressive reforms the parties in California became more programmatic and cohesive.[7]

Now parties, and especially the majority party leadership, determine much of what happens in the legislature. The party leaders are elected by the members of each party, called the caucuses. The assembly speaker is the leader of the majority party in the assembly, and the senate president pro tempore is the leader of the majority party in the senate. Senate and assembly minority leaders represent the minority party in each chamber. One important power the speaker has is the ability to determine which pieces of legislation get on the assembly's agenda by virtue of the speaker's control over the Rules Committee, which schedules legislation. This ability gives the speaker power over legislators and organized interests by controlling their ability to see favored legislation enacted, which in turn increases the party leaders' fundraising capability, and this enables them to either reward or punish members of the caucus as they personally see fit and to influence primary elections so as to bring loyalists into office.

As service in the legislature became more prestigious, competition for legislative seats increased, and costs for media communications rose. Campaign costs began to rise and party leaders used this as an opportunity to gain power by raising and dispensing campaign contributions to other party members. This practice was pioneered by Jesse Unruh and perfected by Willie Brown. The strengthening of parties allowed for stronger legislative leaders with the ability to stand up to the governor and interest groups, which weak leaders of earlier eras had lacked. Unruh was an assembly Democrat, but similar changes were made by Republican Party leaders, and the senate largely followed the path established by the assembly.

These institutional changes and the strengthening of the parties led to a very active, highly competent legislature that the Citizens Conference on State Legislatures often held up as a model for other states wishing to reform their legislatures. California gained a reputation as an innovative state with a legislature that used creative policy solutions to confront problems that other states were ignoring.[8] The reforms Unruh established through his control over the Democratic majority in the assembly set the stage for much of the legislation that created what has been known as the California dream—the quality schools, lush parks, and good roads, and even less tangible things, like respect for civil rights in the form of laws like the Fair Housing and Employment Act, enacted in 1963. Unlike today, the legislature determined the state's political agenda rather than simply reacting to unexpected brush fires. The reforms of the 1960s were, at least initially, a stunning success and the California legislature was held in high regard by experts and much of the public. Admittedly, the legislature during that era benefited from a large postwar economic boom that made these plans a reality, and current policy makers do not have such an advantageous economic situation. Still, the successes were not automatic. They took leadership and organization.

Backlash: The Initiative Revolution and the Erosion of Legislative Power

If the California legislature's heyday began with the Unruh-era reforms, it started to end in 1978 with an organized assault on the status quo, when homeowners and interest groups used the initiative to shift California government in a different direction. The backlash against the establishment is a complicated phenomenon with no single cause, but its effect on the legislature has been profound. Proposition 13 limited property taxes, but by limiting the ability of the legislature to raise any taxes, it also effectively stripped the power of the purse from the legislature and seriously weakened the ability of the legislative majority to shape policy. This was followed by other initiatives with similar effects. The attack on the legislature reached a crescendo with Proposition 140 in 1990, which placed strict term limits on legislators, exacerbating the effects of earlier reforms and creating new problems of its own.

Proposition 13, Its Aftermath, and Legislative Power

Several observers, for example Peter Schrag in *Paradise Lost: California's Experience, America's Future*, have pointed out the irony in the fact that the initiative process has become the mechanism the public uses to register its disapproval of California's political institutions by further restricting their ability to do their job. Proposition 13 is probably the best example of this.

Proposition 13, as we saw in chapter three, limited property taxes to 1 percent of assessed value, limited increases in assessed value to the lesser of 2 percent or the rate of inflation per year, and required a two-thirds vote of both houses of the legislature to increase taxes (California State Constitution, Article XIII). This restriction on the legislative majority's power to raise taxes is quite unusual by American standards. While fifteen states have some supermajority requirement for raising taxes, only seven of these states require a two-thirds majority for all taxes. Most states do not have any supermajority requirements to raise taxes at all, nor does the federal government.[9] This limitation on the majority's power to dictate taxation obviously weakens the legislature's ability to shape policy, since the majority lacks the ability to determine state revenues. This restriction on raising revenue has proven more vexing than the longstanding two-thirds requirement for passing the budget, since it is politically much more difficult to increase taxes than it is to increase spending.

In other cases, initiatives have strictly limited or raised expenditures on particular programs, weakening the legislature's control over the spending side of fiscal policy. Perhaps the most obvious example of the latter type of limitation is Proposition 98, which requires that approximately 40 percent of the state general fund must be allocated to K-14 education (K-12 and the community colleges). Similar initiatives have mandated hundreds of millions or billions of dollars of spending on programs as diverse as high-speed rail, mental health services, and after-school programs. Proposition 98 is, of course, the largest such mandate. This initiative was passed in 1988 in response to Proposition 13's slashing of local governments' ability to fund education and shifting of most responsibility for this spending to the state, which had other priorities. Understandably, the California Teachers

Association advocated Proposition 98 as a response to this deterioration, but this initiative has tied the hands of the legislature in establishing spending levels for K-14 education and has done nothing to improve education.

In theory the 40 percent allocation to K-14 is a floor and the legislature can spend more than this amount, but in practice it has served as a ceiling because provisions of Proposition 98 require increases in expenditures each year. This means that if the legislature had an additional $10 billion of revenue in one year (say due to a tax windfall as occurred in the late 1990s) it could not allocate this money to K-14 spending unless it planned to spend the additional money the next year too. The idea that a large portion of the California budget should go to education is unobjectionable, as should be the idea that California needs to spend more money on education. But Proposition 98 limits the flexibility of the legislature to shape overall amounts of education spending. It can be suspended with a two-thirds vote of the legislature, but this can be difficult to achieve.

Throughout the 1980s and 1990s California spending on education and the quality of its education system rapidly declined despite Proposition 98. For example, in 2007 California ranked near the bottom of the states in its performance on the National Assessment of Educational Progress conducted by the U.S. Department of Education.[10] California is also near the bottom in per-pupil expenditures in recent years, with states like Mississippi and Louisiana.[11] And it spends less on education than most other large, diverse states, such as New York, Illinois, and Florida.[12] This disparity will surely increase as California plans billions of dollars of cuts to its K-12 education system in the coming years. With the massive budget cuts to all areas of government, K-14 will still comprise 40 percent of the budget as mandated by Proposition 98, however.

Many other policies have more subtly tied the hands of the legislature to establish state spending priorities. One example is the provision in Proposition 140 that limits the budget allocation for legislative staff. In the wake of the passage of Proposition 140 the legislature had to cut hundreds of staff positions, with many senior staffers retiring and taking with them years of institutional memory and in-depth knowledge of political issues.[13] To see the implications of this, consider water policy: being able to legislate effectively in this area requires some knowledge of federal, state, and local regulations and agreements among these different levels of government, in addition to the politics of the issue—from the preferences of the governor and state bureaucrats to those of federal politicians and local mayors, farmers, and local water and sewer authority board members. California still has relatively well-developed partisan, committee, and independent staff systems compared to many other states, but the legislature would not have lost many experienced staffers without the passage of Proposition 140. These losses have been a major blow to California's policy-making capacity. Furthermore, legislators are in a better position to judge staffing needs than are members of the public, who have only the vaguest notion of what legislative staff is or does but who voted for Proposition 140, 52 to 48 percent.[14] They presumably supported it for the term limits it provided, without noticing its provision for firing staff.

All of these initiatives struck at two important American traditions—the idea that the legislature should have the power of the purse and the principle of majority rule. One of the potential ironies of democracy thus finds stark expression in California's initiative-driven politics. Majority rule in the votes for initiatives has served to limit majority rule in the legislature and undermine the government's ability to provide for the public interest, which is also a requirement of a democracy.

The Attack of the Killer Term Limits

The erosion of legislative power was merely a side effect of measures like Proposition 13, which mainly sought to limit property taxes, and Proposition 98, which focused on increasing education spending. Unlike them, Proposition 140, with its provisions for the most stringent term limits in the nation as well as cuts to legislative staff and the elimination of legislative pensions, took direct aim at the legislature. The same antiestablishment feeling that animated the passage of Proposition 13 also fueled Proposition 140. Combined with this, however, was partisan animosity toward the Democratic majority and its controversial poster child, Assembly Speaker Willie Brown. The partisan aspect to term limits can be seen in the fact that Republican voters were much more likely to support term limits than Democrats.[15] This time by a relatively narrow margin, the public, led by partisan groups and special interests, lashed out directly at the professional politicians in the legislature by preventing them from keeping their jobs. Like Proposition 13, term limits brought both more and less than the public anticipated.

It would be a daunting task to find anyone who thinks that term limits actually improved the functioning of the California legislature. Therefore, in a very real sense term limits have failed to deliver on what reformers promised, as even a main supporter of Proposition 140, former Assemblyman and L.A. County Supervisor Pete Schabarum, has acknowledged. Limiting terms has had entirely predictable consequences. For example, legislators have less time to develop expertise on complicated issues and, predictably, term-limited legislatures demonstrate less policy innovation than chambers without limits.[16]

It is no longer possible for California to have legislative leaders who build up experience and familiarity with institutional norms, political issues, and politics over long tenures. In the twenty years prior to the enactment of term limits there were five assembly speakers. Ten years after term limits first forced retirements in the assembly, there had already been five. The longest-serving speaker since term limits, Fabián Núñez, was elected speaker in his first term of office, leading one to wonder just how prepared for the job new members of the legislature, however smart and politically savvy, can be. This lack of long-serving leadership certainly weakens the legislature relative to the executive branch, where the governor generally has a seasoned political staff, an abundance of resources, and long-serving agency employees with in-depth policy knowledge. Indeed, Thad Kousser, author of *Term Limits and the Dismantling of State Legislative Professionalization*, finds that since the term limits were enacted, the governor in California gets more of what he wants in the annual state budget than the legislature.

The Contradictions in Action:
The Two California Legislatures

The initiative revolution did not undo all that was accomplished during the Unruh era, but it did greatly change the way that the legislature functions and how it addresses or fails to address the state's most pressing problems. Though many observers consider the California legislature to be a complete failure, it has demonstrated some notable legislative accomplishments in recent years and attempted to tackle important issues. But it has also come up short on big issues, due to its new constraints.

Many of the things that made the California legislature the National Conference on State Legislatures' model in the 1970s remain. California legislators currently have the highest pay and the most staff per legislator, and California's are among the longest legislative sessions of any state.

And the California legislature has had some notable successes. It maintained its leadership role in environmental protection when the legislature passed and the governor signed legislation requiring a 25 to 30 percent reduction in greenhouse gas emissions by 2020.[17] Environmentalists hailed this legislation, the first of its kind in the U.S., as an "historic deal that will jump-start America's fight against global warming" and commended legislators for "leading in the fight on global warming."[18] It also demonstrates a clear response to the public, which favors much greater action on global warming. Whether this legislation ultimately works will depend on implementation, but regardless, it addresses an important issue, embodies the preferences of most Californians, and leads the other states, as we have come to expect of California on environmental issues.

California also continues to be a leader in consumer protection. As concern has grown over the increasing identity theft permitted by new technology, the federal government has done little to protect concerned consumers. Legislation (SB 1386) recently passed in California protects consumers against the mishandling of their personal information by requiring companies to notify them if computers storing personal data are breached. Another bill (SB 1) limits the distribution of consumers' private information. Consumer and privacy rights advocates have touted California as a leader on this issue.

A third area where the California legislature continues to be a leader is civil rights. California, like every other state in the nation, has a contemptible history of racism and discrimination. But California has also often taken the lead in trying to right these wrongs. A recent example of this is the debate over equal rights for gays and lesbians. The legislature passed a law mandating that same-sex domestic partners be entitled to the same legal benefits as married couples (though this legislation stopped short of endorsing gay marriage). The recent passage of Proposition 8 via the popular initiative simply underscores that the California legislature has been largely protective of expanding civil rights in recent years.

A near miss on enacting important legislation, however, captures the problems of today's California legislature. In the early days of 2008, a proposal for universal health-care legislation died in the senate despite passing the assembly and having the support of Governor Schwarzenegger. It was largely killed by the two-thirds requirement needed to raise taxes, according to Senate President pro Tempore Don Perata. Perata stated that because employer contributions and other fees did not cover the cost of the program it would be impossible to fund, since the legislature, requiring a two-thirds vote, would never pass a tax increase to pay for it. Whether or not Perata was merely providing an excuse for his own failure to mobilize support for it, his assessment is probably accurate. California was once a leader in addressing the real problems of average people, but this tradition has been imperiled due to the inability to address basic budgetary problems, which stems in turn from the limitations placed on the majority's ability to control taxing and spending. Universal health care is admittedly a complicated and costly issue, but Massachusetts enacted a bill that covers all residents and other states are in the process of finding solutions. This episode demonstrates that the California legislature can be active as long as its activities require no additional expenditures or taxes. This is clearly a severe, indeed fatal, shortcoming.

In "Federalist No. 58," Madison, drawing on the lessons of British history, wrote that the "power over the purse may, in fact, be regarded as the most complete and effectual weapon with which any constitution can arm the immediate representatives of the people." Since the founding, governors and presidents have come to play a critical role in shaping spending priorities, but the legislature remains the ultimate budgetary authority. In California the legislature's ability to carry out this task has been seriously undermined. What is remarkable about California in recent decades is that the power of the purse has been stripped from the legislature without any broad public discussion of the repercussions of this change for representative government.

The system of Madisonian democracy, with its separation of powers and checks and balances, arose out of Madison's fear of majority tyranny, most forcefully stated in "Federalist No. 10." Madison's challenge was to fashion a republican (i.e., representative) government that also protects minority rights. The result he arrived at, however, is a set of political institutions which make it difficult to translate majority will into an actual change in the status quo. California, like other states, has the same basic Madisonian set of institutions that are adept at thwarting majorities. Remarkably, against this backdrop California has gone even further than the federal government and nearly every other state in limiting the power of the legislative majority to enact its will.[19]

This weakening of the majority has a certain inherent appeal to Americans who revere the Madisonian system. But this system of separation of powers and checks and balances is a relative rarity in modern democracies. No student of American politics has written of the practical importance of majority rule with a greater clarity than E. E. Schattschneider.[20] In modern society, he says, government necessarily concerns itself with issues of the common good, that is, those issues which affect everyone in the community, and not just special interests with a financial or ideological stake in public policy. Majority rule is the best way to fulfill that good, however imperfect it may be. As Schattschneider writes, "The numerical majority has a role to play in modern government because we can no longer wait for the vegetative processes of an infinitely disintegrated system to solve our problems."[21]

He continues that "all that we have a right to expect of any political system is that it will give us a reasonable opportunity to do something effective to protect the great public interests of the community."[22] But the American system of government is one which seeks to stifle majorities. This makes it difficult to achieve action on many problems facing the country. California has raised the ante and imposed further barriers on the legislature, and therefore the people, by limiting the ability of the legislative majority to enact its will. This has led to the inaction of recent years.

What Madison in "Federalist No. 10" called "the republican principle" and what we today call majority rule does not in itself dictate any particular policy outcome. Rather, advocates of a particular policy must gain the support of a large number of voters in order to gain the legislative majority, and then keep the support of those voters while in power through periodic elections. Obviously, reasonable people can disagree about what the most appropriate response to California's budget crisis may be, but the majority should be allowed to fashion and enact a plan. If the public judges it to be a bad one, they can vote in different representatives in the next election.

The initiative theoretically counteracts the federalist model and is a majoritarian tool. However, it does not lend itself well to deliberation over complex subjects and is therefore unlikely to adequately address the major problems facing the state. And the majorities who vote for initiatives have often been mobilized and misinformed by organized interests—that is, minorities. One can certainly make the argument that supermajority requirements and the stripping of legislative discretion over spending and taxing are good things in the abstract, but it is difficult to see how these have been good for California in practice. In fact, initiative governance has caused legislative failure on many issues facing the state.

First and most obvious is the now perpetual budget crisis. With the exception of unusually good tax-revenue-generating years, California has had a permanent, structural budget crisis of several billion dollars for the last twenty years. The recent economic crisis exacerbated this underlying problem, but it is important to remember that the legislature has essentially done nothing to address this problem since it became apparent in the early 1990s. The state continues to accumulate debt to resolve the annual crisis, and with the resulting financial squeeze many successful state programs will be severely cut in the coming years.

To overcome these structural limitations on the majority and on the legislature's ability, through its power of the purse, to address problems like the budget crisis and inferior K-12 education would require skilled political leadership with the willingness to expend political capital. Most people in the state are aware of the decrepit condition of California education, but year after year nothing is done to address this problem. This is a complicated issue that needs some serious thought and study, and careful crafting of policy. Enacting any policy will require real legislative leadership because there are entrenched interests that have a strong stake in disinvesting in education, infrastructure, and public services. As it stands now, there is no incentive for a term-limited legislator, who can only serve a maximum of eight years in a legislative body, to undertake the detailed, hard work necessary to make such changes. It could easily take eight years just to begin to understand the K-12 education system. Better to play it safe, paving the way to run for higher office after you are term-limited out. After the initiative debacle of spring 2009 a *Los Angeles Times* columnist called for the next year's gubernatorial candidates to be "profiles in courage."[23] Courage may not be enough, however. It would require someone like an Unruh to fix these problems, but if Unruh were around today he would not be able to amass the power and knowledge he did in the 1960s.

In addition, since the 1960s the California legislature has become much more polarized,[24] which also makes it difficult to amass the supermajorities required for significant government action. While partisan polarization is common at the state level, it is perhaps greatest in California, which has the liberal Democrats of American coastal areas but Republicans as conservative as any from the Deep South. Admittedly, California is a liberal state on a number of issues, but the extreme conservatives in the legislature have a veto over policy by virtue of the supermajority requirements, so long as they hold one-third plus one of the seats in either chamber of the legislature.

This inability to enact policy that would resolve major fiscal challenges or to address problems which involve a need for additional government resources has sometimes led to trivial and symbolic policies, such as prohibiting state prison inmates from receiving erectile dysfunction drugs. Indeed it is tempting to conclude, as *Sacramento Bee* political columnist Dan Walters did, that the legislature has "lost touch with reality and has become an arena in which economic and cultural interests" fight over nothing and the legislature "distances itself from big issues," leaving them for initiatives.[25] This is true, but the problem is not primarily with the individual legislators. We have seen that there are institutional factors that seriously handcuff the legislature on the big issues facing the state.

California has been putting off the day of reckoning, but that day has finally come. As a result of California's structural deficit and the massive loss of revenue due to recession, the state budget was slashed by over $20 billion in the 2010 and 2011 budgets. These cuts have profound consequences for state programs. One victim of the reductions is the once valued jewel of California's public life, its system of education. Even before the economic crisis of 2008-09, state policies had locked California's two university systems (the California State University and the University of California) in what *Los Angeles Times* staff writer Richard C. Paddock called "a permanent substantial reduction in the quality of the university."[26] Facing continuous budget shortfalls every year, governors repeatedly ordered across-the-board cuts which have eviscerated the state's investment in public higher education. Now the two systems will lose approximately $2 billion more, and hundreds of thousands of community college students will be turned away as well. Higher education can at least raise tuition and fees, though doing that violates the promise of the 1960 Master Plan. But the K-12 system cannot. Student-to-teacher ratios are expected to rise to 43 to 1 in Los Angeles, and student-to-guidance counselor ratios are expected to exceed 1,000 to 1 in Berkeley.[27]

The budget cuts were ultimately bipartisan. Both Democratic and Republican votes were necessary to pass the final budget, given the two-thirds requirement. Rather than pressuring legislators for reasonable compromise between opposing views, that rule operates to permit a relatively small minority to determine the body's outcomes. That minority, mostly Republicans, represents a segment of the population that prefers these disinvestments in the public sector. Peter Schrag suggests that it is because the beneficiaries of public services have shifted from being middle-class whites to nonwhites over the last four decades that white middle- and upper-class voters have withdrawn their support for public services.[28] And he may be right. Still, white liberals and nonwhites make up a large portion of the population and the legislature. So it is only by frustrating majority rule that the proponents of a smaller public sector have prevailed. The existing budget rules permit budgetary policy to wind up being closer to Republican preferences than to the Democrats', though the latter have held majorities in both houses of the legislature in California for decades.

The legislature's dysfunctions have thus produced profound consequences for the state. Angered by rapidly rising tuition costs and overcrowded classrooms, students from around the state gathered in Sacramento in April of 2005 to mourn one of those effects. They mourned the death of the California Dream, which once promised a better life made possible by a bountiful nature, good jobs, and accessible public higher education.[29] There is enough blame to go around for that loss. The governor wields great budgetary power in the state; the legislature failed to act before massive public sector cuts were necessary; and with initiatives like Proposition 13 the voters themselves denied it the tools to do its job.

Can the Situation Be Improved?

Recently, people have spoken of the need for a new constitutional convention for California. If such a convention were able to repair the shortcomings identified above, to remove unnecessary limits on the majority and restore the legislature's power of the purse, it could make a real contribution to the governance of the state. Other proposals have also arisen for remedying the problems of the legislature, some modest and others more substantial.

The more modest reform proposals are for an open primary and for redistricting by an independent commission. Proponents urge that these reforms would reduce the legislature's extreme partisanship, which they believe derives from the way candidates are elected. Californians have a penchant for trying to remedy the results of reforms gone wrong with overly hasty new reforms, and these proposals may provide further examples of that tradition; it is not at all clear that these reforms would accomplish what their promoters anticipate, nor that the problem they address is the right one.

Closed primaries, in which only party registrants can vote, are now said to attract only die-hard partisans who regularly choose the most ideologically extreme candidates to represent their party in the next election. But California has had a closed primary system for decades and only recently suffered the problems of partisan polarization. And no one has explained what the effect of open primaries, in which anyone and everyone can select their candidates, will be on the parties.

The second proposal has already been partially adopted. Redistricting by sitting legislators has always been a questionable practice, and Proposition 11, in November 2008, finally put the job in the hands of an ostensibly independent fourteen-member commission. At best, however, that commission will only be able to produce a handful of competitive districts, because partisans are increasingly clumping themselves in specific geographic areas of the state. It is doubtful this small number of centrists will change the tenor of debates in Sacramento.

Americans have always liked to blame crass partisanship for the problems of legislatures. And extreme partisan polarization has been evident in

California's recent legislatures, giving rise to heated rhetoric and increasingly frequent deadlocks.[30] As noted above, however, this increase in legislative partisanship has often had positive benefits in California. Without an increase in partisanship, program development across a broad range of issues of the kind that was evident in the Jesse Unruh years is simply not possible. Proposals to outlaw segregation in housing, to create bodies like the coastal commission, and to increase consumer protections were all controversial on partisan lines, but that is no reason they should not have been made. Many strongly partisan states have not faced the problems that the California legislature does. More likely the problems of partisanship in California are caused by the two-thirds requirements for passing budgets and raising taxes.

More promising and intriguing is an idea that would more fundamentally alter the state legislature—namely, eliminate the state senate and create a unicameral body. Only one state, Nebraska, has such a legislature. The traditional reason for having two houses was to represent different kinds of constituencies in each, but since the Supreme Court's ruling mandating the apportionment of state senate seats on the basis of population, there has been little representational difference between the upper and lower chambers. Americans are familiar with unicameral legislatures in practice, because most local governments have single-chamber councils. Since California's legislature is extremely small relative to its population, it makes the most sense to have a single body with the same 120 total members, or preferably more, as Mark Paul and Micah Weinberg suggest in chapter ten. Having a unicameral legislature would help eliminate the gridlock in Sacramento since there would be one less obstacle to the passage of legislation, especially the budget. Given all the social and political divisions in California, the threat of gridlock on major issues is greater than the threat posed by an energetic, unified legislature. And major checks on the legislature would remain with the governor and the courts.

Unicameralism would also eliminate the unnecessary conflict within the same party between the two houses that sometimes arises. And a unicameral body would be a great benefit in helping the public keep the legislature accountable, because it would make evident who was to praise or blame for each action. A unicameral legislature will not in itself solve the legislature's problems, but while the state constitution is being revised this change should be seriously considered.

Other proposals have also been made which would substantially change California government. Over the years many people have asked whether California is even governable, given its size and diversity. The state could begin to deal with the problems posed by that size and diversity by devolving more issues to the local level and letting local and regional bodies deal with their more homogenous areas and potentially more manageable conditions. Clearly, the centralization of the K-12 system in the state has not been beneficial to its communities. That is one function that should perhaps be returned to the local authorities. A parliamentary system with proportional representation is another idea some have bruited. It may be worth considering, seeing as that kind of legislature is the norm throughout the world.

But within the state's existing institutional framework, the best chance for realistic reform would be to restore to the legislature its powers of the purse and eliminate the supermajority requirements for the budget and for raising taxes. This would bring California in line with other states and the federal government. To do this and to restore the necessary flexibility and discretion to legislative decision making and budget making will require some revision of the laws established by Propositions 13 and 98, and that will not be easy. Proposition 13 has been called the third rail of California politics, and only the most secure politician would think of challenging this high-voltage measure. And despite all the problems with supermajority requirements and spending mandates, powerful political interests and a significant portion of the public clearly like them. But if the problems of California government are to be remedied and the legislature to recover its effectiveness, the attempt must be made and the public educated about the real consequences of such constraints.

It may seem like a change in the status quo is nearly impossible. At some point, though, when people realize that the California dream of making a better life is becoming a vague memory, they will accept the necessity of serious reforms. The budget debacle of 2009 and the resulting cuts in government services should provide them with a vivid lesson to that end. The prospects of released criminals, shortened school years, and closed state parks reveal the costs of existing arrangements and policies in a way that technical discussions of "structural deficits" and hypothetical warnings did not. When people get fed up enough, political reform is a real possibility. We should remember that the Progressive movement, led by Hiram Johnson, had to overcome entrenched interests to get the initiative placed before voters in the first place. California history teaches that large-scale change is possible, and it is good that it does, for it is that kind of change that California needs now.

FIVE

Reforming the Executive

John Syer

CALIFORNIA'S EXECUTIVE BRANCH is a very influential component of California's government today. It consists of many agencies and bureaus we encounter daily, from the DMV to schools overseen by the Department of Education to the Department of Transportation (Caltrans). This branch also includes more than four hundred boards and commissions, including the Public Utilities Commission (PUC), the Coastal Commission, and the air and water resources boards, among others.

By their decisions these bureaus and agencies determine how the legislature's laws will be implemented and enforced. At the top of this branch are the eight elected constitutional officers John Syer discusses in this chapter, including such positions as the lieutenant governor and attorney general as well as the governor. Tackling the state's daunting political agenda—from limiting climate change and securing a strong position in the global economy to providing affordable medical care, protecting farmlands and timberlands, and more— requires effective state leadership and a team effort among these officers.

California has always had these multiple, independently elected officers (often from different political parties) serving at the pinnacle of state government. With the advent of term limits in 1990 (a maximum of two four-year terms in the same office), the jostling among these elected executives to win new offices has become more intense. Attempting to move to another executive office after eight years in a prior position resembles the game of musical chairs. The nineteenth-century model of multiple elected executives for this branch may well hinder the sort of strong leadership and teamwork that will be needed for California to succeed in the twenty-first century.

John Syer is a professor emeritus of government at California State University, Sacramento, with specializations in California politics and international relations. He was a longtime instructor of state assembly, senate, and executive interns. He is coauthor (with Ken DeBow) of *Power and Politics in California*, now in its ninth edition.

S INCE CALIFORNIA WAS admitted to the Union in 1850, there have been at least seven (currently eight) statewide executives elected by the voters of the state. Considering the political turbulence of late, is it now time to reconsider the number of statewide executives to be elected in California?

How did California come to have eight statewide elected officials serving simultaneously at the top of the executive branch? When James Marshall discovered gold in the foothills east of Sacramento in January of 1848, there were only 27,000 residents in California. Due to the gold rush, California's population quadrupled to 107,000 persons in 1849. At the same time, the area was undergoing a shift from Mexican to American control with the ratification of the Treaty of Guadalupe Hidalgo by the U.S. Congress. During the period of transition, it was not clear whether Mexican jurisprudence, American laws, or mining camp rules were in force.

With the prospect of public order declining to dangerous levels, U.S. General Bennett Riley (de facto governor of California) issued a proclamation calling for the election of delegates to participate in a constitutional convention to be held in Monterey in September and October of 1849. Like the delegates to the national constitutional convention in Philadelphia in 1787, delegates attending the Monterey meeting did not represent all the inhabitants of California. "In keeping with the practices of the era, there were no women, Native Americans, African Americans, or anyone of Asian descent."[1] To expedite their task, the delegates in Monterey used the U.S. Constitution and the constitutions from the thirty existing states of the Union in preparing the document for California.

The forty-eight delegates in Monterey spent little time deliberating on the composition of the executive branch. With only brief dissent, the convention delegates agreed upon the following seven elected statewide executives: governor, lieutenant governor, controller, treasurer, attorney general, surveyor general, and superintendent of instruction (California Constitution of 1849, Articles V and IX). In essence, the convention delegates in Monterey accepted the executive provisions contained in the constitutions of other states. "The criticism and mistrust that was leveled at the colonial governor and the British monarch eventually led to the governor of the states...being deprived of significant authority."[2] The governors of California would thus share executive power with six other statewide elected officers, and the term of office initially would be only two years. A secretary of state was to be appointed by the governor.

The constitutional convention in Monterey completed its work on October 13, 1849, and forwarded it to the U.S. Congress, and California was admitted as the thirty-first state of the Union on September 9, 1850. In 1862, the governor's term of office was lengthened to four years, and the post of secretary of state was made elective. With the elimination of surveyor general as an elective office and the addition of an elected secretary of state, the number of elected statewide executives remained at seven in the subsequent California constitution of 1879. Over a century later, in 1988, the office of insurance commissioner was made the eighth member of the statewide elected executive.

The Seven Seekers

The California constitution of 1879, currently in force, declares: "The supreme executive power of this state is vested in the Governor" (Art. V, Sec. 1). Despite this language, as mentioned above the state constitution also establishes seven additional elected statewide executive positions. Elected executives include a chief law officer (attorney general), a chief elections officer (secretary of state), a chief fiscal officer (controller), a chief banker (treasurer), a chief schools officer (superintendent of public instruction), a chief insurance regulator (insurance commissioner), and a chief stand-in (lieutenant governor). In short, executive power in California is now, and always has been, decentralized.

What are the responsibilities of the various elected executives? As to law enforcement, it is customary for county district attorneys to initiate criminal prosecutions in California. Should there be appeals arising from trial court convictions, the state attorney general's staff handles them. With responsibility to supervise county sheriffs and district attorneys and to see that state law is enforced throughout California, the attorney general may also bring a criminal case in any county in the absence of legal action by local prosecutors. The attorney general also publishes "Opinions" in reply to legal inquiries from persons throughout state government. The chief law officer decides upon the titles of ballot measures and prepares the summaries of ballot propositions in voter information pamphlets.

California's secretary of state is responsible for the orderly conduct of the state's elections. Upon receiving sufficient signatures from voters, the occupant of this office qualifies initiatives, referenda, and recalls for the ballot. The secretary of state's staff prepares the voter information pamphlet, which contains the text of the measures, the attorney general's summaries, financial impact statements by the legislative analyst, and pro/con arguments on the proposals. Records of donations to candidate races and ballot measure campaigns, as well as amounts of various types of campaign expenditures, must be filed with the secretary of state in a timely manner. After receiving vote tallies from each of the fifty-eight counties in the state, this office publishes the statewide record of the vote for candidate races and ballot measure contests.

The accuracy of the state's financial accounts is the responsibility of the state controller. The controller creates an account for each specific type of spending the legislature has authorized. The controller must be able to provide accurate balances for all state accounts on a daily basis. If legislative appropriations to specific accounts are lacking, there is no legal basis for a controller to pay obligations from such accounts. When the legal deadline for the adoption of the state budget (June 30) was missed in 2009, the state controller issued IOUs in payment of the state's obligations since there was no authorized basis to issue regular checks.

The state treasurer is both an investor and a borrower on behalf of the state. The stream of revenues from taxes and fees that accumulates in the state's treasury is not constant from month to month. Sales tax proceeds spike during the holiday season in December. Likewise, revenue flows increase when personal income and corporate taxes are due. When idle funds are amassed for which there is no immediate need to expend the moneys, it is the treasurer's responsibility to place such funds in interest-bearing accounts with banks on a short-term basis. The objective is to earn the highest possible interest from the investment of these idle state funds, especially in light of the chronic budget deficits faced by the state of California. The treasurer also borrows funds for the state and its localities. Borrowing is needed to pay for long-term capital improvements such as the construction of canals, highways, schools, universities, and prisons. After voters have approved a certain government indebtedness, it is the treasurer's responsibility to arrange for the sale of bonds for state or local construction projects.

The superintendent of public instruction (SPI) has several competitors in the area of K-12 education. This contributes to confusion within the executive branch. The SPI heads the California Department of Education, but is required to implement the policy guidelines of the State Board of Education (a body appointed by the governor). There is a secretary of education as well, on the governor's cabinet, who reflects the chief executive's view on educational issues. Elected local school boards also are involved in decisions on facilities construction and personnel management. One obvious constraint upon the superintendent of public instruction is that while he or she nominates the deputy superintendents to help manage the Department of Education, it is the State Board of Education which actually makes the legal appointments to these posts.

California's executive branch consisted of seven statewide elected officials for over a century. It was not until 1988 that a successful ballot measure (Proposition 103) created the post of insurance commissioner as the eighth elected statewide executive. In addition to managing the Department of Insurance, the commissioner has several powers to oversee insurance rates in the state. The insurance commissioner certifies insurance companies to conduct business in the state and registers the names of corporations. Insurance companies themselves decide which type of coverage they want to offer (e.g., auto, homeowners, or medical); but the insurance commissioner establishes the maximum rates of the various kinds of coverage.

Finally, there is the lieutenant governor. Compared with those of the other elected executives in California, the duties of the lieutenant governor are relatively scant. Unlike the executives discussed earlier who lead large agencies such as the Department of Education or Insurance or Justice, the lieutenant governor supervises only a small personal staff. Without the responsibility to implement a major section of California's statutory codes, a lieutenant governor may focus on a particular policy objective, such as improving higher education, or may simply bide his or her time and raise money for a future election campaign. The California constitution designates the lieutenant governor as president of the California State Senate (Art. V, Sec. 9), but the lieutenant governor can only vote in this capacity when there is a 20-20 tie in the chamber, which rarely occurs.

The most intriguing thing about this office is that whenever the governor is absent from the state (or temporarily disabled or undergoing impeachment by the legislature), the lieutenant governor becomes the acting governor of California with full powers of that office. Should a governor of California die in office or resign the position (as Hiram Johnson did in 1917 to become a U.S. senator and as Earl Warren did in 1953 to become chief justice of the U.S. Supreme Court), then the lieutenant governor becomes the full-fledged governor of California. The order of succession when the governorship is vacant is: lieutenant governor, senate president pro tempore, assembly speaker, secretary of state, attorney general, treasurer, and controller.

Musical Springboards

Governor Ronald Reagan (1966–1974) and Governor Arnold Schwarzenegger (2003–2010) ascended to the top office in California without any prior experience in public office. These two celebrity governors are the exception to the rule in attaining the governorship in California; the overwhelming bulk of California's governors have served in public office (often several offices) before entering the so-called "corner office" on the first floor of the State Capitol.

Some public offices serve as better springboards to the governorship than others. During the first five decades of statehood there were six governors who had earlier served in the California legislature or the U.S. Congress.[3] Such offices were not common stepping-stones to the governorship in the twentieth century, although Governor Pete Wilson (1990–1998) did enter the corner office after serving in the U.S. Senate. With the exception of Governor James Rolph, Jr. (1930–1934), who had served as mayor of San Francisco for twenty years, leaders of big cities in California have not yet succeeded in winning the governorship. Mayor Tom Bradley of Los Angeles lost two battles with George Deukmejian for the governor's office in 1982 and 1986, while Mayor Dianne Feinstein of San Francisco was defeated by Pete Wilson for the state's top office in 1990. Ms. Feinstein rebounded by winning a seat in the U.S. Senate in 1992.

As is reflected in Table 1, the most common launching pad historically for winning the governorship in California has been the office of lieutenant governor. Nine lieutenant governors have risen to the office of governor, but the incidence of this post being a successful stepping-stone to the corner office has declined substantially since the 1930s. Although Gray Davis did manage to use the lieutenant governor's office as his springboard to the governorship in 1998, the post of attorney general served as the stepping-stone for Governor Earl Warren (1942–1953), Governor Pat Brown (1958–1966), and Governor George Deukmejian (1982–1990). Elevation from the office of attorney general to that of governor is by no means a certainty, however. Attorneys General Evelle Younger in 1978, John Van de Kamp in 1990, and Dan Lungren in 1998 all lost bids to become governor. One

TABLE 1. **Executive Springboards to Governor of California**

Name of Governor	Inaugurated as Governor	Executive Office Prior to Governorship
John McDougall	1851	Lt. Governor
John Downey	1860	Lt. Governor
Romualdo Pacheco	1875	Lt. Governor
Robert Waterman	1887	Lt. Governor
William Stevens	1917	Lt. Governor
Friend Richardson	1923	Treasurer
C. C. Young	1927	Lt. Governor
Frank Merriam	1934	Lt. Governor
Earl Warren	1943	Attorney General
Goodwin Knight	1953	Lt. Governor
Edmund G. (Pat) Brown	1959	Attorney General
Edmund G. (Jerry) Brown, Jr.	1975	Secretary of State
George Deukmejian	1983	Attorney General
Gray Davis	1999	Lt. Governor (previously Controller)

SOURCE: E. Dotson Wilson and Brian S. Ebbert, *California's Legislature: 2006*
(Sacramento: California Assembly, 2006, p. 253)

state treasurer (Friend Richardson) and one secretary of state (Jerry Brown) have used their respective offices as stepping-stones to the governorship.

The term-limits provisions enacted in 1990 restricted the length of service in any one statewide executive post to eight years. Before 1990, a secretary of state or a state treasurer sometimes served twenty or thirty years without ever attempting to rise to the governor's office. Such longevity in one position is no longer possible due to that eight-year limit. A person might now hold two or three elective offices in the executive branch before running for governor.

Term limits prevent Arnold Schwarzenegger from running for governor again in 2010. Several elected executives were originally mentioned as possible candidates to replace Schwarzenegger, including Attorney General Jerry Brown (former secretary of state and governor), Lt. Governor John Garamendi (former insurance commissioner), Treasurer Bill Lockyer (former attorney general), Superintendent of Public Instruction Jack O'Connell, and Insurance Commissioner Steve Poizner. Several of the above individuals ultimately will decide not to run for governor in 2010. However, there is an old saying in the State Capitol: "California has one governor and seven wannabes."

Gubernatorial Powers: Small and Large

The most coveted elected position in the executive branch possesses a broad array of powers. Some of the governor's responsibilities are constitutional and other powers have evolved through the years in an extralegal manner. Some duties are very influential, while others are much less so.

Some aspects of the governor's job do not have particularly broad impact. California's governors decide whether to pardon those convicted of crimes and commute prison sentences. While important to selected individuals, these decisions do not have a broad impact on most residents of the state. Governors may call the California legislature into special session to address a single problem. Making such a call is no guarantee that the legislature will resolve the issue in question. Governors may call special elections to place matters before the California electorate rather than wait for regularly scheduled contests during even-numbered years. Governor Arnold Schwarzenegger called for special elections in 2005 and 2009, but the ballot propositions he supported were rejected by the voters. The costs of the special elections ($70 million in the latter year) and their uncertain outcomes may dissuade future governors from using this option. In addition, governors command the state militia (also known as the California National Guard). In the event of natural disasters or civil disorder, the governor may dispatch the state militia to provide security and assistance.

Much more important than these functions are the governor's other powers in budget making, legislative matters, and designating appointees. Governors have major responsibilities throughout the budgetary process. They initiate the process by submitting a proposed state budget (containing expenditures and revenues) to the legislature within the first ten days of each calendar year. Thereafter, representatives of the Department of Finance and the directors of other executive departments testify before legislative committees in support of the proposed budget. Once the annual budget has been passed by both houses of the legislature (the deadline is June 15), the governor may use the line-item veto to reduce (not increase) specific appropriations within the budget.

Though they are not members of the legislative branch, California's governors are major players in the legislative process. They are constitutionally required to address the California legislature during an annual State of the State speech. Executive departments track the progress of bills and try to influence legislators and legislative committees to support the governor's proposals.

A major power of California governors is that which permits them to veto any legislative measure they oppose. (While the line-item veto mentioned earlier applies only to dollar amounts in specific budgetary appropriations, the general veto eliminates entire legislative enactments.) In the middle of a given legislative term, governors must use the general veto within twelve days of a bill's passage, or the bill in question will become law without the governor's signature. At the conclusion of a legislative term, the governor has thirty days in which to cast a general veto.

Gubernatorial vetoes may be overridden by two-thirds majority votes in both chambers of the legislature, but such overrides are very rare. The last governor to experience veto overrides was Jerry Brown in 1979. Governor Arnold Schwarzenegger has employed the general veto in a robust manner. During his first four years in the corner office, he vetoed nearly one-quarter of all the measures sent to him by the legislature.[4]

In addition to strong budgetary and legislative influence, California's governors have sweeping powers to appoint individuals to a wide variety of public offices. Even though 99 percent of the state of California's 235,000 employees (excluding university personnel) are in the civil service and are not hired or fired by the chief executive, governors still make well over two thousand high-level political appointments during each four-year term in the corner office. These appointments give governors substantial leverage in constituting California's executive and judicial branches. With the power to appoint staff to the heads of departments and agencies and members of a wide assortment of boards and commissions, the governor has considerable impact in the executive branch. Although California's trial court judges and appellate justices are technically elected to office, governors make appointments to the bench when retirements occur between elections. During the eight years of a two-term governorship, it is possible for a governor to significantly alter the composition of California's judiciary.

Beyond the constitutionally derived powers of office already discussed, modern California governors have developed a number of additional roles. With the growth of mass media and the availability of high-speed transportation, a governor today can become an agenda setter well beyond the borders of California. Governor Arnold Schwarzenegger has visited Washington, D.C., to lobby both the U.S. Congress and the White House on several matters. He has asked for federal moneys to upgrade California's deteriorating highways and bridges and to strengthen levees to forestall possible flooding. Governor Arnold Schwarzenegger has also become a global messenger on the threat posed by emissions of greenhouse gases, promoting California's strict limits on emissions in Washington, D.C., and negotiating "compacts" to reduce them with provinces in Canada and Mexico.

Governors of California can also be campaigners and candidates. They recruit members of their political party to run for public office, and they may endorse presidential candidates in California's primary elections. They also run themselves. Earl Warren in 1952, Ronald Reagan in 1968, Jerry Brown in 1976 and 1980, and Pete Wilson in 1996 all mounted unsuccessful presidential campaigns while serving as governor. Ronald Reagan eventually did win the presidency in 1980, six years after leaving the corner office in the State Capitol. Having been born and raised in Austria, Arnold Schwarzenegger is not a "natural born citizen" and, therefore, could not run for president, under the language of the U.S. Constitution (Art. II, Sec. 1.5).

Leadership in the Corner Office

What distinguishes an ordinary officeholder from a true leader? Leaders clarify the goals of government and then mobilize the citizenry in support of them. Leaders possess the courage to undertake difficult tasks that are necessary for society to address. In other words, leaders distinguish pressing needs from routine matters. Leaders relate facts to the public regarding imminent challenges and then summon sacrifice from the people as needed. Leaders have a long-term perspective which allows them to leave the state of California in better shape than they found it.

Leaders customarily possess a mixture of skills which they employ to attain their goals. They know how to build consensus and to form winning coalitions. In particular, governors must be able to develop harmonious and productive relationships with the California legislature. The ability to bring highly competent appointees into managerial positions in state government is also a sign of leadership. Leaders clearly delegate responsibilities to their subordinates. After deciding among the various options for dealing with a pressing problem, real leaders make sure to follow through on a given plan until closure is reached. By observing ethical standards and avoiding scandals, leaders focus on the job at hand rather than wasting their energies and few years in office with distractions. True leaders also acknowledge their mistakes and return to solving critical problems as quickly as possible. What follows is a summary of gubernatorial approaches to leadership since 1938, in preparation for a discussion of executive branch reforms that might be considered by a new constitutional convention.

When an influx of laborers moved to California during World War II to work in the state's shipyards and aircraft assembly plants, they were governed by the most popular politician in state history. At that time, the institution known as cross-filing permitted candidates to run (i.e., file) in both the Democratic and the Republican primary elections at the same time, if they so chose. In 1938, Republican Earl Warren won the primary elections of both major political parties to become state attorney general with no major opponent in the November general election. Thereafter, Warren won the races for governor in 1942, 1946, and 1950 to become the only three-time winner of the governorship in California history. Warren successfully cross-filed for a second time in 1946 by winning both the Democratic and Republican primary elections for governor. Three years into his third term as governor, in 1953, Warren left the corner office to become chief justice of the U.S. Supreme Court.

As demonstrated by his winning the primary elections of both major political parties, Warren was a nonpartisan figure. He appointed individuals from both parties to senior positions in state government. To prepare for the growing population, Governor Warren expanded highway construction and university facilities. He had the courage to regulate major professions and industries in California on behalf of the general public. When Japanese Americans were interned during World War II on orders from the national government, he initially supported this repressive action against U.S. citizens but later acknowledged that this was a mistake. After Warren's appointment as chief justice, the remainder of his third term as governor was served by Lt. Governor Goodwin Knight.

Except for Democrat Culbert Olson's governorship (1938–1942), only Republicans served as governors in California from 1899 until the election of Democrat Edmund G. (Pat) Brown to the governorship in 1958, when the Republican grip on the governor's office was broken. With a majority of Democrats in control of the legislature, Governor Brown eliminated cross-filing in 1959. He instituted major construction projects involving highways and university campuses. His most challenging task was winning approval of the State Water Project despite the opposition of organized labor and

Northern California. Small farmers and union members opposed the canal system because they believed it would advantage corporate agriculture over the smaller operations; unlike federal water projects, the State Water Project did not limit the size of farms which could receive state-subsidized water.

By winning the governorship in 1966, Republican Ronald Reagan denied Pat Brown a third term in the corner office. Reagan's victory was aided by reaction against the student protests on the Berkeley campus of the University of California in 1964 and by the racial strife in the Watts neighborhood of Los Angeles in 1965. In addition to his law-and-order message, Reagan advocated small government and low taxes. After obtaining cuts in funding for higher education, mental health, and Medi-Cal (health services for the poor), Governor Reagan still found it necessary to sign tax increases in 1967 and 1971 in order to balance the state's budget.

Shortly after the Watergate affair brought down President Richard Nixon in 1974, Democrat Edmund G. Brown, Jr. (Jerry Brown) assumed the governor's office his father had left eight years earlier. In defiance of corporate agriculture, he supported the ten-year struggle of the United Farm Workers union and won legislative approval to establish the Agricultural Labor Relations Board. The ALRB thereafter conducted secret-ballot elections at locations throughout California to determine whether or not workers wanted to unionize. This was a victory for some of the lowest-paid workers in the state. Governor Jerry Brown also was a strong supporter of environmental protection, opposing the construction of nuclear power plants in California and limiting the use of some pesticides. A supporter of diversity in government, he appointed women and people of color to senior positions, including Rose Elizabeth Bird as the first female chief justice of the California Supreme Court.

Governor Jerry Brown initially opposed Proposition 13 (discussed in chapter three), but he reversed his position upon its passage in June of 1978 in time to assure his reelection to the governor's office in November of that year. In cutting property taxes by 57 percent, Proposition 13 reduced funding for school districts and other local governments by some $7 billion per year. In future years, it would be up to state government to replace this lost funding. While Governor Jerry Brown can be credited with important innovations, he failed to act in time to safeguard California from the harsh effects of this substantial property tax reform. Like his father before him, he eventually lost the support of the Democrat-controlled state legislature. After his reelection as governor in 1978, Jerry Brown spent over 170 days out of state seeking the Democratic presidential nomination for 1980. Not only did this quest fail, but several of of his general and line-item vetoes were overridden in 1979 with the help of Democratic votes in the legislature. Such an affront to a governor has not occurred since.

In the general election of 1982, former Attorney General George Deuk-mejian (Republican) narrowly defeated Mayor Tom Bradley of Los Angeles (Democrat) to win the governorship. Governor Deukmejian had extensive prior experience in state government, having served in both houses of the state legislature and also as the state's chief law officer. As a proponent of strong law-and-order policies, he preferred to appoint former prosecutors (not defense counsels) to the judiciary. In conjunction with his successful reelection campaign in 1986, Deukmejian was instrumental in winning the removal of three of Jerry Brown's appointees to the California Supreme Court during a judicial retention vote. He viewed Rose Bird, Cruz Reynoso, and Joseph Grodin as too sympathetic to criminal defendants in their rulings. With three openings to fill on the state's highest court as well as numerous appointments to the lower courts, Governor Deukmejian recast the California judiciary to reflect his views. He also instigated a major prison construction program and a dramatic increase in California's inmate population. Outside the judicial and correctional areas, Governor Deukmejian did not initiate new programs, as he abided by his pledge not to increase taxes in California. In the years to come, his expansion of the state's correctional system came to be a heavy financial burden that surpassed the annual budget for the University of California and the California State University combined.

In the gubernatorial election of 1990, former U.S. Senator Pete Wilson (Republican) defeated Mayor Dianne Feinstein of San Francisco (Democrat). Given his support for women's right to choose, Governor Wilson was viewed as a more moderate Republican than Governor Deukmejian. Having inherited a budgetary deficit from his predecessor, Governor Wilson fashioned a balanced financial plan in 1991 by advocating budget cuts as well as increased taxes. Unlike George Deukmejian, who resisted tax increases, both Ronald Reagan and Pete Wilson did permit them when the need was compelling.

With the opposition party in firm control of the California legislature, Governor Wilson decided to pursue some of his projects by supporting initiatives on the ballot. His support of Proposition 187 to terminate the funding of state services for the families of undocumented workers was passed by the voters in 1994 during his successful reelection campaign, though it was later invalidated by the courts. With vocal support from Governor Wilson, Proposition 209 in 1996 eliminated affirmative action in state hiring, selection of contractors for state projects, and college admissions. Though he was initially seen as moderate, Governor Wilson's views on affirmative action and on state services for the families of undocumented workers ultimately alienated many Latino voters from the Republican Party.

Despite Republican Dan Lungren's occupying the usually helpful stepping-stone office of attorney general, Democrat Gray Davis, emphasizing his lengthy service in state government, easily won the 1998 governor's race. Given his prior posts of chief of staff to Governor Jerry Brown, member of the California State Assembly, two terms as state controller, and one term as lieutenant governor, Gray Davis likely had more experience inside state government prior to becoming governor than any other person. Even with this lengthy experience in state politics, he did not foresee the serious problems taking shape. Gray Davis did not exercise the qualities of leadership described above nor effectively address the energy and budgetary problems facing California. With his popularity waning, Davis was fortunate to win reelection in 2002 over a low-profile Republican candidate named William Simon.

Almost immediately after winning reelection, Gray Davis became the focus of a recall effort. Some 55 percent of the voters on October 7, 2003, decided to remove him from the corner office. With slightly less than a majority, Arnold Schwarzenegger was the highest vote getter among the replacement candidates and, therefore, became the next governor of California.

The contrasts between Davis and Schwarzenegger could hardly be greater. Davis had lengthy experience in elective office; Schwarzenegger was a body builder and a movie star with no experience in elective office. Davis was a bland government functionary lacking in radiance; Schwarzenegger was an international celebrity with charisma. Davis drew his electoral support largely from Democrats; Schwarzenegger was a centrist who appealed to independent voters and across party lines. Though Schwarzenegger was a pro-business, anti-tax Republican, his support of women's right to choose and strong protection of the environment were welcomed by Democrats. Schwarzenegger's marriage to Democrat Maria Shriver, niece of President John F. Kennedy, also contributed to his bipartisan image.

After Democrats and public employee unions succeeded in defeating his four Republican-oriented ballot measures in 2005, Governor Schwarzenegger admitted that he should have listened to Maria Shriver's advice that he avoid divisive partisan conflicts. Claiming to have learned his lesson, he embarked upon what he called a post-partisan agenda through which he aimed to find good ideas in either major political party. In cooperation with the Democratic legislative leadership, Governor Schwarzenegger signed the Global Warming

Solutions Act of 2006 mandating a 25 percent reduction in greenhouse gas emissions by 2020. The Republican governor easily won reelection in November of 2006 by defeating Democratic Treasurer Phil Angelides. Once Schwarzenegger won his second year in office, however, he became more partisan, resisting tax increases and reducing public services.

In the summer of 2008, the longest budget deliberations in state history became a major test of Governor Schwarzenegger's leadership. The governor finally signed the state's budget on September 23, 2008, eighty-five days into the new fiscal year, which had begun July 1. After a nearly three-month delay in adopting the budget for fiscal year 2008-09, there followed one of the most painful and contentious budget deliberations ever, for the 2009-10 spending plan, before it was signed on July 28, 2009. Due to the Great Recession (bank failures, mortgage foreclosures, and massive unemployment) the revenues collected by the state had declined dramatically. Neither Republican legislators nor Governor Schwarzenegger would agree to raise taxes, so substantial cuts were made to state spending. Spending for California's K-12 schools and community colleges was cut $6 billion, and the state's university systems lost $3 billion in funding. Some $4 billion were cut from in-home services and medical care for the elderly, the disabled, and the indigent. Despite these large reductions, the 2009-10 budget incorporated gimmicks in an effort to achieve balance. For example, the date for releasing paychecks for state workers was changed by one day, from June 30, 2010, to July 1, 2010, thereby shifting $1.2 billion in spending to the following fiscal year. The effects of the spending cuts were not shared by the entire population of the state: industry and affluent residents were spared tax increases, while the neediest in California suffered major cuts in services.

Unifying the California Executive

After 160 years of living with multiple elected executives in California, it is time for a change. Some of the elected executives may be eliminated, or executive powers can be fully consolidated in the governor's office. There are numerous reasons for unifying executive power in California.

In 1996, subsequent to hearing testimony and deliberating for nearly two years, the California Constitution Revision Commission put forth its final report. The commission recommended that the number of separately elected executives in California be reduced from eight to four: the lieutenant governor would be chosen in conjunction with the governor as part of a two-person ticket, and the treasurer, superintendent of public instruction, and insurance commissioner would be appointed by the governor instead of elected.[5] From 1978 to 1998, and during Governor Schwarzenegger's tenure from 2003 to 2009, the governor and the lieutenant governor were of different political parties. (Governor Schwarzenegger appointed a Republican, Abel Maldonado, to the post in 2010 after John Garamendi left the State Capitol for Congress.) The use of a ticket (similar to the presidential–vice presidential model on the national level) would assure that these two offices were held by people in the same party. Candidates for lieutenant governor could be named before or after the results of gubernatorial primary elections are known.

Beyond the matter of whether or not California should institute a two-person ticket, there is the question of whether California needs to elect a lieutenant governor at all. The office itself has few responsibilities, but as acting governor a lieutenant governor could create mischief in the absence of the governor from the state. With rapid methods of communication available, in a time when California's governors travel widely, should chief executives be deprived of their constitutional powers when they are outside of the state? As shown in Table 2, five states (Maine, New Hampshire, New Jersey, Tennessee, and West Virginia) do not have lieutenant governors. Either the president of the upper house or the speaker of the lower house of the state legislature may serve as chief executive should a governor leave office.

As indicated in Table 2, elected controllers (12) are much less common than elected treasurers (36), despite the California Constitution Revision Commission's recommendation to retain the former as an elective position. The superintendent of public instruction (14) and the insurance commissioner (10) are not especially common offices in other states. Since the SPI is not independent of the State Board of Education appointed by the governor, is it essential that this office remain elective?

Despite the Revision Commission's recommendations in 1996 to reduce the number of elected executives in California, the legislature never presented any constitutional amendments for consideration by voters in the state. In any event, reducing the number of elected executives from eight to four is only a partial corrective.

Comprehensive unification of the executive branch has more to recommend it than half-measures that would not completely consolidate executive power in California. By having the governor be the only elected executive in the state (with the power to make appointments to formerly elective posts), a unity of command would be established that clarifies ultimate accountability. When power is dispersed among eight elected executives, incumbents may pass the buck on thorny issues and avoid responsibility for problem solving.

TABLE 2. **Numbers of Elected Executive Positions throughout the U. S.**

Type of Position	Number of States with Position Elected
Governor	50
Lieutenant Governor	45
Attorney General	43
Treasurer	36
Secretary of State	34
Superintendent of Public Instruction	14
Controller	12
Insurance Commissioner	10

SOURCE: *The Book of the States* (Lexington, KY: The Council of State Governments, 2006, pp. 169+)

Would it be the members of the State Board of Education, the governor's education secretary, the superintendent of public instruction, or the actual governor who is accountable for the quality of education made available to youngsters in California?

With eight elected executives in California, it is too easy for that branch's powers to get embroiled in internal conflicts or a governor's functions to be stymied, perhaps by an executive officer from the opposition party. Democratic Treasurer Phil Angelides frequently disputed financial statements issued by Governor Schwarzenegger's office preceding their contest for the governorship in 2006. When Governor Schwarzenegger proposed cutting the K-12 education budget by $4 billion in early 2008, SPI Jack O'Connell commenced a speaking tour around the state to encourage opposition to the governor's reductions in school funding. Then late in 2009 Insurance Commissioner Steve Poizner (a fellow Republican) threatened to take the governor to court to prevent the sale and privatization of part of the workers' compensation fund. And in early 2010 Controller John Chiang and the governor squared off in court after an earlier fight over furloughing state employees, because Chiang refused to cut correctional officers' pay as Schwarzenegger ordered. Upon his return to elective state office as attorney general in 2006, former Governor Jerry Brown had commented as follows on his role.

New York Times: How do you feel about having to answer to a Republican governor?

> Jerry Brown: You don't answer to a governor. The attorney
> general is autonomous.
>
> *New York Times:* But isn't Schwarzenegger over you?
>
> Jerry Brown: No. The attorney general reports only to the
> people and to his conscience.[6]

The possibility of friction between a governor and an attorney general cannot be lightly dismissed. Except for departments with their own counsel, attorneys general are supposed to provide legal representation for departments and agencies that are under the governor's supervision. It is clear that Attorney General Brown did not believe he was bound by Governor Schwarzenegger's instructions. In American jurisprudence, clients ordinarily get to pick the attorney they wish. Because the state attorney general does not always provide the legal counsel that a chief executive might wish, governors have hired their own lawyers at extra expense to the state.

Electing eight separate executives has other drawbacks as well. It is no surprise that candidates for governor receive the bulk of the electorate's attention. Even if we assume that voters clearly grasp the responsibilities of each executive office, it is an open question whether candidates for the multiple elected executive positions have the necessary expertise to succeed in office. Controllers need not be CPAs, nor must state treasurers possess MBAs or advanced training in investments. Bill Lockyer did have a law degree when he served as attorney general (1998–2006), but what was his level of expertise regarding the duty he had in his role as treasurer to sell government bonds? The case of former State Senator Joe Dunn (D-Santa Ana) is instructive. Termed out of the state legislature in 2006, Dunn expressed interest in running for attorney general until Jerry Brown declared his candidacy for the position. Dunn then considered running for state treasurer, but former Attorney General Lockyer announced his intention to run for that office. Finally, Dunn decided to run in the Democratic primary for controller in 2006, which he lost to John Chiang. Joe Dunn obviously wanted to occupy executive office regardless of the qualifications needed in particular positions. Mr. Dunn finally was named the CEO of the California Medical Association, which lobbies for physicians at the State Capitol.

The limit of two terms (eight years) in each elected executive position leads officeholders to play musical chairs. Staffers on the state payroll are not allowed to engage in electioneering during work hours. Raising campaign funds and preparing political advertisements on state time are forbidden. On the other hand, answering constituent inquiries promptly and generating publicity for an elected executive's programs are permissible. The stepping-stone offices provide useful opportunities to improve an incumbent's visibility and name recognition. Holding an elected executive office is obviously an advantage when it comes to raising funds for future campaigns. When all is said and done, should the state of California be subsidizing elected executives on each step of their attempted journey to the corner office?

Having governors make appointments to the seven executive positions that are now elective has several advantages. First, governors are able to name appointees with the skills and expertise necessary for a particular office. Second, without seven would-be governors planning their routes to the corner office, there is less likely to be friction within the executive branch itself. Third, when a person who serves at the pleasure of the governor fails to perform up to expectations, the chief executive can remove him or her from office, which is much less cumbersome than forcing an elected executive to quit. Fourth, appointed executives need not devote attention to reelection to their present positions or to campaigning for another post in the future. Fifth, with seven fewer elective offices, fewer campaign funds would be needed and greater attention could be focused on the race for governor. Last, there is the problem of agency capture by outside interests, such as bond houses contributing heavily to candidates for state treasurer, or insurance companies giving large sums to campaigns for insurance commissioner. The chance of one group capturing the corner office, which receives funds from a multitude of interests, is less likely than in the case of the aforementioned offices.

An argument for retaining many elected executives is that it enhances diversity at the top ranks of state government. Upon examination, however, this viewpoint is not very convincing. Lt. Governor Cruz Bustamante (1998–2006) was the only Latino elected executive during the entire twentieth century. SPI Wilson Riles (1970–1982) and Lt. Governor Mervyn Dymally (1974–1978) were the only African American members of the elected executive, and there have been no others for over a quarter of a century. It is true that three Asian Americans and seven women have served in various offices of the elected executive (e.g., secretary of state, controller, treasurer, and SPI), but no women have ever held the elective offices of governor, lieutenant governor, or attorney general. By the use of gubernatorial appointments, California's chief executives have been able to diversify the upper levels of state government more quickly than through elections to the executive offices. Governors have appointed women to head such major entities as Caltrans, the Health and Human Services Agency, and the Air Resources Board. Women have served as chiefs of staff to governors of California. As mentioned earlier, Governor Jerry Brown appointed Rose Elizabeth Bird to be chief justice of the California Supreme Court in 1977. Today, three of the seven appointees to California's highest court are women. Unlike aspirants to positions in the elected executive, high-level appointees need not raise large amounts of campaign money for themselves or bother to hit the campaign trail.

Leadership in Troubled Times

The differences between the nineteenth and twenty-first centuries in California are profound. When the elected executives were written into the California constitution of 1849, there were only 107,000 residents of California. By 2009, some 38 million people resided in the state, with a total of 60 million inhabitants projected by 2050. We cannot anticipate comparable increases in precipitation levels, agricultural acreage, miles of beaches, or timberlands. While fears of a unified state executive can be traced to colonial times, the multiple-elected executive is now outmoded. What with recall elections, impeachment proceedings by the state legislature, and veto overrides, there are adequate means to deal with despotic governors. Given checks and balances provided by the legislative and judicial branches, there is no need for seven independently elected executives to limit the power of a governor still further. Moreover, organized groups and the press corps keep a close eye on governors as well. Considering the extraordinary challenges facing California today, the state's chief executive needs a unified administration.

The tasks confronting the state are immense. Some challenges arise within California itself, while others are the result of global developments. Educational achievement in the state's schools must be strong enough for California to compete in the global economy. Can the state train sufficient math and science teachers? Will the state develop the environmental and alternative energy industries of the future? Will immigrants be integrated into society and public safety be maintained? Will California manage to remedy its chronic budget deficits while avoiding costly long-term indebtedness? Will California's highways, bridges, and levees be maintained properly? Will the clarity of California's mountain lakes and the cleanliness of the state's beaches be preserved so that tourism can flourish? After water is allocated to urban users and to agriculture, will river flows still be sufficient for fish to spawn? With oil and gas less affordable and with traffic congestion more prevalent, will California build an effective mass transit system? Will California be able to save its wildlife habitats and agricultural land? And, what about the state's capacity to deal with catastrophes such as wildland fires, floods, and earthquakes?

The Global Warming Solutions Act of 2006 mentioned above is an example of the complex administrative challenges facing California. After Governor Schwarzenegger signed the bill, the Air Resources Board was assigned to write the regulations needed to implement it. The regulations took some two years to prepare, given the concerns of various carbon dioxide producers. Despite much consultation, the auto industry, energy companies and utilities, and cement makers may well file suits against the law's implementation. The executive branch in California will need to be highly skillful, persistent, and disciplined to achieve the objectives of this legislation.

Eliminating seven elected offices does not guarantee that solid candidates will run for governor in the future. The stronger the governorship is, however, the more likely it is to attract talented leaders. As world supplies of food, water, and oil become more scarce, Californians must select governors who are willing to speak hard truths, willing to resist entrenched interests, and willing to forego short-term popularity. Governors of California must be able to direct administrative teams that know how to solve complex problems. The justification for a fractured executive in California is no longer persuasive; the need for a unified executive is more apparent than ever.

Voting, Elections, and the Failure of Representation in California

R. Jeffrey Lustig

THE LEGISLATORS AND EXECUTIVE officers discussed in the last two chapters are elected to office and accountable to the state's citizens. That's what makes California a democracy. The different steps in the process that accomplishes this are familiar. Candidates are nominated, funds raised, campaigns run, primary and general elections held, and once representatives are chosen, laws are made and enforced. This chapter explains how this representative process is working today and argues that much of the state's current crisis can be traced to its flaws—from the way electoral districts are drawn to the overly expensive ways campaigns are run to the artificially narrow range of options offered by the two parties on election day. The result of it all is that one-half to two-thirds of the potential electorate does not feel inclined to vote in any given election. And this, I will propose, is the product rather than the cause of the system's problems. In conclusion the chapter proposes constitutional reforms to remedy the problems and expand the range of choices open to voters, ranging from a multiparty system to serious campaign contribution limits.

> *"The most powerful and perhaps the only means that we still possess of interesting men in the welfare of their country is to make them partakers in the government."*
> —TOCQUEVILLE, *DEMOCRACY IN AMERICA*

REPRESENTATION IS THE HEART of American democracy. And voting is at the center of representation. Governments derive their just powers from the consent of the governed, and Americans see the vote as conveying that consent. Each vote is supposed to count equally for one, and furthermore, no more than one. In the United States, as Tocqueville noted, "a majority governs in the name of the people."[1] Beyond voting, the process of representation also includes a number of other steps noted in chapter one: drawing electoral districts, formulating the ballot options, picking candidates, campaigning, lawmaking, implementing programs, and more.

California suffers a crisis of representation today. The most obvious sign of that crisis is the fact that most of its people do not vote. And those who do vote are distinguished from those who do not by factors of class and race. Any solution to the state's problems that overlooks this exclusion of the West Coast's blacks and Latinos and the poor of all races would not be a real solution to California's current political problems. Beyond nonvoting, the crisis of representation also derives from recent changes in party organization and campaign processes that have weakened the vote for everyone and begun to invert the representational relationship. Instead of the electorate picking the representative, the representative in many ways picks the electorate.

These flaws produce two paradoxes. First, although California is usually seen as a liberal state because of its policies on the environment, civil rights, and gay rights, its U.S. senators and most of its legislators, it remains in the grip of conservative politics on taxes, crime, affirmative action, and term limits. The second paradox is suggested by the remarks of one scholar that California's initiative-driven politics make the goal of "balanc[ing] the rights of the minority against those of the majority" impossible. "Measures that would protect...a minority against the majority's will" are defeated by the methods of initiative governance.[2] That sounds right at first; it is sometimes hard for minorities to protect themselves. And yet some minorities do prevail against the majority. We saw in chapter one that a minority of wealth, the top one hundred and fifty thousand people in the state, have increased their share of state income from 13.8 percent in 1993 to 25 percent today. And a small number of corporations got large tax breaks even in the midst of general economic distress in 2008 and 2009.[3]

How can conservative politics prevail in an ostensibly liberal state, and a minority thrive in a majoritarian era? These are paradoxes this chapter attempts to resolve. But first let us see how disenfranchisement works in California, how new party and campaign methods have bled voting in California of its expected power, and how the underrepresentation of some people's interests skews the formulation of the public good, which it is the responsibility of a republic to fulfill.

Parties in California

Political parties are the most visible promontories on the terrain of representation. Neither the federal nor California constitutions say how voting is to be organized, but political parties arose historically to fill the gap. The parties are private associations that perform crucial public tasks. They recruit candidates, frame platforms, run campaigns, propose bills for legislators to write, and round up the votes to pass them. They set up a linkage between citizens and government which offers a public alternative to the more hidden and exclusive linkage created by interest or pressure groups—mainly businesses and business groups, but now also unions, local governments, and a few public interest groups. Parties and pressure groups have been characterized as creating "two contrasting kinds of politics," "two different strategies of politics and two different concepts of political organization."[4]

Historically parties have collected, or "aggregated," different interests, an especially important function in as balkanized and disintegrated a place as California. In their internal caucuses, platform committees, and task forces they unite disparate interests into coherent platforms that can be represented by officeholders, and that also shape voters' political identities. They transform a multitude of private outlooks into a provisional statement of the public good.[5]

What enabled parties to do this historically in the U.S. and California, to attract a variety of groups to be unified in the first place and mobilize voters to support their platforms, was that they were mass organizations. Scores of local precinct workers were deployed by platoons of party operatives in places like San Francisco, San Jose, and downtown Los Angeles to rally the faithful, spread the word, and deliver an occasional turkey or sinecure to constituents. A network of clubs, newsletters, and local rallies surrounded these activities and provided the milieux in which thousands of people acquired an understanding of politics on a face-to-face basis.

California once had a lively collection of these sorts of parties—seven, for example, in 1854, including not only the Whig and Democratic but the intriguingly titled Customs House Whig, Citizens Reform [the Know-Nothings], Independent Citizen's, "Floating," and "Ciudado" parties. Twenty years later it had a different seven.[6] The class-conscious Workingman's Association issued the first call for the state's second constitutional convention, in 1879, and wound up with 51 of its 152 delegates. California passed the first primary law in the country in 1866, providing an option for party members, instead of backroom elites, to select candidates.

Under the electoral system described below and the effects of Progressive reforms, however, the number of California's parties declined and their powers ebbed. Angered by the complicity of party bosses with the Southern Pacific Railroad (the SP), the graft and corruption in which the parties were awash, and the gutting of the Railroad Commission that the 1879 constitution created to regulate the SP, Hiram Johnson and his colleagues defeated the SP's candidates via a strengthened law for holding primary elections. Coming into office in 1910, they immediately took aim at the parties, the tools of the predatory interests, rather than at those interests themselves. And they were thorough. They made city and county elections and the election of judges and school officials nonpartisan. They introduced cross-filing, which permitted a candidate of one party to run in the primaries of other parties, win the general election in the primary, and thereby deprive other parties and the populace of a general election. This cross-filing gave an overwhelming advantage to incumbents. It allowed Progressive and regular Republicans to maintain a hold on the governorship, except for one brief term, until 1959.[7]

But political nature abhors a vacuum and as California became a weak party state it also became a strong interest-group state, with the private power system distinctive of the latter. The state legislature of the 1940s provided for the full flowering of the private interest system dominated by the legendary Artie Samish who, Carey McWilliams noted, was a new kind of boss with a new type of machine. The old machines had been party organizations, "but in California [in 1949] there are no party machines; in fact, it is almost true to say that there are no parties":

> What Mr. Samish has done, therefore, is to convert the [system of] interest-group[s] into a machine which functions independently of the party...A party can be challenged at the polls, but as long as Artie controls the interest-groups his power is beyond dispute....Businessmen, not ward-heelers, are the lieutenants in the Samish machine."[8]

McWilliams added that "given the cross filing system and the trade association machines he controls, [Samish] can nominate and elect candidates in many districts...[for] nominal sums." Samish was eventually transferred to a less influential position in federal prison, but elements of his system lived on. That was made clear by the FBI "Shrimpgate" sting in the 1980s, and the conviction of Clay Jackson, chief lobbyist for the American Insurance Association, in 1993.

California's parties recovered some of their strength after World War II. Cross-filing was abolished in 1959 and the federal "one person/one vote" ruling in 1964 equalized representation in the state senate, substantially help-ing otherwise underrepresented urban populations and minority groups.[9] But even though the state's parties have become multimillion-dollar businesses today, with permanent staffs and a new group discipline, if not belligerence, in the legislature, the Progressive reforms have cast a long shadow. The par-ties remain weak in the electorate. They do not provide vital anchors for Californians' loyalties or identities as they do in other parts of the country, like New York, Massachusetts, and Illinois. In 2009, 44.6 percent of the California electorate was registered in the Democratic Party, and 31 percent in the Republican. Almost 25 percent of the electorate had no interest in affiliating with either major party.[10]

The Diminished Electorate

The starkest sign of California's flawed system of representation is that only one-third of Californians eligible to vote usually do, though up to one-half may turn out for presidential elections. In 2008, 23 million Californians were eligible to vote, but only 16.2 million were registered (70 percent). In the abnormally high-turnout Obama election of that year, only 60 percent of eligible Californians voted (78 percent of the registrants). In the presi-dential election of 2000, only 51.9 percent of those eligible voted. In 2002, when Gray Davis was reelected governor, only 35 percent of the eligibles voted, and the same percent cashiered him a year later and replaced him with Arnold Schwarzenegger.[11] The latter's slapdash initiatives to resolve the budget collapse of 2009 drew only 28 percent of registered voters. By contrast, characteristic voting rates elsewhere are: Italy, 90 percent; New Zealand, 88 percent; Israel, 80 percent; France, 76 percent; England, 76 percent; and the state of Minnesota, 78 percent.[12]

And the percentage of registered voters in this shrunken electorate keeps shrinking further. California's population has increased by almost 25 percent since 1990, but voter registration has grown by only 15 percent. While 65 percent of the adult population was registered in 1994, only 56 percent were in 2006.[13]

Equally troubling is the fact noted above that this diminished electorate is not representative of the population. Demographically, it differs from the larger population by factors of class, race, and age. Most of the usual voters in 2006 were homeowners (77%) with household incomes of over $60,000 (56%) and were college graduates (53%). But of the nonvoters, 66 percent were renters, 72 percent had household incomes less than $60,000, and only 17 percent were college graduates. The increasing economic inequality of the 1990s expanded the turnout gap between rich and poor from an insignificant 2 percent in 1988 to a full 20 percent by 1996.[14] That means that the ghettos and barrios of the state, the immigrant colonias, and poor white neighborhoods of the city are only sporadically represented.

In 1970, whites made up 74 percent of the state's population but almost 90 percent of the electorate. By 2006, as Ronald Schmidt notes in chapter seven, they were only 43 percent of the population but still counted for 67 percent of the electorate. Although whites will be only one-third of the state's population in 2040, if current trends hold they will still be a majority of the voters. At the same time, 32 percent of the state is Latino, but only one-sixth of the electorate is. About 6 percent of the turnout is African American and 7 percent Asian American.[15] Until the late 1990s more than half of the state's voters were over fifty, while only a third of its population was that old. The average age of voters dropped recently, but in 2006 almost 40 percent of the voters were still over forty. Thus, most of California's young are not voting. People over sixty, whose interests have turned to matters of security and health care rather than schools and public services, make up the bulk of the electorate.[16]

As might be guessed from these bare facts, those who vote also see things differently from the larger population. Those who do not vote regularly, for example, include more people who would prefer increased government services and would accept higher taxes to pay for them (66%), would like to see more spending on health and human services and public higher education (70%), and disapprove of Proposition 13 and term limits. At the local level they favor more funding for low-resource schools, even at the cost of other expenditures. "By far the top priority for Asians, African Americans, and Latinos is improving jobs and the economy; whites were the least likely to mention those issues as well as creating a more equal society," write Mark Baldessare and Jonathan Cohen in a Public Policy Institute of California report. Nonvoters are also more troubled by the lack of affordable housing. They favored a 2006 affordable housing bond by 80 percent, while less than half of homeowners (49%) did. Job programs and affordable housing are not, however, the topics one hears reported on the evening news. The scope of issues on which people in different income groups diverge is, one national study concludes, "much larger and more widespread" than previously thought.[17]

In a republic a majority is entrusted to govern in the name of the people. But all this means that California is governed today by a de facto minority—

a "majority" of only a third of the population eligible to vote (perhaps 17 percent) speaking in the name of the whole. This is hardly what people mean when they talk about a democracy. By not recording the needs of all the groups in the population this process also prevents the system as a whole from accurately determining the common good. What is called "public policy" winds up not being fully public but representing a range of more private interests—in tax policy, environmental programs, public services, and more. "A public sphere from which specific groups [are] excluded," the German political theorist Jürgen Habermas notes, is "less than merely incomplete; it [is] not a public sphere at all."[18]

There are two Californias, then, and a minority sets the political and social agendas for the majority. Leon Bouvier and Philip Martin's 1985 prediction about the emergence of a two-tier economy finds complementary confirmation in the rise of a two-tier polity, one group possessing effective political voice while the other does not. Political leaders are also put in a fix of having to win votes and maintain support from a narrowing top tier while also being expected to resolve the problems of the whole society, which includes a broad though unrepresented bottom tier. The result is obvious, though only noted by the rare political scientist: instead of equal representation there is an "inequality in the response of government policy-makers to the...different subgroups in the population." Policy outputs "differ from what a more democratic system would produce."[19]

Small surprise, then, that California leaders for the past twenty years have given short shrift to the needs of the poor, the young, and the disadvantaged during annual budget negotiations. Nor is it a surprise that long-term racial disparities persist, belying the expectations kindled by the election of minority legislators. At the moment of triage because of inadequate funds, the system cannot provide for each person to count for one and only one. Some people's votes count for a good deal more than one at that point, while others' votes count for nothing.

California began as a state by formally barring African Americans and Chinese from the vote, informally excluding Mexican Americans and, until quite recently, imposing racial restrictions in housing and other areas. Even though such overt racism no longer exists on the West Coast, institutionalized racism remains. And the election of an occasional black, Latino, or member of another marginalized community does not change that. It does not change it because the problems are structural, not individual. A single elected leader may look like others from his or her community and provide an instance of what Hanna Pitkin calls "descriptive representation." But that does not mean that the community has been empowered. In Pitkin's terms, the new legislator may *stand for* his or her constituents without necessarily *acting for* them.[20] The only real remedy for the situation is to get rid of the structural conditions which prevent the community from having the power to have its interest represented in the first place. And that's much harder than electing single candidates, or even getting others to be tolerant, for that matter.

What causes the low voting rates and prevents equal representation in California? Explanations over the years have suggested everything from apathy to ignorance to the nonvoters' supposed happiness with things the way they are. It is more fruitful to look at what the vote actually is in the current context of representation—to look at where it is cast, how it is cast, and what it is cast for. Once we understand the electoral district, the winner-take-all system, and the changing character of California's political campaigns, we will understand how the vote has been weakened for everyone in the Golden State, and why some of its communities do not expect much from the voting booth.

The Context of the Vote

Districting and redistricting. Voting is often said to be the first step on the road to representation. But that is not quite right. The first step is the creation of the district in which the vote will be cast, the building of that road. That determines how the individual vote will be counted, and what it will mean for the system as a whole.

California's 120 legislative districts and its congressional districts are redrawn every ten years according to criteria of shared community, continuity of boundaries, compactness, and rough equality of numbers. A decennial redesign is necessary because California's population reshuffles itself so often. During World War II immigrants poured into Los Angeles, Oakland, and San Francisco to work in shipyards, airplane factories, and branch plants of General Motors and Goodyear Tire. In the early nineties, in the wake of plant closures in defense and other industries, many moved into the Central Valley and Inland Empire. The redistricting criteria sound technical and scientific. But determining which "communities" count and what is "compact" are highly political decisions. For example, even after the one person/one vote ruling was made in 1964, exclusionary racial districting continued in California. Los Angeles County, with three million Latinos making up a third of its population, lacked a Latino county supervisor for over a century because districts were intentionally drawn to break up the voting power of the Latino community. After a U.S. District judge finally ordered this changed in 1990,

Gloria Molina was elected, the first Mexican American to belong to the body governing the largest county in the nation.[21]

What makes the situation especially questionable in California is that the redistricting process has always been done by sitting legislators. And these have an interest in drawing "safe seats" to benefit themselves or their party. Lumping the bulk of the other party's votes into curiously shaped districts that resemble Rorschach tests will save a future candidate a lot of money at campaign time. It will also assure that all but one or two sitting legislators in California will always be returned to office. This "partisan gerrymandering" has been upheld by the courts, though racial gerrymandering to remedy the effects of past discrimination and benefit minority candidates has been struck down as unconstitutional.

This incumbent-oriented redistricting is objectionable on a number of grounds besides the obvious one of permitting individuals to rig the game for themselves. It insulates the parties from changing trends in the society. In the new districts where there is little competition, extremists may be elected who can win office without ever having to talk to voters from the other party and who may then create partisan stalemates in the legislature. Instead of helping conduce to the representation of the society as a coherent whole, the effect of this kind of redistricting, according to political scientist Bruce Cain, is to "move in the direction of incoherent, self-interested particularism."[22] State voters in 2008 created an independent commission to take over the redistricting, as described in chapter four. Whether or not it will be able to chart a different course, given its complicated structure and required methods, remains to be seen.

One last development is affecting how these districts are formed in California. State electoral districts in America have always been geographically based. And political researcher Frédérick Douzet finds strange things happening to California's political geography. The state is becoming balkanized by residential mobility into small, relatively homogenous electoral enclaves. These exurbs, ghettos, barrios, and gated communities wind up isolated in their political views from their contiguous regions. As a result, though more ethnically and economically diverse as a whole, California is paradoxically becoming more segregated in its parts. Not only poor immigrants but long-term residents and the wealthy are self-segregating. Douzet points out that the notably diverse Bay Area is "one of the most segregated places in California." Levels of voter turnout are also shifting in the state's different regions, rising in the increasingly conservative inland counties and falling in coastal areas like Los Angeles.[23] Douzet predicts that the tendency for districts to produce extremists who are not used to speaking to a diverse constituency will therefore increase, especially in the Central Valley, where conservative self-segregation is pronounced. This trend will consign the electoral losers in those enclaves to political insignificance and, she predicts, "contribute...to the increasing gap between California's electorate and the state's population."[24]

All of these things affect the electoral district and how the individual vote will be weighted by the larger electoral system before the voter even steps into the voting booth.

The electoral system and party system. The eventual significance of votes is also dramatically affected by the single-member plurality electoral system that California and the rest of the nation use. It is "single-member" because the districts each elect only one representative. It is "plurality" because the candidate with the most votes represents *all* the voters. If there are only two candidates in a race, the candidate with 50 percent of the votes plus one wins. Those who vote for the losing candidate are not guaranteed any representation: their votes are usually wasted. Nor do the issues they might have raised get a hearing. The minority communities of the state often suffer from problems others do not (for example, the siting of environmentally hazardous incinerators in their neighborhoods). And some of these problems will soon be suffered by other citizens more widely (like cancer from certain agricultural pesticides). In both cases the problems should be heard in the legislature. But if those who suffer from them lack a political voice, they will not be.

This electoral arrangement virtually guarantees a two-party system as the French political scholar Maurice Duverger noted long ago, likening the causal relation to a "law."[25] Political recognition is denied third or fourth parties that get smaller fractions of the vote, even if they reflect real segments of public opinion. That is not the way it is in most democratic countries in the world. If the Greens in Germany attract only 10 percent of the vote, they get 10 percent of the seats in the national legislature. That is because Germany has a multiparty proportional representation system. In the 1980s, this permitted the Greens to seat legislators, join a governing coalition, and have a real influence on national legislation. If the Greens in California, by contrast, get 10 percent of the vote they get no representation in the legislature, accomplish nothing institutionally, and lack the opportunity to grow into a majority party. To put it differently, even though Californians are increasingly dissatisfied with the state's Democrats and Republicans, they will have no chance to choose a viable new party to represent their needs as long as the state retains the present winner-take-all electoral procedure.

This also indicates something about the party system as a whole. So far we have been discussing the state's two major parties. But they are linked together into a party *system* that also has important functions. Over the course of the nation's history different party systems have offered voters different menus of choices so the voters could make their preferences known. The political scientist Walter Dean Burnham identified five successive party systems in national politics, each lasting for about thirty-six years—the Experimental System of 1789 to 1820, the Democratizing system of 1828 to 1860, and so forth.[26] Such movements from one party system to the next keep the electoral process flexible and, by periodically offering voters new menus of choices, make it possible for them to express their changing priorities. In one period people may be divided by disputes about regulating corporate power, in another desegregation and school busing, in a third, taxation or immigration.

If periodic shifts in the mix of options do not occur for some reason, then this two-party dynamic freezes up, the electoral choices cease to represent people's real concerns, and the parties cease to be seen by the voters as real vehicles of their consent. When that happens a gap opens up between the campaign issues and the society's real problems. Solutions to people's real problems are kept off the ballot. This is what has happened in California. The state's two-party monopoly has prevented an airing of many people's real political concerns. Aside from global warming—the remedies for which have yet to be implemented—California's party agendas remain mostly what they were in 1975, before deindustrialization and the budget crisis occurred. Lacking effective competition, the major parties have no reason to alter their basic platforms to represent the state's new issues.

The New Campaign. Eighty years ago, California pioneered the media-based, candidate-centered, and expensive methods of campaigning used now by the whole nation. Clem Whitaker launched the new era in 1933 with Campaign, Inc., which he created to help harvest votes for candidates and initiatives from the arriving crop of immigrants who lacked established loyalties in a state with weak parties. Central to Whitaker's effort was the new occupation of campaign consultant, a political mercenary who would plan campaign strategies for a fee, write speeches, prepare press releases, and dig up needed facts, pseudo-facts, and wholly spurious facts as needed. The latter were inaugurated by false newsreels scripted in Hollywood's back lots to discredit socialist Upton Sinclair, the 1934 Democratic candidate for governor. The model behind it all was marketing, with the new consultants boasting they could sell a candidate like a bar of soap. Communications technology was central to their effort.

Buying advertising in California media markets and producing photo opportunities and staged video clips costs hundreds of thousands of dollars, especially when accompanied, as these campaigns are, by extensive polling and focus groups that slice and dice the electorate into narrow niches defined by wealth, race, age, job, and social tastes (e.g., soccer moms, NASCAR dads, "waitress moms," and Starbucks habitués in contrast to the folks at Dunkin' Donuts) in order to manipulate their political buying habits.

The victors in the 2008 state senate election cycle in California raised an average of $1.1 million each. Assembly victors raised an average of $800,000.[27] That was an average and includes lower amounts for safe districts. One assembly candidate for a competitive district spent $4.5 million in 2004, for a job that paid only $99,000 a year. One senate contender raised $2.2 million and another raised $1.6 million, in addition to what their political parties contributed. In 2006, two gubernatorial candidates together spent $56.9 million in unsuccessful races.[28]

These are immense amounts of money. No ordinary working person can afford them. In fact, the parties cannot afford them either. The task has therefore fallen to wealthy candidates and interest groups. This leads in California, as nationally, to candidate-centered rather than party-centered campaigns. Modern election campaigns focus on candidates' personalities rather than on party platforms. A Gray Davis, Arnold Schwarzenegger, Jerry Brown, or Meg Whitman is relatively independent of the parties. Candidates like them win their nominations because of the size of their electoral war chests, though they may occasionally be beaten by lesser millionaires. It is these wealthy candidates and their consultants—not the parties—who now define the platforms. But to maintain sufficient funding even they need to supplement their own reserves from the only source they can—industries and interest groups. California Republicans look to organizations like the chambers of commerce, the utilities, and the Farm Bureau. Democrats look to unions, Hollywood, and minority-group organizations. And both parties look to real estate developers, oil interests, high-tech and biotech industries, and AT&T. (In 2008, the latter donated directly to 111 of the state's 120 lawmakers, of both parties.)[29] This explains why fund-raising has become a continuous activity for incumbents and would-be incumbents.

The situation alters the function of modern campaigns, however, from what citizens expect and democratic theory proposes. According to those expectations, campaigns are contests in which candidates present their positions to electors, a lively give-and-take occurs, and the voters—perhaps even the candidates—acquire an education in the course of choosing the most reasonable and promising positions. Television and radio, which help in this, are called communications media.

But communication is a two-way process, whereas the media actually provide for only a one-way process. This latter is therefore more accurately understood as *transmission*. The media's function in the new campaign is to transmit a sales pitch by the clever use of images rather than real information about the quality of the product being sold. One sign of the new situation is that political consultants regularly instruct candidates to keep their terms vague and avoid substantive explanations so as not to alienate independents and crossover voters. The young Governor Jerry Brown mastered the technique early and called the key terms "buzzwords." James Lorenz, an official in his administration, explained that buzzwords, "when spoken to a particular audience, would summon up in their minds a series of associations that were never directly stated by the speaker." They amounted, Lorenz went on to say, to a form of hype. And the purpose of sales pitches and hype is not, it must be noted, to sustain a democratic relationship between citizens and representatives. A democratic relationship involves a conversation, an education, and ultimately the constituent's authorization of the representative's actions. The essence of a sales approach is manipulation, and the salesman sets the goals before he ever meets his mark.

The effect of this new campaigning in California, as could be predicted, has been to further hobble party structures already weakened by the Progressives' measures. They not only no longer control nominations. They also are no longer mass organizations. They do not have active and ongoing precinct organizations and workers that can attract new generations of voters. And rather than aggregating different interests, their method of sending simplified pitches to different niches of the population has disaggregated and atomized those interests more seriously. The parties have ceased to play any educational role. For most people they are no longer organizations in which members can learn as part of their daily activity about the larger society of which their concerns are part.

As a result of these various changes California's party system has wound up not as an alternative to the interest-group system but as an expression of it. And that means that the main choices offered on the ballot are limited to a narrow spectrum of social possibilities acceptable to the private interests. "[T]he public face of politics," two seasoned Capitol hands explain, "the campaigns that pander to various constituencies, the legislative hearings, the debates on bills, the news conferences and media events—are just for show.…[L]obbyists represent the real focus of the Capitol that most of the public doesn't even know exists."[30] One proof is the fact that despite the hard-fought public battle to preserve funding for schools and health services in the 2008–09 budget negotiations, Democratic legislators joined Republicans in approving corporate tax breaks, further depleting already paltry state coffers.

The solution to the paradoxes noted at the beginning of this chapter begins to become clear. A conservative minority has been able to maintain its power in California despite the Republican Party's low registration, not only because of the two-thirds rule for passing budgets and new taxes (discussed in chapter three), and not only because their mastery of the initiative process (addressed in chapter four) has led to the enactment of conservative measures on tax limits, criminal sentencing, term limits, affirmative action, immigration, and same-sex marriage. Conservative power is maintained more fundamentally by the nature of the electorate itself as refracted through a dysfunctional party system. In the absence of changes to the state's electoral procedures and party structures, that power may be expected to increase in the near future because of changes in the state's political geography. Conservatives' cohesiveness in the inland counties will enable them to act more effectively than the fragmented Democrats on the coast.[31]

Because the cost of campaigning in California is so high and private funders are necessary to help pay it, California's party system is failing to present real choices on the issues of central concern to large sectors of the population. No politician in recent years has raised the eminently desirable proposal for public works jobs, despite the state's exceptionally high rates of job loss and poverty. No politician has promoted a public takeover of the private utilities to prevent profit-taking off of necessities, once a live issue in the state. And when a few leaders in 2008 raised the idea of charging oil companies royalties for resources taken from the public domain, as do all other oil-producing states, the proposal was quickly defeated.

Some commentators, wishing to appear evenhanded, spread the blame for this broadly, from intransigent anti-tax Republicans on one hand to the state's unions on the other. But most unions cannot really afford this game. The California Teachers Association and the Service Employees International Union are exceptions. They are among the top twenty current contributors to candidates' campaigns. And California has a higher rate of unionized labor, at 18 percent, than most other states, and did have notable organizing victories in the 1990s, launched by a revived Los Angeles Central Labor

Council.[32] But labor strength in recent decades has been confined to a few sectors and its actions have been mostly defensive—trying to prevent wage and benefit cuts and the deregulation of labor laws. Whatever its imputed strength, labor has not been able to stop the wealthy interests' increased control of the state's income nor impede the class polarization described in chapter one. And most of the unions involved in efforts to raise minimum wages, prevent further cuts to school funding, and maintain checks and balances on the job are not special interests strictly speaking, but are working in the public interest.

Summary: The Citizen as Subject

The powers of the California voter are thus quite circumscribed. The coalescence of the party and interest-group systems has greatly limited the choices available on the ballot. Individual voters do not determine the electoral district in which they vote, the electoral system that vindicates or nullifies their vote, or what they vote for. On the model of the marketplace, they are essentially consumers of others' products. They are what older political thinkers called "subjects," not citizens. Subjects only obey laws; citizens also help create them.[33]

The German poet and playwright Bertolt Brecht once imagined a situation in which the people had "forfeited the confidence of the government" and asked:

> Would it not be easier
> In that case for the government
> To dissolve the people
> And elect another?"[34]

California's governing elites have come up in effect with the same idea and have been trying to accomplish the feat for years. Instead of being picked by the voters, they reach into the electorate and, aided by polling, focus groups, and targeted ads, pick the voters who support their positions.

That, finally, also explains the state's incredible shrinking electorate. To bring the point into sharper focus it helps to remember Burnham's widely noted explanation for the aftereffect of the famous 1896 presidential election, in which Democrat William Jennings Bryan, who was supported by the populist movement, lost to William McKinley. Electoral turnout for presidential votes in the United States, which until then averaged 79 percent and reflected "the most thoroughly democratized [political system] in the world," after 1896 plummeted to 66 percent, and then descended to 50 percent by 1920. Burnham attributed the post-Populist voting decline to the rapid exclusion from the electoral agenda of issues of central concern to small farmers and the new urban working class. The loss of voters, he concluded, transformed what had been a democratic system into "a rather broadly based oligarchy."[35]

A similar process is happening more slowly in California today. Large parts of the population are effectively disenfranchised because the issues that are of critical importance to their lives—jobs, affordable housing, restored public clinics and hospitals, and more—are excluded from the ballot as the elites "dissolve the people and elect another." The lack of active parties that would involve people in their meetings and activities adds to the alienation. The conclusion that emerges from this analysis is that nonvoting is not the cause of California's problems of representation but their product. Parties are not weak because voters don't vote; voters don't vote because the parties are weak. And people don't appreciate the aura of manipulation that surrounds electoral activities. The problem, again, is fundamentally institutional. And no amount of scolding nonvoters, no quick fixes like "motor voter" registration or rapid registration of newcomers will resolve it. The only hope for improving voting levels and reviving a genuine democracy lies in structural reform of the state's electoral institutions.

Direction for Change

It is clear from this account that California needs to do two things to remedy its crisis of representation. It needs to engage all groups in the population in its politics and to strengthen the power of the vote. Without the "habit of self-government," furthermore, the perceptive Tocqueville observed, "it is difficult to conceive how men...should make a proper choice of those by whom they are to be governed." In order to accomplish the above two things it is also necessary, then, to resuscitate habits of self-government, and the place to do that, as the pre-Madisonian, civic republicans knew, is in local participatory forums—the sole place it is also possible for people to acquire an education in the public good. Thomas Jefferson followed their lead and greatly admired the local wards in Virginia because they let "people be partakers in government" and provided the political education necessary for republican government. They provided ways for "the mass of the people [to be raised] to the high ground of moral responsibility necessary to their own safety and to orderly government."[36] Similarly, Tocqueville saw the New England townships teaching people "the nature of their duties and the extent of their rights" and culminating in "the art of being free."

Some of California's small towns and independent big-city neighborhoods always provided for this kind of involvement and education. And California's famous experimental colonies and cooperative societies sought to provide for them historically.[37] But such participation is no longer provided in the mainstream of the state's political life, and its absence is taking a toll on the state's character as a democratic political system.

Some may doubt that the face-to-face discourse involved in people's handling of their public affairs is really necessary in the computer era, given the speed with which large volumes of information can be transmitted electronically and by the Internet. But democratic citizens need more than mountains of information. They need a frame of mind that can think intelligently about politics, and organize and interpret what information they get. And that can only be learned by participation and interaction in the public sphere. The intellectual historian Christopher Lasch made the point when he noted, "What democracy requires is public debate, not information.... We do not know what we need to know until we ask the right questions, and we can identify the right questions only by subjecting our own ideas about the world to the test of public controversy."[38] Without local forums for public debate, Californians will not be able to learn what they need to know and will not be able to take charge of representation, and the existing electorate will continue to shrink.

What else might provide for participation on the West Coast today? Strengthened party organizations for one thing—and parties open to the concerns of the whole population. Campaign finance reforms are also needed to stanch the influence of private power.

Some have also urged that the state adopt open primaries. In these people vote in the primary election of any party no matter what party they are registered in. The general election then pits the top two vote-getters against each other, regardless of their party affiliations. Proponents of this reform say it would cure the partisan deadlock that has paralyzed the legislature because moderates, instead of extremists, would then be elected. Before such a reform is adopted, however, Californians need to decide what they want for the future of their political parties. If they want to strengthen parties and party competition, open primaries are not the way to go. Letting people who are not registered in a party, and may even oppose it, perform its core function of nominating candidates is a sure way to destroy, not strengthen, the state's Democratic and Republican organizations. This idea is heir to the state's Progressive anti-party tradition and reminiscent of cross-filing.[39] It would also effectively abolish the private and autonomous status of political parties in the state. If successful, open primaries would produce a bland agenda in the middle of the current electoral spectrum. What is needed by contrast is a broader agenda that includes the new policy options noted above.

Rather than constricting its electoral options, California needs to expand them. The way to do that is not with open primaries but through a multiparty system with proportional representation. A larger number of parties would open up the system to new ideas, new political formations, and increased citizen participation. With proportional representation, legislative seats would be awarded according to the percentage of the popular vote a party wins (see chapter ten). All but three of the world's democracies use a form of this system. These systems also introduce multiple-member districts, which provide a reprieve from the gerrymandering which is inevitable with single-member districts, Lani Guinier notes, because they require "the arbitrary allocation of disproportionate political power to one group." The latter also arbitrarily decides "whose votes get wasted."[40]

Many forms of proportional representation exist, but all provide recognition for many points of view, avoid wasting votes, and avoid the arbitrariness of redistricting. People *group themselves* on the basis of their political orientation, rather than being grouped by others according to where they temporarily reside.

The most basic reform necessary to increase participation, however, is to strengthen local government. A system of representation cannot exist without a politically experienced public; and active political parties and local participatory bodies are the ways to acquire that experience. The American founders themselves received their education in politics by participating in colonial Houses of Burgesses and revolutionary state governments, as limited and exclusionary as those forums were. In the framework they designed for the nation, however, they did not provide means for such participation to their successors. This is an oversight for which California, with its great size, social heterogeneity, and current challenges, finally needs to provide a remedy. A new constitution needs to return to local governments many of the powers removed from them in the wake of Proposition 13.

A true republic represents not only private interests but also the public good, and requires that citizens appreciate not only private needs but mutual obligations. The fact that California in recent years has done a poor job of eliciting this sense of shared responsibility among its citizens and leaders should be of major concern to constitutional reformers. To rekindle a concern for the common good—indeed to elicit that concern in the first place in such a heterogeneous and constantly unsettled society—people need to participate in public affairs. That is the essential precondition for repairing California's flawed system of representation.

PART III

Effects of the Crisis:
A Changing California

SEVEN

Immigration, Diversity, and the Challenge of Democratic Inclusion

Ronald Schmidt, Sr.

THE LAST THREE CHAPTERS explained the flaws of three basic institutions of California government—its legislature, executive, and party system. We can also see the depth and extent of California's political crisis by looking beyond these institutions to policy efforts to tackle the state's key problems. The next three chapters take that look and show how the state's political dysfunctions undermine its ability to successfully address a problem of changing demographics, a problem of settled community, and a key problem of the natural environment. We will examine the issues of immigration in chapter seven, of urban development in the barrio of East L.A. in chapter eight, and of water allocation in chapter nine.

In the first of these Ronald Schmidt describes how the constant arrival of new people has added to the diversity, energy, and cultural richness of California society but has also led to ongoing problems of providing services, jobs, and inclusion for the newcomers. This has been the case particularly when the immigrants were members of racial or ethnic groups who suffered discrimination in California. The politics of immigration in the state have long been interwoven with those of racial discrimination. The problems are also aggravated when the newcomers lack the formal documents for entry, though the state was historically lax about such things, especially for the original Anglos, and immigrants who worked in the state's agriculture.

The conflicts that surround inclusion have arisen historically not only between insiders and outsiders, like the current battles at the border, but also within those groups over matters of civic membership, group identity, and economic justice. They have erupted in recent years sporadically over language policy, provision of benefits to the undocumented, and affirmative action. In this chapter, Schmidt explains the current makeup of immigration into the state, the political questions it poses, and why—faced with the certainty of a continuing influx and the reality of diminished resources—California needs to design a new constitutional approach to immigrant inclusion.

Ronald Schmidt, Sr., is a professor of political science at California State University, Long Beach, author of *Language Policy and Identity Politics in the United States*, and coauthor of *Newcomers, Outsiders, and Insiders: Immigrants and American Racial Politics in the Early Twenty-First Century*. He writes on immigration, Latino politics, and language policy in the U.S. and Canada and is a former president of the Western Political Science Association.

California's Political Demography

RACIAL AND ETHNIC diversity, racial discrimination, and migration have all been prominent parts of California's story throughout its history. The story in this chapter, however, begins with an important change in U.S. immigration law, adopted in 1965. This new law eliminated an older immigration policy that had discriminated in favor of immigrants coming from Northern Europe, and the 1965 revision ushered in a period of high migration to the United States. In addition, it brought a dramatic change in the origins of U.S. immigrants: from mostly European to mostly Latin American and Asian.[1] Nowhere in the United States have these changes been more pronounced than in California. According to the U.S. Census Bureau, California's population in 1970 was 77 percent (non-Hispanic) "white," 12 percent Latino, 3 percent Asian-origin, and 7 percent black.[2] But about a decade ago, California became the first "minority majority" state in the mainland United States. By 2005, California's "white" population had dropped to 43 percent of the state's residents, while the Latino/Hispanic population had grown to 36 percent, and the Asian American population had increased to more than 12 percent. The African American population remained fairly constant at 6 percent.[3] Demographers estimate that within the next couple of decades, California's Latino population will exceed the European-origin population.

This dramatic increase in California's ethnic and racial diversity in recent decades has been driven primarily by international migration. Indeed, those keeping track of the upsurge in immigration to the United States following the 1965 revision of the country's immigration law quickly noticed that California had become the primary destination state for immigrants in the late twentieth century. While the U.S. Census Bureau found that California's foreign-born population made up 8.8 percent of the state's residents in 1970,[4] by 2005 it had increased to 27.7 percent, compared to 12.4 percent for the U.S. as a whole in that year. That was nearly 10 million people.[5] Further, while California has about 10 percent of the country's population, it has been home to at least one-fourth of the nation's foreign-born population since the 1970s.

Another dimension of the state's ethnic diversity is that California is the state with the largest number and the highest percentage of homes in which English is not the language usually spoken. Thus, the same 2005 U.S. Census Bureau survey found that nearly 14 million California residents—some 42 percent of the state's population—usually speak a language other than English in the home.[6] Two-thirds (66.7%) of these usually speak Spanish in the home, making it by far the dominant non-English language spoken in California. The next largest language group is Chinese speakers, who comprise 6.6 percent of those who usually speak a language other than English in the home.[7]

As a result, California also has the largest number of public school students coming from non-English-speaking homes. The California State Department of Education found that in the 2005-06 school year, 43 percent of the state's 6.3 million public school students (K-12) were from homes in which English is not the language usually spoken, and of these 79 percent were native Spanish speakers. And 85 percent of the public school students who had not yet been certified as "English language fluent" were Spanish speakers.[8]

These rapid demographic changes in the state have helped generate a large gap between what journalist Dan Walters once referred to as the "sociological" and the "political" populations of California.[9] As Table 1 indicates, in the 2006 California state election over two-thirds (67%) of the state's voters were "white," or Anglo, while this group made up only 43 percent of the state's overall population. Meanwhile, California's Latino and Asian/Pacific Islander populations were significantly underrepresented among voters, with Latinos making up 36 percent of the state's population but only 17 percent of its voters, and Asian/Pacific Islanders making up 12 percent of the population but only 9 percent of the voters. Only the black population's number of voters was similar to the group's proportion of the state population.

Table 1 shows this and also indicates that the California legislature is somewhat more descriptively representative of the state's most significant ethno-racial population groups than are the state's voters. (By "descriptive

TABLE 1. **California Political Demography, Voting, and Representation (2006)**

Group	Percentage of Population	Percentage of Voters (2006)	Percentage of Legislators
Whites	43	67	52
Blacks	6	6	7
Latinos	36	17	22
Asian/Pacific Islanders	12	9	5

SOURCES: Census Bureau, Current Population Survey; Census Bureau, American Community Survey; California State Legislative Caucuses.

representation," we mean that the legislature is proportionately similar to the general population, reflecting the major ethnic and racial groups in the state.) This is due mainly to two factors. First, judicial rulings have required that all "persons" be counted (not just citizens or voters) for purposes of drawing up legislative districts, which means that noncitizen immigrants are "represented" by legislators even if they cannot vote for their legislators. Thus, even though many immigrants are not citizens, and therefore cannot vote, they are still counted for purposes of drawing up legislative districts. And second, judicial interpretations of, and congressional amendments to, the Voting Rights Act of 1965 have required California to draw legislative district boundaries so as to maximize the chances of black, Latino, and Asian American voters of electing representatives of their choice. Since Latinos and blacks live in relatively segregated residential neighborhoods throughout the state, this means that California has a number of so-called "majority minority" legislative districts (not true for Asian/Pacific Islanders because they tend to be much more integrated residentially). But while California's racial minorities enjoy a greater degree of legislative representation than in the past, this does not mean that the problem of democratic inclusion has been successfully addressed in the state, a point that will be discussed below.

To summarize, California continues to experience a situation in which large numbers of Latinos and Asian/Pacific Islanders are not able to participate formally in the state's political processes. To a large degree, this exclusion is due to the immigrant origins of many of the state's Latinos and Asian/Pacific Islanders. Thus, nearly 60 percent of California's foreign-born population—some 4.5 million people—remained noncitizens in 2005 and therefore were excluded from voting as well as from a variety of other formal means of political involvement under current California law,[10] though

California in the past and some states today let noncitizens vote in some local elections.

What's at Stake?

Does this exclusion of major segments of California's populace from voting matter? Yes, for at least three reasons. First, despite the fact that there is a higher proportion of Latinos and Asian/Pacific Islanders in the legislature than among the state's voters, these groups continue to be *underrepresented among public officials*. As Table 1 indicates, Latinos in 2006 made up 36 percent of the state's population, but only 22 percent of California's state legislators. Similarly, Asian/Pacific Islanders made up 12 percent of the state's population, but only 5 percent of its legislators. While there is no guarantee that descriptive representation will lead to effective substantive representation, it seems hard to imagine that effective substantive representation can be achieved in a diverse political community when politically important groups are disproportionately absent from among its public authorities.

And the matter is not helped by having legislative representatives who are elected by only a small percentage of their districts' residents because many people in the district are ineligible to vote (an outcome of the requirement that districts be made up of equal numbers of persons, whether citizens or not). This sort of representation all too easily leads to a distortion in the political priorities of the state, as electoral accountability is confined to a small proportion of those represented.

A second cause for concern is that the *public policies* adopted by the state may not match the needs of its people and their future when much of its population is barred from formal political participation. That is, it is important for all segments of a polity to be represented in deliberations about public policy because it is impossible for public authorities to know what is best for the community's people and those authorities lack ways to understand and communicate with all segments of the polity's population. How can those who control the state's public policy-making institutions, if they are, for example, disproportionately old, white, and economically well-off, possibly know how to craft policies that meet the needs of the state's people as a whole? And what incentive do they have to pay attention to the needs of those with whom they have little personal contact—for example, those who are relatively young and have young children, those whose life experiences have included ethno-racial stigmatization and discrimination, those who have great difficulty finding and keeping jobs that provide adequate resources for housing, transportation, food, health care, etc.? And this does not take account of an additional obstacle to good public policy: the all-too-human propensity to believe that one's own experiences and understandings are "normal," while those of others who are "different" are less true or important or meaningful.

Third, as noted above, in a political culture based at least in part on the value of democratic consent, *regime legitimacy* must be undermined by this divergence between California's population as a whole and those eligible to participate in its formal political processes. Indeed, the combination of the lack of political representativeness and the lack of responsiveness to policy concerns of a growing segment of the population is a sure-fire formula for diminished legitimacy in *any* political culture. To the extent that California's political system becomes perceived as unrepresentative of its population, its legitimacy and future stability must surely be in doubt.[11] In the absence of democratic consent and inclusive public participation Californians cannot claim to have a government that lives up to its own public values of democratic equality and fairness.

California's Political Reaction: Forty Years of Failed Inclusion

How has the politically engaged portion of California's population reacted to becoming the country's core destination for immigrants, and the associated increased ethnic and racial diversity? I will examine the subject by exploring the reactions of California's voters through the initiative process established by the Progressive reforms adopted in the early twentieth century.[12] This is the process enabling California's citizens—or, at least the political entrepreneurs among them—to circulate petitions calling for a vote on a proposed new state law or constitutional amendment (see Christopher Witko's explanation in chapter four). A sufficient number of valid signatures places the proposed policy on the next state ballot, thereby enabling a majority of "the people" (who vote) to establish state law without going through the relatively elaborate legislative checks and balances of the State Capitol.

Some of California's most far-reaching and important public policies on immigration and ethnic and racial diversity have been adopted by way of voter initiatives. It should be noted here that the federal government has exclusive authority over immigration policy. The states, however, do have considerable control over how immigrants are treated by state and local governments once they have become residents.

TABLE 2. **California Voter Initiatives Approved**
         on Immigration or Racial/Ethnic Subjects

Year	Proposition Number	Initiative Subject	Percent Approval
1964	14	Repealed Rumford Fair Housing Act	65
1972	21	Restricted Mandatory Public School Integration	63
1984	38	Restricted Voting Materials to English Language Only	71
1986	63	Made English CA's Sole Official Language	73
1994	187	Eliminated Public Services to Unauthorized Immigrants	59
1996	209	Eliminated CA Affirmative Action Policies	55
1998	227	Eliminated Bilingual Education in CA	61

In any case, for purposes of this book it is of central importance that nearly all of the voter initiatives on the subjects of race/ethnicity or immigrant settlement have been adopted by a majority of California's white voters, but have been opposed by a majority of the state's Latino, black, and Asian/Pacific Islander voters. Given the continuing overrepresentation of California's white population among the electorate, as depicted in Table 1, this is a highly significant pattern. Table 2 provides an outline of the most important voter initiatives adopted since the 1960s in which the primary subject of the initiative was either immigration or a matter pertaining to race/ethnicity.

Elaborating briefly on the main aims and/or impacts of these voter initiatives:

- *Proposition 14* (1964) attempted to rescind a law passed by the state legislature and approved by the governor that outlawed racial and ethnic discrimination in the sale and rental of housing in California. Proposition 14 was subsequently overturned by the courts on grounds that it violated the state and federal constitutions.

- *Proposition 21* (1972) also dealt with the subject of ethnic and racial segregation and integration. It was drafted to overturn court decisions requiring the Los Angeles Unified School District to bus students for purposes of school integration. Those decisions had held that California's constitution prohibited de facto school segregation, not just de jure segregation intentionally created by explicit school district actions. Proposition 21, upheld by the courts, changed the state's constitution to ensure that the more restrictive federal doctrine applied in California: school districts were required to racially integrate *only* if it could be proved that officials had *intentionally* segregated schools.

- *Proposition 38* (1984) expressed California's opposition to a federal law, the Voting Rights Act (VRA), which had been amended in 1975 to require that "language minorities" (i.e., Latinos, Asian Americans, and American Indians) be protected under that law and to require state and local election officials to provide ballots and official election materials in languages other than English where there are geographic concentrations of minority language speakers. This initiative required the governor of the state to send a letter to the president of the United States calling upon the federal government to rescind the VRA language requirements.

- *Proposition 63* (1986) made English the sole official language of the state of California. The state's first constitution, adopted in 1850, required that official state documents be printed in both English and Spanish, but this requirement was eliminated in 1874, leaving California with no official language policy. So California moved from being officially bilingual (1850) to being linguistically "neutral" (1874) to being officially monolingual in English in 1986, just as millions of immigrants began to arrive from around the globe. Like the Proposition 38 effort two years earlier, the campaign for this initiative was spearheaded by U.S. English, the country's largest and best organized "official English" interest group.

- *Proposition 187* (1994) sought to bar unauthorized immigrants in California from having access to the state's public schools, public health-care facilities, and other public services designed to help low-income residents. It also required public employees in California to check the documentation status of their clients and/or students, and to report any lacking the proper documentation to federal immigration authorities. Overturned as unconstitutional by the courts before it could be enforced, Proposition 187 nevertheless had a major impact on the country's immigration debate by purportedly leading then-President Clinton to adopt increasingly aggressive efforts to "seal" the border between the U.S. and Mexico. And it led to the passage of the 1996 law excluding non-U.S. citizens (including both authorized and unauthorized immigrants) from receiving federal social welfare funds.

- ***Proposition 209*** (1996) put an end to California's state-initiated affirmative action programs,[13] most of which were designed to increase ethnic and racial minority participation and success in California's public system of higher education. Most tellingly, Proposition 209 eliminated special admissions and student services programs that aimed to increase the number, and graduation success rates, of ethno-racial minority students in community colleges, the California State University system, and the University of California system.

- ***Proposition 227*** (1998) eliminated most of the state's bilingual education programs in the public schools, replacing them with a one-year "English immersion" approach to linguistic diversity on behalf of the state's large number of "limited English proficient" students. This initiative too was supported by U.S. English, though it was bankrolled by a politically active Silicon Valley computer entrepreneur, Ron Unz.

Debating California's Exclusionary Approach to Ethno-Racial Difference

It seems fair to say that taken in combination, these voter-approved initiatives dealing with several aspects of California's ethnic and racial diversity have expressed and reinforced a consistently chilly climate. What underlies this series of negative responses to the state's immigrant newcomers and its ethnic and racial minorities? There is not space here to thoroughly examine this question, so I will sketch out the contours of the debates over immigration in California (and nationally) that provide the rhetorical contexts for the political decisions made by a majority of California voters on these initiative measures.

Three themes have been predominant in these immigration-centered debates: (1) the problem of "illegal" immigration, (2) the economic effects of immigration (both documented and undocumented), and (3) the cultural effects of immigration (again, both documented and undocumented).

Theme 1: The Problem of "Illegal" Immigration. The debate over unauthorized immigration has become much more shrill in recent years, in part at least because U.S. Census Bureau data indicates that the number of unauthorized immigrants has surged, despite increased efforts to seal the border between the United States and Mexico. The most widely cited studies reaching this conclusion have been the Pew Hispanic Center's analyses of Census Bureau data, the most recent of which found that nearly twelve million residents of the United States in 2005 were unauthorized migrants, and that nearly half of these had arrived in the country in the previous five years.[14] This apparent surge in unauthorized immigration, about 80 percent of which comes from Latin America, has become one of the most controversial aspects of the immigration debate in the last several years, and it has been the focus of much discussion in Congress. And, as California has been the most popular destination state for immigrants (including the unauthorized), this trend was the subject of sharp debate in this state.[15]

The debate has focused primarily on additional steps designed to seal the border (e.g., building a seven-hundred-mile fence and increasing the size and technological sophistication of the Border Patrol) and on whether to authorize the status of the undocumented through a guest worker program or in some other way. The most prominent rhetorical strategies deployed by immigration restriction groups have centered on the perceived "lawlessness" engendered by unauthorized immigrants. The undocumented have been depicted increasingly as criminals, drug smugglers, gangsters, and potential terrorists.

Those favoring immigrant groups, in contrast, have sought to portray immigrants (even those who are unauthorized) as hardworking people who are simply seeking opportunities to help their families out of (often) desperate economic circumstances, and who have the potential, given the chance, to be outstanding citizens of California and the United States. In addition, pro-immigrant groups argue that there is no realistic and humane way to seal the border, given the lure of family connections and economic opportunities (including businesses here that depend on immigrant labor, even unauthorized immigrant labor), as well as the deteriorating economic situations in the homelands of many migrants. All that can be accomplished by draconian measures such as building a border fence is to make unauthorized border crossings more dangerous and more expensive for the most vulnerable of migrants, who will be driven to find a way to get here in any case.

In terms of California politics, immigration restrictionists have urged the state (and local governments) to take steps to remove the perceived incentives for illegal immigration by making it ever more difficult for those who are unauthorized to work, to find places to live, to gain access to public services (e.g., emergency medical care), to have their children educated in California public schools, and so on. That was the major aim of Proposition 187, as noted above, and despite its unconstitutionality, anti-immigrant groups and public officials have worked to get local governments (city councils, police departments, public hospitals) to implement policies of this nature. Pro-immigrant groups, in contrast, argue that undocumented workers make a net positive contribution to the state's tax base, and that policing the border is an exclusive responsibility (and power) of the federal government. State and local governments, they argue, should not play a part in deporting unauthorized immigrants.

Theme 2: The Economic Effects of Immigration. The second theme in the contemporary immigration debate has been focused primarily on (a) whether immigrants make a positive or negative contribution to the economy as a whole, and (b) whether immigrants are a fiscal burden on governments and taxpayers or whether they pay their way in the balance between taxes and benefits received.

Regarding economic impact as a whole, the question is whether immigrants add to economic growth, and whether they stimulate the kinds of growth that ensure a healthy future for the state's (and nation's) economy. Critics of immigration generally argue that too many current U.S. immigrants have too little human capital (that is, education, job skills, etc.) to contribute positively to the kind of economy we need to develop in order to ensure the future prosperity of the state and nation. Immigrants, they say, tend to stimulate the development of the wrong kinds of jobs and industries—that is, low-paying jobs and low-profit-producing industries. They will drag the economy in a direction that will not contribute to our future prosperity in a globalized world. Other critics emphasize that immigrants are increasing the ranks of poorly educated, low-income workers to the point that they are displacing native-born workers, and the competition for low-skilled jobs drags down wages to the point that most Americans cannot afford to work at them.

Immigration supporters, on the other hand, argue that the economic changes being blamed on immigrants are not being caused by those immigrants but by global economic changes driven by corporate leaders who increasingly dictate the movement of capital and industries in ways that reflect their own lack of concern for the economic well-being of California and the United States. In many cases, these are the same economic forces that have devastated the economies in the homelands of the people who have been forced to become immigrants. To blame immigrant victims of globalization for the growing economic dislocations and inequalities being generated in California, the United States, and many other parts of the world is short-sighted indeed. And it creates a false conflict between low-income (mostly nonwhite) immigrants and low-income native workers in which both sides will lose, while the real perpetrators of the problem will continue to amass ever more wealth for themselves.

The other aspect of this theme in the immigration debate concerns the economic effects of immigration on governmental budgets and public services. Here the question is whether immigrant workers and entrepreneurs pay more in taxes than they receive in benefits from the governments collecting the taxes.

Those who claim that there are too many immigrants in California—and particularly too many unauthorized immigrants—argue that these newcomers are sucking dry the public resources of the state, creating a severe drain on public institutions such as public schools, hospital emergency services, other social services, and the physical infrastructure of the state (parks, recreation areas, roads and highways, water supplies). And this, it is claimed, is because immigrants pay far less in taxes than the value of the public services they receive. This claim is frequently employed to oppose any increases in taxes or increased spending levels on California's public institutions and infrastructure. Improving our public resources, critics say, will only provide new incentives for even more immigrants to come to the state.

In contrast, those taking a more hospitable line toward immigrants argue that most are here to stay, whether Californians like it or not, and the future well-being of our state requires that *all Californians*—those born here, as well as those who have migrated here—become well educated, healthy, and able to live in decent surroundings. Starving public institutions of badly needed resources until the immigrants go away is a losing strategy that will handicap the state's future in a multitude of ways. Children who grow up without access to good schools, health care, recreational facilities, adequate living spaces, etc. will not be an asset to the state's future, whereas investing in our own future—in the form of all the children and young people in the state—will pay dividends in a healthier and more robust economy. And it will create a more humane and decent society. Besides, the pro-immigrant groups claim, their data show that overall, when all levels of government are taken into account, immigrants actually pay more in taxes than they receive in public services, use public services less than citizens, and keep many hard-pressed businesses afloat. Rather than taking advantage of native Californians, immigrants are actually *receiving less* than their fair share of public resources.

Theme 3: The Cultural Effects of Immigration. But the theme with perhaps the greatest emotional impact concerns immigrants' effects on California's cultural cohesion. This theme has deep roots in the past and figured prominently in earlier efforts to reduce the number of immigrants to the country, particularly from countries perceived as culturally alien from the United States.

The basic argument has been quite consistent over a long period of U.S. history: culturally different immigrants (variously described in religious, racial, and ethno-cultural terms) threaten to undermine and/or corrupt the cultural integrity and vitality of the American people. The underlying assumption here is that the United States is a monocultural country and that one of its greatest challenges (and historical accomplishments) is the successful assimilation of immigrants from different cultures. Numerous contemporary scholars and political activists have made this a prominent theme in their public rhetoric.[16] As some see it, it is not just a nation that is threatened by immigration; civilization itself is at stake.

The issue of language plays a very prominent role in this theme. Many immigration restrictionists express the belief that the presence of multiple languages in the public spaces of the contemporary United States, and especially the increasingly prominent public fact of the Spanish language, threaten a permanent partition of the American population into two competing and mutually hostile camps. This is a primary theme, for example, in Samuel Huntington's critique of the effects of immigration from Latin America on U.S. culture as a whole, and with respect to California, in Victor Davis Hanson's writings on *Mexifornia*. A classics scholar who maintains a family farm near Selma in the Central Valley, Hanson writes poignantly about the bucolic pleasures of his childhood on the same farm and in his hometown, depicting a time in the 1950s and 1960s when Anglo farmers were respected as the primary agents of economic prosperity, and respectful farmworkers of Mexican origin were grateful for the opportunities given to them by their employers, and urged their children to assimilate into the dominant and unifying culture.

All that has changed, Hanson laments, as a result of the combined effects of the onslaught of mostly illegal immigrants, whose sheer numbers have overwhelmed the peaceful and cohesive community of his childhood memory, and the oppositional efforts of multiculturalist educators and nationalistic Chicano and Latino political activists. After noting the alarming increase in poverty among California's (and the country's) Latino population, for example, Hanson cited the following causes in a 2002 journal article on *Mexifornia*:

The true causes of such checkered progress—continual and massive illegal immigration of cheap labor that drives down wages for working Hispanics here; failure to learn English; the collapse of the once strong Hispanic family due to federal entitlement; soaring birthrates among a demoralized underclass; an intellectual elite that downplays social pathology, claims perpetual racism, and seeks constant government largesse and entitlement; and years of bilingual education that ensure dependency upon a demagogic leadership—are rarely mentioned. They cannot be mentioned. To do so would be to suggest that the billions of public dollars spent on social redress did more to harm Hispanics than did all the racists in America.[17]

In a 2007 update of his *Mexifornia* analysis, Hanson wrote that "the flood of illegal immigrants into California has made things worse than I foresaw." While much of his depiction of California "five years later" is focused on negative economic consequences and the increased criminality of unauthorized immigrants, his update focuses on this cultural theme when he describes the spring 2006 immigrant marches in opposition to the December 2005 passage of a highly restrictive bill by the U.S. House of Representatives:

> In contrast, this spring Americans witnessed millions of illegal aliens who not only were unapologetic about their illegal status but were demanding that their hosts accommodate their own political grievances, from providing driver's licenses to full amnesty. The largest demonstrations—held on May Day, with thousands of protesters waving Mexican flags and bearing placards depicting the communist insurrectionist Che Guevara—only confirmed to most Americans that illegal immigration was out of control and beginning to become politicized along the lines of Latin American radicalism. I chronicled in *Mexifornia* the anomaly of angry protesters waving the flag of the country they vehemently did not wish to return to, but now the evening news beamed these images to millions. In short, the radical socialism of Latin America, seething in the angry millions who flocked to support Venezuela's Hugo Chávez, Bolivia's Evo Morales, and Mexico's Andrés López Obrador, had now seemingly been imported into our own largest cities.[18]

In short, in California—and increasingly elsewhere in the country—immigration opponents raise "cultural threat" as a reason both for reducing immigrant numbers and for insisting that those who do become permanent members of the country's population assimilate to the dominant culture. Very prominent in this campaign is the language issue. Three of the voter initiatives described above focus on trying to preserve the cultural unity of California by protecting the status of the English language.

Embedded in this cultural threat argument against immigration are four specific charges. First, immigration critics argue that immigrants *resist* learning English; second, that they *are not*, in fact, learning English; third, that by retaining their home languages and cultural ties to their homelands, immigrants are failing to integrate into American society and are creating conflicts and political divisions with "real" Americans; and fourth, and finally, that immigrants are refusing to be Americanized, thereby turning their backs on the language and culture that have made this country great.

The claims that many immigrants are resistant to learning English and are not learning English seem sensible in that the number of people living in the United States who normally speak a language other than English at home has been steadily increasing for over three decades (as we saw above), and this is due largely to the influx of new immigrants. The increase has been even more dramatic in California.

However, those groups and political activists who take a more pro-immigration and multiculturalist perspective cite data indicating that these seemingly sensible perceptions are actually false. While the number of non-English speakers—and especially Spanish speakers—living in California (and the country) has increased dramatically in recent decades, this does *not* mean that they are resistant to learning English or that they are not trying to do so. Indeed, surveys of Latinos, including immigrants, have consistently found that virtually all members of these groups (over 95%) think it is important for them to learn English.[19]

Moreover, studies by linguists and sociologists show consistently that the traditional trajectory of English assimilation among immigrants (that is, the first generation speaks its home language most frequently; the second generation is bilingual, but English-dominant; the third generation is only able to speak English) seems to be replicating itself among contemporary immigrants at an even faster pace than was true a century ago.[20] One important study faults Huntington's assertions about immigrants not learning English by showing that Southern California—which has the largest concentrated pool of speakers of non-English languages in the country, and an extensive network of non-English language resources (television and radio stations, newspapers, etc.)—is, in fact, "a graveyard for languages." The "life expectancy" of even the Spanish language in Southern California is barely three generations, and that of other languages is only two generations.[21] In short, multiculturalists and linguistic pluralists argue that few immigrants in general, and virtually no Latinos, are resistant to learning English, and in fact are doing so at a faster rate than previous generations of immigrants.

At the same time, it is true that most (more than 95%) Latinos—immigrants and nonimmigrants alike—also believe that it is important for members of their families to retain (or gain) the ability to speak and read the Spanish language.[22] And this leads many assimilationists and those resistant to immigration to conclude that Latinos especially want to maintain a separate and foreign culture in California, and that this is the cause of political division and conflict, and proof that Latinos are resistant to becoming real Americans (the third and fourth claims in this theme of the immigration debate).

To those provoked by the cultural threat of immigrants, it seems obvious that history has made both California and the United States English-speaking political communities with a single and cohesive and British-derived national culture. From this perspective, hanging on to another (and "foreign") language and culture not only divides that community in politically dangerous ways, but also prevents Latinos from fully achieving the social mobility necessary for newcomer groups to make progress and become truly integrated into American society. It is this line of thinking that apparently leads many Californians to support voter initiatives that proclaim English the sole official language of California, and that eliminated most bilingual education classes in the state. And it is this line of thinking that led the state to oppose the federal rules requiring ballots and election materials in languages other than English.

Proponents of immigration and of ethno-linguistic pluralism respond to these concerns on several levels. For example, while they agree that English has been the dominant language of the United States since its inception as a country, they point out that it is *not true* that English has been the sole language of the country at any time in its history. Other languages and language groups have been present at all times in our history, and some of these groups were initially incorporated into the country through violent, coercive means. This is particularly the case in California, which was taken from Mexico by force following the Mexican American War (1846–1848). Those Mexicans who chose to stay in their homes and communities in Alta California following this annexation became U.S. citizens, but there was no requirement in the Treaty of Guadalupe Hidalgo, which ended the war, that they learn English. Indeed, as mentioned above, the first state constitution made both English and Spanish the public languages of the state. The presence of Spanish in California is not best understood, therefore, as simply derivative of the current period of relatively high levels of immigration.

Given our state's history, it is not surprising that many of its place names (e.g., California, Los Angeles, San Francisco, San Diego, San Jose, Fresno, Santa Ana) are Spanish. In view of these realities, it seems at least ironic, if not absurd, that recently arrived Anglos from the midwestern, eastern, and southern regions of the United States have the temerity to command Spanish speakers to speak English since they are in "America."

This is one of the ironies of Hanson's writings on *Mexifornia*. His idealized depiction of the San Joaquin Valley of California during his childhood in the 1960s fails to recall, for example, the bitter dispute during that decade between the Cesar Chavez–led National Farm Workers Association (NFWA) and the growers who had long dominated their workers' lives. In its organizing work in the San Joaquin Valley during that period, the NFWA operated almost exclusively in the Spanish language and employed symbols that derived mostly from Mexico (e.g., Our Lady of Guadalupe), even though most of the Valley's farmworkers at that time were U.S.-born and U.S. citizens. Many were migrants from Texas; few at that time were migrants from south of the U.S.–Mexico border. In short, the Spanish language has played a formative and constitutive role in the formation of California's multicultural reality, and the immigrants who have arrived in the state since 1965 have greatly expanded the presence of the Spanish language, but *they have joined an ongoing reality* in doing so. Again, then, the notion that Spanish is a foreign language in California is fundamentally wrong.

It is also false, multiculturalists claim, to assert that immigrants' desire to maintain their non-English languages and cultural communities means that they are somehow separatists who want to hold back their own from social mobility and cause division and conflict in the state. This claim overlooks the fact that most speakers of other languages want to be *bilingual*, which means that they want to become fluent in English—and most do. Given their fluency and their evident desire to participate in mainstream institutions and jobs, there is no reason to believe that these immigrants and their ethnic descendants have any desire to maintain "separatist" enclaves in California. They simply want to live in a culturally and linguistically pluralistic society, one in which they can fully participate in mainstream society and its public and civic institutions while also retaining their ties to a valued heritage. It is the inability of many monolingual English speakers to comprehend the possibility and reality of bilingualism and biculturalism that leads to social and political conflict, multiculturalists claim, and not any desire by immigrant and cultural minority communities to foster separatism.

Toward a More Inclusive Future for California

Though a clear majority of California voters has consistently sided with the assimilationist and restrictionist positions in these political debates, this writer believes that the arguments and facts marshaled by cultural pluralists and those favoring a more proactive approach to dealing with questions of immigrant settlement are much more persuasive.[23] I will accordingly close this chapter with some suggestions for a more effective and appropriate approach to issues concerning the settlement of our state's immigrants, and to our longstanding cultural diversity. As noted at the beginning of this chapter, democratic values require that we find ways to encourage newcomers to become integral members of the state's political community.

A more successful and democratic policy approach needs to be characterized as inclusive, proactive, and pluralistic in relation to ethnic and racial diversity. Immigrants will come. Californians can try to intimidate and harass them, but stopping them is not a real possibility. The course consistent with a democratic society is to encourage newcomers and racialized outsiders, in a way that reaches out to them and is respectful of the ethno-cultural attachments that remain meaningful to them, to be active members of the political community. More specifically, I suggest three major changes in the state's approach to immigrants and California's cultural diversity:

A Proactive and Inclusive Approach. Rather than adopting a "hands-off"—or even hostile—approach to the efforts of immigrants to become part of the state's political community, why not reach out and actively try to encourage newcomers to adapt productively to an often challenging environment? Why not, for example, provide public funds to community-based organizations that are working to help newcomers get settled in the community? Such groups provide a wide array of services: English-language classes, help with paperwork, assistance in preparing for citizenship exams, networks for mothers concerned about their children's health and education, etc. There is much that California could do to make immigrants feel more welcome in their new communities, and to assist them to develop social and personal resources that would ensure quicker adaptation and more productive contributions to the state's well-being.

A Bilingual-Bicultural Pluralistic Approach. Rather than punish newcomers and longtime Latino and Asian American residents for not having assimilated into the Anglo culture and English language, why not encourage them to become fluent and comfortable in English while supporting their efforts to retain their home languages and cultural ties? Bilingualism and biculturalism would enable individuals to retain a richer sense of their community's contributions to the state's well-being and history. It would also enable them to be more socially mobile and contribute more smoothly to the state's political development by comfortably interacting with and participating in the state's dominant cultural and linguistic community. Indeed, bilingual education that aims at an educated and bilingual citizenry should be available to *all* members of the state's population, not only to immigrant groups. To this end English-only laws should be removed from the state's constitution.

Political Incorporation through Political Participation. Finally, as noted in this chapter's introduction, it is vitally important that the state's newcomers and racialized outsider groups become active participants in the state's politics. The Progressive Movement's decimation of the state's political parties in the early years of the twentieth century helped to undermine one of the few institutional avenues facilitating the political incorporation of newcomer groups. Other institutions have failed to fill the gaping hole left by the parties' demise.[24] One way to fill this hole is to permit resident noncitizens to vote in local, and perhaps even in statewide, elections. It was done here historically.[25] A second constitutional change, therefore, should declare that noncitizenship is no bar to voting rights. This would encourage newcomers to become involved in choosing their representatives in local and state government and would give them greater incentives to become full-fledged citizens. Other steps might be taken as well, but this would be one step that would encourage political organizations to be more active in promoting the political incorporation of the state's huge immigrant population.

In short, California has not done well by its immigrant and ethno-racial minority populations. This failure has undermined our democratic values and the state's commonweal. Coming to a better understanding of what is necessary to meet the challenges generated by large-scale immigration would help us achieve and preserve a democratic future for our state.

EIGHT

The View from East L.A.

José G. Arias

THERE ARE MANY Californias in the regions, rural towns, and exurbs of the Pacific Coast. A constitutional crisis affects them differently, hitting hardest in the ghettos, barrios, and other underrepresented communities of the state. Californians once expected that prosperity would spread naturally to these communities, and racial discrimination would cease as their residents rose into the middle class. But the barrios and ghettos remain fixed parts of the state's social terrain and are now, indeed, acquiring new sister communities in other parts of California.

José G. Arias reveals the state's oldest barrio, East Los Angeles, to be a product not only of the discriminatory practices of the larger society, but more positively of the vitality and creativity of the people who live in its neighborhoods. Despite all their efforts toward stability and revitalization, however, Arias shows this community to be still buffeted by statewide booms and busts and hindered by patterns of investment and redevelopment policy. Rather than viewing the prospects for East L.A. as shaped simply by inevitable economic forces or immigration, he shows that they are largely the products of political choices and local government organization. Arias raises the question how much the state's underrepresented communities like East L.A. can be changed therefore without changes in the larger society. He concludes by proposing reforms for job creation, housing, health, and local government organization.

> **José G. Arias** is a Ph.D. student at UC Berkeley's School of Education and a scholar at the Institute for the Study of Social Change. He has been an organizer with Barrios Unidos of San Mateo County and Homies Unidos of El Salvador. He is a licensed wood-destroying pest inspector.

"You don't have to be a genius to figure out what's in front of you,"
Chente said. "Yet this is the hardest thing to do precisely because what
we see is not always expressing what's beneath it."
— LUIS RODRIGUEZ[1]

SEATED AT A MAKESHIFT picnic table to the east of the L.A. River I find myself sipping an earthy distillate of the agave plant, hoping to talk to some of the guests who have gathered for Timo's family's fifty-somethingth Fourth of July barbecue. I, like many other people, am trying to understand California's recent politics and want to see what a long-marginalized community can teach me about it. What might a new constitutional convention mean for the barrios and ghettos of the state? My friend Timo has invited me to his aunt's house in East L.A., suggesting that the fireworks would resemble the first days of Operation Iraqi Freedom. After a little background research into the day's menu, I have accepted and brought my bottle of mezcal for them.

Surveying the neighborhood outside the brick and wrought iron fence from my metal folding chair, I think about what it means to celebrate our country's day of independence in California's oldest barrio. Much of what we have come to think we have a right to has been planted, cultivated, harvested, canned, washed, cooked, built, repaired, and delivered by people around here who lack ready access to what they plant, can, and build for others. But despite everything, the 125,000 predominantly Mexicans and Chicanos of East Los Angeles continue to toil as the necessary ground troops of America's largest manufacturing hub and fastest-growing service industry center.[2] Over 40 percent of all families around here scrape by on less than $25,000 a year, approximately half the U.S. median,[3] while a full quarter live below the federal poverty line. They provide the cheap labor necessary to keep many marginal businesses afloat, enabling people beyond the 7.4 square miles of the barrio to maintain relatively high standards of living.[4] As I pour a round into the plastic cups of Timo's family, I think of Frederick Douglass's question from 1852, "What to the slave is the Fourth of July?"

It was a provocative question and appropriate for the audience who listened to the fiery abolitionist more than a decade before emancipation. But was it fitting for the people at this family's barbecue? From Timo's fifty-eight-year-old punker uncle to the young woman cradling a dog in her arms, the folks seated around the well-manicured lawn do not show the signs of fetters that would indicate a life of bondage. Still, 60 percent of the barrio's inhabitants are employed in the same poorly paid and generally hazardous service, construction, manufacturing, and transportation jobs that were once widely described as wage slavery.[5] And it is hard to move out of those jobs. The large Mexican American working class lags far behind the national average in upward social and economic mobility, both within and across generations.[6] The constant reproduction of racialized poverty in their ranks led some scholars to once liken the community to an internal colony.[7]

A colony? Maybe. But for my friends there is nothing more American than firing up a propane grill in the front yard, chewing on carne asada, and eating potato salad whose recipe dates to World War II. Much as European immigrants did throughout the nineteenth and twentieth centuries, Mexicans and their Chicano progeny currently provide much of the labor that keeps America's economy going. They are also recreating California's cultural landscape in ways that infuse its collective consciousness with a *mestizo* sensibility that, despite nativism and reaction, has always represented its future. I walk over to the porch to see if Timo's uncle, who's known for his savvy and ability to see the big picture, can help me make sense of the contradictions posed by East Los Angeles.

Changes in the Barrio

> Parado en la esquina, sin rumbo sin fin
> Estoy en El Lay, no tengo donde ir
> Un hombre se acercó, mi nombre preguntó
> Al no saber su lengua, con el me llevó
> Esto es el precio que pagamos
> Cuando llegamos a este lado?
> Jalamos y pagamos impuestos
> Migra llega y nos da unos fregasos
> El Lay, L.A....
> —LOS ILLEGALS[8]

With an eclectic style that draws from both sides of the *frontera* (the U.S.–Mexican border), Jesús "Xiuy" Velo may be the closest thing to East L.A. incarnate I have met. His long graying hair, yellow-lens sunglasses, off-white guayabera, faded blue jeans, and worn leather guaraches celebrate Chicanismo with pocho pride. At the same time, this *veterano* of both the 1968 school blowouts and the Chicano Moratorium riot of 1970 (the former a protest against a racist L.A. school district, and the latter a famously bloody demonstration against the Vietnam War[9]) now seems a little out of place in his own neighborhood. He is a representative of an older barrio, remembered fondly as the largely tight-knit Belvedere that eventually evolved into the perennially troubled, divided, and violent "East Los" of today. How and why did the barrio change? When did things go wrong? How might a constitutional convention off in the future and four hundred miles north possibly provide substantive relief to an area poor in resources and political capital, yet rich and resilient in other ways? I hoped Xiuy would be able to provide some insights.

"What are you looking for?" Xiuy asks in a rhythmic way of talking reminiscent of the rock music he created as a bassist for Los Illegals. "Because I could tell you a lot about this corner right here." He extends his arms outward with his palms up, then looks out at the row of houses across the street. "My family moved here in 1940 when it was pretty much a mixed area. It was like New York at the turn of the century." He begins to point out every building. "You had Russians, Irish, Armenians, Japanese...It was like everyone was looking for the American dream and we were the Mexican American, the Chicano family."

Historically, immigrants and people of color in Los Angeles had been driven into the less desirable urban industrial areas in part by restrictive covenants that allowed only white families entry to the suburbs built during and after World War II. The effects of the covenants were reinforced by numerous federal policies under the auspices of the Home Owners Loan Corporation and the Federal Housing Administration, which institutionalized redlining practices that denied loans to people of color and their communities as risky mortgage recipients.[10] Russians, Irish, Armenians, Japanese, and even a few Latinos were eventually able to move out of the increasingly crowded barrio by jumping on the freeways that tore through East Los Angeles in the "urban renewal" projects during the middle of the century. Beginning in the 1940s, a corporate consortium made up of General Motors, Firestone Rubber, and others purchased and subsequently destroyed the city transit system, rerouting people into the concrete channels of congestion that helped to open mature suburbs to a few Eastside families.

But the urban renewal displaced 10 percent of the barrio's inhabitants and cut its housing stock considerably.[11] Nonetheless, the middle-class and largely white exodus toward higher-paying jobs, higher property values, and better schools allowed new immigrants from Mexico and Central America (the latter escaping civil wars) to move en masse into the relatively affordable Eastside rentals during the last decades of the twentieth century. In

2000, approximately half the barrio's inhabitants were foreign-born, with close to 99 percent having arrived from Latin America. Only a little over a third owned their homes, compared to a national average of 69 percent.

Despite the smooth integration between old and new that might be suggested by the census bureau's terms "Latino" and "Hispanic," tensions quickly developed between the older established families and the recent immigrants from El Salvador, Guatemala, and Honduras, along with the Mixtec and Zapotec peoples from southern Mexico. (The settled East Los Angelenos had already experienced similar tensions with the Mexicanos. Xiuy felt those tensions as a young musician traveling through Mexico. "Look," he tells me, "our family has been in this country since 1914, escaping the revolution. Whenever Mexicans come up here they look down on us. They expect us to talk like they do. We have to do their customs. We can never do anything that is ours.")

Xiuy offered his perspective on all the changes in his barrio. "Voting-wise, there is no power here anymore. Two-thirds of everybody in this huge neighborhood are renters now. It is a place for immigrants to come. We have had an influx of people who can't vote, don't vote, and are confused about the vote."

And this was more than a decade after the historic 1995 case that finally forced the Los Angeles County Board of Supervisors to stop diluting Chicano voting strength through racial gerrymandering. Once permitted to really vote their interests, the locals elected Gloria Molina, the first Mexican American to serve on the county board in over a century. East L.A. is under the jurisdiction of the largest county in the nation because East L.A, never having been incorporated, lacks its own city government. Dating back to at least 1960, a "Citizens Committee for the Incorporation of East Los Angeles" circulated a petition that listed five goals of self-governance that would be aided by cityhood. Two dealt with the perennial issues of air pollution and unemployment.[12] Cityhood has been regularly sought by lay people, local politicians, and real estate interests as a necessary step for improving East L.A. Three times over the past fifty years—in 1961, 1963, and 1974—efforts at incorporation ended in defeat at the ballot box. The efforts were met by staunch resistance from a variety of sectors, including merchants wary of additional taxes, county officials concerned with decreased oversight, and companies nervous about local authority, as well as the AFL-CIO's Committee of Political Education (COPE) and a few building trades unions who sought to protect existing contracts and business partnerships.[13] The barrio therefore currently suffers the same confusion of local jurisdictions and the same complex relations with state funding agencies—especially for schools after the passage of Proposition 13—as other unincorporated cities in the state.

I asked, "Is the loss of voting power the greatest challenge East L.A. faces?" As Xiuy thought about my question, my mind wandered to the movements that won the right to vote for people of color in the 1870s in California, and for women in 1919. Although these were important victories, *full* equality—measured, at a minimum, by equal treatment under the law and equal pay for equal work—has despite the formal provisions continuously escaped both groups.

"Listen," Xiuy pauses to make sure that I am with him, "America is in love with the cheap labor that millions of immigrants represent. It is the heroin of the United States. They love it...and they love to hate it." He looks over toward the grill. "187, 209, those propositions....They make it hard for undocumented immigrants in the barrio to survive. At the same time they won't raise wages to hire Americans for the jobs these people are willing to take....Our greatest weakness, however, is also our greatest strength. Although many are here without papers, we have numbers. When we march and actually apply ourselves toward something important, we do it in a number that is huge."

Since at least the first decade of the twentieth century, when rapid industrial growth and development around the L.A. Central Plaza forced residents out of "Sonora Town" around Olivera Street, Mexican migrants have steadily moved into the land around the manufacturing plants, meat packing buildings, and railroad yards east of the L.A. River. Now, with an average family size of four and a half people and more than one person per room in 50 percent of all homes, East Los Angeles is one of the most densely populated areas in the county.[14] This crowded barrio, as Xiuy proudly indicated, has historically been active in local, state, national, and even international politics. Most memorable, of course, was its central place in the Chicano Power movement of the late sixties and early seventies. Largely forgotten is the role this barrio played in the Mexican Revolution. Beginning in 1907, the Partido Liberal Mexicano and its leader Ricardo Flores Magón organized aggressively from its East Los Angeles headquarters against the dictatorship of Porfirio Díaz. It was from East L.A. that Magón went on to lead his short-lived revolt in Baja California in 1911. Interestingly enough, during a Fourth of July gathering in 1914, he touched on many of the same problems facing Mexicans in the U.S. that concern Xiuy close to a hundred years later.[15]

"Is the barrio still politically active?" I wonder, loud enough for Xiuy to hear.

"Not really." He looks down the block at the crowd awaiting dusk to fire off the large surface-to-air missiles they have dragged outdoors. He adds, "The law has found a way to cage us, trap us, and keep us where they want. The Chicano forefront, those of us who grew up in the sixties and seventies and were legal, have become artists, professionals, and even major city and state politicians..." Xiuy is interrupted by a long Caprice Classic, radio blaring, lumbering past us and up the street while lazily avoiding the children running after each other with sprinklers. "My generation, because we were legal, had the wherewithal to do what we had to do and we made our mark. The generation that followed, because they lack papers and are suffering from a massive drop in wages as a result of Reaganomics, are only interested in survival. People just want to make a living and try to get out of here."

"So you still live here?" I look up and down the street, trying to guess which house Xiuy now calls home. The last few rays of light reveal a neighborhood filled with stucco buildings painted a cornucopia of color—the community is not shy about expressing itself in every shade imaginable, or, possibly, on sale.

"I'm in...Orange County now...." Xiuy's voice trails off as he stares at the dark and lime green house in which he grew up. After a few minutes he looks around the yard and stops when he sees his daughter. "You see mijita over there?" I look over at the preteen girl playing with my dogs near the hedges that line the right side of the yard. "She won first place in the annual spelling bee at her school. Out of a group of *puro gabachos,* my daughter was the best English speller! Can you believe that?"

Xiuy dropped out of nearly every school in East L.A. during his rebellious youth and largely escaped a district that had, since at least the Progressive Era of the early twentieth century, attempted to Americanize its Mexican students through segregated vocational tracks and a curriculum that presented Anglo-American culture as the paragon of industry and virtue. Now he is a civil rights analyst/investigator for the U.S. Department of Housing and Urban Development. How could I blame him for moving? He was not alone in wanting to leave an area where schooling was poor, over two-thirds of all adults lack a high school diploma, and approximately 40 percent of all students drop out of, or are pushed out of, high school. In an era in which education credentials are thought to provide access to the middle class, the school your children attend takes on central importance. The schools must be well equipped and communities must invest heavily in them so their children are prepared to score well on the standardized tests that determine if they qualify to continue on for a college degree, and where that degree will ultimately be from. With professionals and wealth now largely concentrated in the suburbs, the relatively new schools serving those suburbs are able to tap into their plentiful resources, and students from their families are able to earn the degrees that will help them maintain and increase their family's wealth. Most of the older urban schools, however, such as those in East Los Angeles, face the daunting challenge of educating students who have serious needs, without equipment, supplies, or fully repaired buildings, and with ranks of not-yet-credentialed teachers. Because many of these students leave school without the high school diploma necessary to secure even a living wage, they will continue to live in the underclass.[16] That the current avalanche of high-stakes testing may produce a (presumably) merit-based social stratification has not yet struck the residents of "East Los," any more than it has the rest of the state's citizens.

I begin to wonder about the future of this barrio and the people sitting around me. "Yo!" Adrian, a friend from college who has returned to Los Angeles after graduation, hollers as he climbs onto the porch with the bottomless bottle of mezcal. We sit on the stairs and toast East L.A. "What did you think about Dolores?" he asks. "She's on point, right?" I nod my head and remember the interview he arranged for me that morning.

East Los Angeles in My Pocket

> Somewhere else is the place of life.
> There I want to go,
> there surely I will sing
> with the most beautiful birds.
> There I will have
> genuine flowers,
> the flowers that delight,
> that bring peace to the heart,
> the only ones that give peace to man,
> that intoxicate him with joy....
> —NAHUA POET[17]

I am in Adrian's sparsely decorated fourth-floor corner apartment serenaded by car horns, construction rattles, and loud conversations floating up from the street below. Built in 1906, the Alexandria Hotel was an extravagant monument to the fevered early-twentieth-century development of the city center. It drove up rent in the downtown area, which helped push Mexican migrants east across the L.A. River. Once host to numerous Hollywood legends, U.S. presidents, and foreign dignitaries, the Alexandria first hit hard times in 1923, when the grandiose Biltmore Hotel replaced it as the hub of the city's social scene. As capital increasingly moved out of the city and into the surrounding suburbs, the Alexandria fell into disrepair and became notorious as a transient hotel during the last few decades of the century. But following a $14 million facelift that began in 2006, the rejuvenated building became emblematic of the downtown renaissance. Luxury lofts, high-end restaurants, and exclusive nightclubs have appeared.[18] History repeats itself as the parts of the population deemed less desirable—the largest concentration of homeless people in the country—have been forced to move elsewhere in the name of public safety.[19]

Alarmed at the voracious gentrification, activists working with the largely black Skid Row community of some ten thousand people, over 40 percent of whom lack adequate shelter, have been organizing over the past few years against a number of development projects and policing strategies that are driving the poor out of downtown.[20] Do the current battles for the future of downtown Los Angeles portend what might take place across the river in a few years? With an eagerly anticipated six-mile Metro Gold Line extension opening any day now in East Los Angeles—one that will provide the area with transportation by train through downtown and into Pasadena—the land surrounding the Eastside rail lines has already been targeted for redevelopment and many working-class apartments lie in the line of fire.[21]

"We need to revitalize East Los Angeles!" Dolores leans out the window and observes the frenetic energy of a downtown area changing even as we talk. I sit down in one of the two chairs Adrian owns and watch something more intriguing than anything on television. Down below, clusters of young white professionals navigate silently around small sections of sidewalk claimed by weathered and vociferous groups of homeless black men sitting on milk crates. Dolores turns around and leans on the windowsill. "We need policies favorable to local businesses and landlords. They have already committed themselves to the neighborhood, so we need to know how to support and protect them."

Dolores Chavez is forty-eight years old and has the confidence of a barrio homegirl who has done well. Educated both in California and abroad, she is adorned with clothing and trinkets that suggest world travel, although some, she admits, came from the neighborhood Ross. She sits down, pushes the bracelets bunched around her forearm down toward her wrists, and says, "So you want some *native* insights about the future of East Los Angeles? Well...East Los Angeles is right here in my pocket! I carry it wherever I go! Even though I left the Eastside for school in England,...in the back of my mind I always knew that I would return home and settle down in the barrio." Now, having worked with the arts and small business communities in East Los Angeles for the last twenty years, Dolores has come to the conclusion that "neighborhood revitalization and the building of infrastructure" are of utmost importance.

I was surprised at the idea. Given the Eastside barrio's close proximity to the historic heart of Los Angeles's economic and social worlds, real estate investors have routinely seen it as a prime site for the kind of redevelopment schemes that have repeatedly displaced Mexican working-class families. One of the giants of post–World War II East Los Angeles politics, Edward "Eddie" Roybal,[22] built his initial reputation organizing the community in the huge Community Services Organization (CSO) against developers who were clearing out prized low-income neighborhoods under the guise of urban renewal. It is an unfortunate irony that the entire six-mile Metro extension, which many see as the first step toward Eastside gentrification, has been named in his memory.[23]

"What do you mean, revitalization?" I ask, suspicious of any policy framed in the language of redevelopment.

"Well...we all want our neighborhoods to be safe and clean....And when I was growing up I felt like it *was* clean and we were more united. I didn't see a division between cultures even though there was a lot of diversity. Now, there are all these problems and they tend to escalate quickly because anyone can get a gun these days. That is a problem."

She had a point. Many people are familiar with the violence that has plagued East Los Angeles over the past few decades. The stereotypical image of Eastside *vatos locos* and barrio wars reached a broad audience through widely distributed Chicano exploitation movies like *American Me* and mainstream caricatures of gangbangers as in *Colors*. Although exaggerated in such films, violence and homicides involving firearms do occur at dramatically higher rates in East L.A. than elsewhere. In 1992 the homicide rate in the LAPD Hollenbeck area of East Los Angeles was double the city's average and a remarkable six times the national average.[24]

Dolores had also touched on a topic that has been a relatively well kept secret. After the shutdown of large assembly-line factories during the 1970s and 1980s, many low-tech, labor-intensive, and high-polluting industries took over their sites in the relatively inexpensive, industrially oriented, and politically weak Eastside and South Central neighborhoods. As a result, a majority of Los Angeles County's postindustrial factories and incinerators producing airborne toxins are located in the densely populated barrios and ghettos that surround the city's downtown.[25] Combined with the exhaust from ever-present freeway traffic, this produces some of the worst air quality in the entire state. As could be expected, constant exposure to this environmental hazard has resulted in a variety of respiratory problems, including a disturbingly high 8.8 percent rate of asthma for East Los Angeles children.[26] The barrio's residents, unfortunately, are some of the least equipped in the state to deal with these serious health issues. Due to their precarious position as the region's low-skilled and undocumented labor force, many lack the insurance necessary to secure adequate health care.[27]

"Self-empowered and self-motivated...." Dolores interrupts my train of thought. "We need to educate ourselves on the issues that impact our community and act on them in a way that is effective. Local meetings are great, but they are somewhat inadequate when it comes to dealing with our major issues." She grabs Adrian's promotional hip-hop CD and hands it to me. "For instance, a number of artists like Adrian are now activists and entrepreneurs. We need a political force that can support these artists and make their work accessible to everyone in East L.A." Adrian nods his head in agreement. "We could begin by making sure children learn in school how to express themselves through the arts, but for that we would need to have more control of school resources." I could see where Dolores was headed.

Three decades after the last campaign, the East Los Angeles Residents Association (ELARA) is currently organizing what many feel is the strongest effort to date for city incorporation.[28] With support from one of the state's most powerful politicians, Senate Majority Leader Gloria Romero, and a less militant political climate than what may have alienated conservative residents in the past, ELARA feels that incorporation is finally within reach.[29]

Although it could represent one of the greatest victories in the history of the barrio and let East Angelenos more fully control local land use and school funding, cityhood would not, in and of itself, automatically assure help for those I had been thinking about, the most vulnerable within the barrio—those in need of good jobs, affordable housing, safe streets, and control over the cycles of gentrification and decay bred elsewhere in the state's economy. There is also irony here, since historically it was the white suburban communities of Southern California that most often used municipal incorporation, to insulate their investments through building codes and other restrictions from working-class and minority newcomers.[30]

The State of East L.A.

"Until you can do everything yourself, you'll always ask,
What more can brown do for me?'"
— GEORGE LOPEZ[31]

The barrio, in many ways, is a community of exiles—individuals and families that have for a variety of reasons been forced out of or off their land, yet managed to find refuge and a degree of comfort on the east side of the Los Angeles River. Like residents of other neighborhoods throughout the state, East Angelenos work and relax, mourn and celebrate as they try to cope with the issues bred of economic marginalization and social stigma. It is a complex and contradictory picture Xiuy, Dolores, and my own studies have given me. Concentrated poverty and racial/ethnic segregation caused by white flight, limited formal political participation due to a large undocumented population, underequipped schools, environmental hazards, the absence of a civic political apparatus to develop local remedies—this is the visible face of the state of East L.A. But the creativity and resilience of the people also endure. And the growth of the Latino population (from two to over four million in Los Angeles between 1980 and 2000) is a sign of great political possibility.

What could state political reform possibly provide for such a place? Of the many problems of a people converted by a confluence of factors into one of the most expendable and denigrated ethnic working-class communities in the state, which are the most important? And which might be addressed by those who would improve the state's institutions—perhaps the delegates to a statewide convention from East Los? I can think of a few solutions for East L.A. as a concrete place in space and time. But I have a harder time with East L. A., the symbol for the state's many refuges for the victims of its shifting fortunes.

There are obvious reforms that could help the concrete community, and the ghettos and barrios around the state like this one. First, given the importance of jobs to provide sustenance in a business society, means for getting ahead for immigrants, and also a sense of pride within the community, a Works Progress Administration, similar to the agency created by the federal government during the New Deal, could provide jobs to the barrio's unemployed and working poor. Such an agency could also supply the labor necessary to begin addressing East Los Angeles's air pollution by having the state purchase the toxin-emitting factories and then pay local workers to dismantle them and convert their lots into urban green spaces and parks.[32] A constitutional amendment could give California state government formal authority to create such an agency.

Also crucial, second, is the expansion of adequate health care to all sectors of the community. The barrio is home to many who are either unemployed or underemployed (countywide the rates for Latinos are 14.3 percent and 15.1 percent respectively, approximately double those of whites and Asians.)[33] Many of its residents are also undocumented individuals and employed in the informal economy, accounting for about 8 percent of East L.A.[34] For most of these, health insurance and health care are currently out of reach. A right to health care should be included in the state constitution's Declaration of Rights, and the state's population as a whole taxed, on a progressive scale, to pay for public clinics and improved public health care.

Third, avenues of political participation could be created for the undocumented of East L.A., giving them, for example, the right to vote locally, as was once done in Southern California communities and other places in the country, as Ronald Schmidt recommended in chapter seven. No reason local residents should not be able raise their concerns publicly and participate in the decisions which affect their lives, particularly about their children's schooling. In fact there is a good and democratic reason why they should. Most of the undocumented do pay social security taxes (even if not in their own name).

Finally, the matter of schooling is an essential piece of the puzzle in places like East L.A. The barrio's schools need more resources for the renovation of their buildings, development of their academic support programs, creation of arts programs like Dolores proposes, and provision of college scholarships. Students need the support to graduate from high school and scholarships to go on to the state's increasingly expensive higher education institutions. If the movement toward incorporation is successful, the barrio will enjoy greater control over school funding and curriculum decisions, which may lead to more culturally relevant education and less student alienation. But places like East L.A. need to be granted control again over their own property taxes for their schools to flourish; and given Proposition 13, that will take constitutional reform of state/local tax relations.

Such reforms are sensible and logical, even if they would be difficult to implement now politically. That implementation would require the mobilization of those "numbers" Xiuy talked about, in an organization like the CSO which Roybal helped build and which remained a force in Los Angeles politics for years.

But what about the barrio as symbol? How do the recommendations change if I think of East L.A. as representing the places in the state where the exiles produced by changing social and economic arrangements find a refuge and raise families? The recommendations offered above would resolve many of the problems found in East Los Angeles proper, but might they produce new East Los Angeleses if this city's current residents were unable any longer to afford to live east of the L.A. River? Even if Dolores's revitalization were to occur, could the barrio keep control of it and share in its rewards? Or would the improvements and revitalization create new exiles in the state, people unable to afford to live in a community with full employment, clean land and air, a strong city government, and good schools? Many of the Eastside's current residents came here originally as exiles. Can this one community be saved if others aren't?

Two of the programs I think about—jobs and health—would clearly help everyone in the state, not just East Los Angelenos. But the condition of the barrio, I begin to see, is inseparable from that of the larger society that created it and recreates it every day in response to its needs and its carelessness. Can the barrio really be changed without also changing those needs and that carelessness?

The first fireworks start to shatter the night sky as Adrian, Timo, and I straddle the roof ridge of Timo's house, and I look again at this community, trying to spot the contradictions hidden in plain sight and see where they might lead me.

California's Water Crisis: The Delta and Beyond

Osha Meserve and Erik Ringelberg

CALIFORNIANS HAVE BEEN fighting over water since the state began. Access to water determines which of California's cities will flourish and which will fail, as it decided historically which farms and ranches would boom or bust. The two massive aqueduct systems, the federal Central Valley Project and the State Water Project, which were once seen as providing answers to all the state's water problems, are now raising new questions about energy use, environmental side effects, and water quality and quantity.

The Sacramento–San Joaquin Delta, Osha Meserve and Erik Ringelberg explain in this chapter, is the heart of the state's water system not only geographically, but politically. The multitude of issues raised around management of its water, and of interest groups with a stake in their resolution, carries to an extreme the dynamics evident with other resource conflicts in the state. The extent to which matters often assumed to be purely environmental are also suffused with questions of historical precedent and legal rights, as illustrated by the Delta, is also a measure of how intrinsically political all these conflicts are. Chapter nine explains this and raises rarely posed questions about the relationship between the granting of rights over common resources, the needs of a place like the Delta, and the requirements of a democratic society. Meserve and Ringelberg also offer a range of farsighted constitutional proposals for improving the management of Delta water and of all the state's streams, aquifers, and natural resources.

Osha Meserve is an attorney in Sacramento. Her practice focuses on water resources, land use, and other environmental matters. **Erik Ringelberg** is a consulting ecologist specializing in public policy and listed species recovery in Sacramento.

WATER IS A PRECIOUS RESOURCE in an arid land. And most places where Californians live and grow crops are arid, receiving less than ten inches of rain a year. The state therefore relies on a vast, publicly funded infrastructure to deliver water throughout its regions. As its population grows, its citizens are increasingly faced with the challenges and problems raised by the need for long-distance delivery of water. How the often-competing demands on water resources are balanced in the years to come will have profound impacts on the future of the state and its environs.

Water availability has always been a limiting factor for development of civilizations, and struggles over water resources have a long history in this state. Mining required water diversions to remove the placer gold deposits in the rivers, and later for hydraulic mining of whole hillsides. These interests encouraged development of water laws that protected appropriative rights—those enabling the physical diversion of water for use anywhere. Alternately, American farming traditionally relied upon riparian rights to assure access to water that was to be used on land abutting the watercourse. Later, large-scale agriculture in California secured publicly funded regional redistribution of water. Today, agriculture still uses the bulk of water exported through the state's aqueduct systems although provisions for urban, and, to a lesser degree, "environmental" purposes have been increased. Most important for the next century, the easily accessed water resources from the San Joaquin, the Colorado, and Owens Valley rivers are now fully allocated, leaving only the Sacramento River watershed and perhaps the northernmost watersheds to exploit.

Massive redistribution systems with dams and canals define the landscape of the Central, San Joaquin, and Imperial valleys. Because of these redistribution systems, high-quality water remains readily available in California. It is, however, allocated inefficiently—water that should be used for drinking, for example, is still used to flush toilets and water lawns. Today, however, because of economic, environmental, and social costs, this approach to water management is being rethought. California's zero-sum approach has given us winners and losers, but the slow and clumsy hammer of the federal Endangered Species Act has the last say: fish do not grow where no water flows. The individual and collective tragedies that arise from these battles reveal a pressing need to rethink our approach to water management. Among its other tasks, a constitutional convention would need to consider water management and other related natural resource questions.

To illustrate the need for dramatic change consider the latest chapter in the controversy over management of water resources in the Sacramento–San

Joaquin Delta, including the renewed calls for massive new infrastructure to deliver water to the Bay Area and points south. The continuing controversies over Delta water resources illuminate the failures of our current system and the need for core, constitutional changes. After identifying key barriers to appropriate management of essential water resources, we will describe several ways that a constitutional convention might address and improve water management.

First, a Little History

Even more so than elsewhere in the United States, water is the lifeblood of the West, a region which, on average, receives less than half the precipitation that the rest of the country gets. How water is parceled out in a dry land determines not only which crops can be grown, but also who can grow them, and who cannot. It also determines where people can live and which species can survive.

Despite water being arguably California's most important natural resource, the California constitution says very little about it, leaving most of the heavy lifting to statutory schemes scattered throughout California's code system. Article X of the California constitution includes several water-related provisions, the most important of which is its Section 2, which requires that all water used under state-conferred rights be devoted to reasonable use, regardless of source or user. While this concept may sound obvious, its inclusion in the constitution did not come easily.

Nearly a century ago, water wars between users who held appropriative rights and those who held riparian rights disrupted the water rights system. The riparian system had been imported to California from the water-rich eastern states of the U.S., while the appropriative system had arisen in the goldfields of California's Mother Lode. These conflicts peaked in 1926, when the California Supreme Court unleashed a furor with the *Herminghaus v. Southern California Edison* case.[1] While preceding decisions had generally upheld the rights of riparian right holders over appropriative right holders, *Herminghaus* went so far as to state that a dam could not be operated if it would obstruct the natural flooding that occurred on a downstream rancher's riverside lands, whatever the needs of the upstream appropriator.[2]

The ensuing public outcry culminated in a referendum to amend the California constitution. Conferences and discussions took place throughout the state, and a long series of legislative hearings hammered out the language of the proposed amendment. While Californians agreed that change was needed, they disagreed about how much. In the end, the legislature took the middle ground, drafting an amendment that adopted conservation and the elimination of waste as explicit policy goals, but also continued protections for "riparians," who used water reasonably and who had gained their right legally. The new amendment stated that water rights "shall be limited to such water as shall be reasonably required for the beneficial use to be served" and "shall not extend to the waste or unreasonable use" of water.[3]

Although this section of Article X has provided a foundation to guide all water use, it has not ended water conflicts. Conflicts over proper water allocation continue today with no end in sight, while offering little clarity on respective rights short of court chambers. Hence, the main strategy of water rights holders has become a dogged defense of their current rights, no matter how murkily defined.

To understand how these conflicts play themselves out today we must first understand the basic facts about the state's water supply. Half of California is arid—receiving, as noted, less than ten inches of rain per year. About 75 percent of its rain falls in the north, while two-thirds of its population lives in the south.[4] California's typical answer to the lack of water in any particular location is to ship it there as needed. The resultant water infrastructure is massive and affects every major river in the state. The state's complex plumbing system supplies 15 million acre-feet (maf) of water to the state's homes, farms, and industries.[5] In 2005, the state used an estimated 43.2 maf of water, and 80 percent of it went to agriculture.[6]

A truth that applies to any water system, no matter how well designed, is that "from wherever water is taken, life will be altered and diminished."[7] Today the Sacramento–San Joaquin Delta, for example, receives only about half the flow it did in predevelopment times. Let us look more closely at this Delta, where yet another water war is brewing.

The Sacramento–San Joaquin Delta: Heart of California's Water World

Geographically and politically, the Delta is the heart of the state's natural and managed water supplies. The water of the Delta is not only critical to maintain local farming and communities, but is also transferred through a vast water system to supply the burgeoning populations of Southern California. The Delta water mainly irrigates the farmland of the San Joaquin Valley, "the most productive unnatural environment on Earth."[8] The eight counties of the San Joaquin Valley grow more than $20 billion worth of crops each year,

Regional Imports and Exports, 1995 Level of Development

1995 Level of Development (taf)

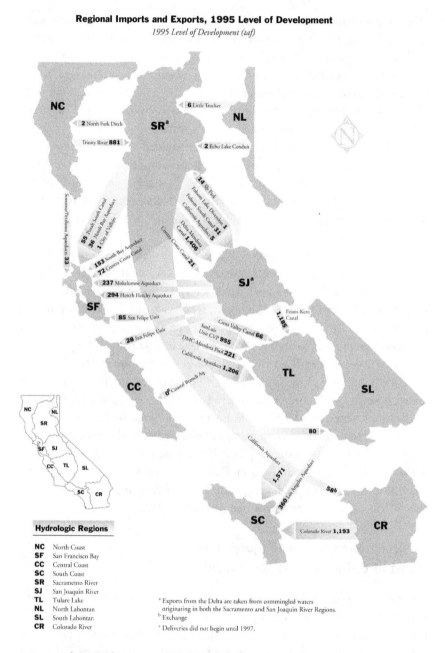

Hydrologic Regions

NC	North Coast
SF	San Francisco Bay
CC	Central Coast
SC	South Coast
SR	Sacramento River
SJ	San Joaquin River
TL	Tulare Lake
NL	North Lahontan
SL	South Lahontan
CR	Colorado River

[a] Exports from the Delta are taken from commingled waters originating in both the Sacramento and San Joaquin River Regions.
[b] Exchange
[c] Deliveries did not begin until 1997.

FIGURE 1 from California Water Plan Update Bulletin 160-98, California Dept. of Water Resources more than the rest of California combined, and more than any other state. This massive water transfer has economic, political, social, and environmental impacts that have transformed California's landscape and established the basis of conflicts for the foreseeable future.

Whatever tenuous balance is sometimes achieved between different water users and groups with claims on Delta water is all too frequently destabilized by such things as drought, shifts in climatic conditions, diversion of the Delta's freshwater to Southern California, unmanaged population growth in the desert regions, the introduction of invasive species, and evolving economic needs. The different water claimants—farmers of competing crops, utilities, environmentalists, and others—are still engaged today in struggles over allocations of Delta resources, and assigning one another blame for the current troubles.

Sources of Strain in the Delta

The Delta is a major switching yard for some 6 to 7 maf of pumped water per year, including a portion of drinking water supplies for 23 million people, from the Bay Area down to San Diego, as well as irrigation water for over 7 million acres of agricultural land.[9]

Combined, the projects divert from about 20 to 70 percent of the natural stream flow into the Delta, depending on the rainfall per year. In addition to these exports, some water that historically flowed into the Delta is also diverted upstream for agricultural and other uses, and lost by evaporation/transpiration. The system is difficult to manage because the relative amounts of water contributed by the Sacramento and the San Joaquin rivers vary greatly by year, season, and tide.

From the State Water Project pumps, water enters a labyrinth of pipelines, tunnels, and canals (including the 444-mile-long California Aqueduct) that carry it to farms and residential users. The Central Valley Project pumps, meanwhile, primarily divert water to the sprawling farms of the San Joaquin Valley, the core of U.S. fruit and vegetable production. Southern California relies on the Delta for 30 percent of its water supply, while the San Francisco Bay Area relies on the Delta for 33 percent of its supply.

Hindsight provides a striking perspective on past water distribution choices, and a lesson on how ideas that once seemed infallible now prove deeply flawed. An unanticipated consequence of placing the CVP and SWP pumps in the South Delta has been that it changes water circulation patterns throughout the estuary, causing saltwater intrusion and reverse flows on the

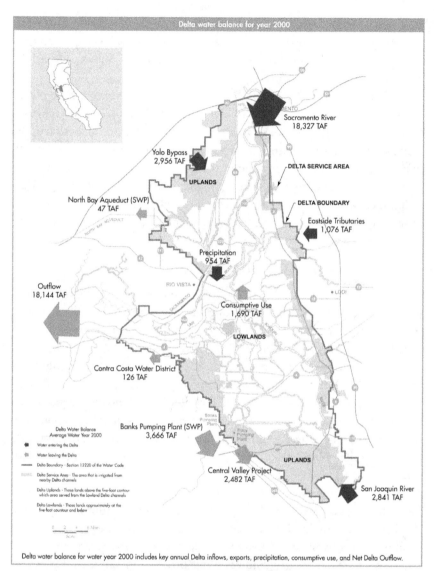

Delta water balance for water year 2000 includes key annual Delta inflows, exports, precipitation, consumptive use, and Net Delta Outflow.

FIGURE 2. Freshwater from the Delta rivers (Sacramento, San Joaquin, Mokelumne, and Calaveras) is channeled to two massive distribution systems—the Central Valley Project (CVP) and State Water Project (SWP). California Water Plan Update, California Dept. of Water Resources.

San Joaquin River. The massive unscreened pumps also entrain and kill fish. These problems are now being used to justify construction of new, upstream diversion and conveyance infrastructure for the projects that would fundamentally alter flow patterns and water quality in the Delta yet again.

Within the Delta's watershed there are also thousands of existing diversions along the length of the Sacramento and American rivers, upstream of the Delta, as well as thousands of agricultural diversions within the Delta. A total of about seven thousand permitted diverters receive water from the Bay-Delta estuary. While fraught with accounting challenges, information compiled by the State Water Resources Control Board for the recent Delta Vision process revealed that water rights granted on paper far exceed estimated annual diversions, as well as the total volume of water known to flow through the Delta in even its wettest years.[10] Potential future diversions upstream of the Delta would only worsen the situation.[11]

When surface water (from the Delta, for instance) is not available, groundwater is the next choice for water users. Although most scientists and many farmers recognize the connection between surface water and groundwater, the state and state law do not. This permits local "mining" of groundwater, which leads to irreversible subsidence and drying-up of streams reliant on groundwater replenishment during months of drought.

The lack of comprehensive regulation over groundwater has contributed to the depletion of what was once a seemingly endless water supply. Some areas of the San Joaquin Valley have literally sunk dozens of feet as a result of over-pumping.[12]

Reliance on groundwater also occurs when surface water rights in the wetter areas of the state are transferred to other regions. In 2009, for example, the state's implementation of the Drought Water Bank transferred water to points southward from farms with Sacramento River water rights; those farms then pumped groundwater instead. Each year's use of groundwater in the state exceeds replenishment by 2.2 maf.[13]

In addition to questions of water quantity, major dangers are posed to the Delta's water quality. Water pollution from historic gold and cinnabar mining, urban runoff, and municipal and agricultural wastewater pose major challenges to the health of the Delta, exacerbated by removal of freshwater flows by water diversions. While scientists are still attempting to clarify the connections between specific contaminants and the decline of aquatic species, the role of water quality is undeniable.

A more subtle, but profoundly destructive, impact on the Delta has been delivered by invasive species brought in through ship ballast water, agricultural crop seeds, and deliberate transplanting. Much of the biomass in the Delta is now made up of plants from around the world, clams from Asia, and fish from Europe.[14] These species compete for food with the native species, occupy their habitats, and consume them, contributing to severe declines in native species.

Looming Stress Factors and Effects in the Delta

California is subject to earthquakes that can occur at any time, and is also subject to sea level rise and other impacts as the global climate changes. The California Department of Water Resources is concerned that an earthquake could cause several levees to fail at the same time, potentially necessitating emergency actions and restoration projects when the state lacks the resources for them. (For a map of Delta topography, see the Calfed Program's *State of Bay-Delta Science* report, p. 104, at http://science.calwater ca.gov/pdf/publications/sbds/sbds_2008_final_report_101508.pdf.) With a warmer and wetter climate, runoff during the winter may increase as much as three times and there could also be significant sea level rise. Such changes could, for instance, greatly increase the salinity of the entire Delta.[15]

During the 1992 floor debates in the U.S. Senate regarding the Central Valley Project Improvement Act, Senator Bill Bradley (D-New Jersey) asked what would happen if California did nothing to change the way the Delta and its resources were managed. In answer to his own question, he postulated a list of perils:

- Several species could become extinct, not the least of which might be California fishermen.

- Many Northern California coastal towns could collapse due to the demise of the fishing industry.

- During droughts people will pay hundreds of dollars for every acre-foot of water they use while just over the hill in the Central Valley hundreds of thousands of acres of subsidized cotton and rice will flourish in the desert.

- Federal courts and state courts will run the CVP and SWP.[16]

Many of the results Senator Bradley feared have come to pass despite several efforts to address the core ills of the Delta since 1992. One such effort was the CALFED[17] Bay-Delta Program agreement of 1994, which reflected a widespread consensus that the Bay-Delta system was in crisis and a twenty-five-agency coordinated effort was needed to reduce conflicts in the system and rationally address its multiple problems. CALFED was the "largest and most comprehensive ecosystem restoration and water management program in the world."[18]

One Delta plumbing fix considered by CALFED, as well as in previous years, was the construction of a new upstream diversion point near Sacramento leading to a canal around the Delta to facilitate diversion of CVP and SWP water. In 1982, Proposition 9 proposed funding for the construction of such a "peripheral canal," but it was defeated by popular vote, 62 percent to 38 percent. Voting patterns were clearly divided between north and south, with areas north of Kern County voting overwhelmingly against the proposal.[19] Due to growing controversy on the topic, CALFED did not include the canal as a component of its final program in 1998, but listed it as a Preferred Program Alternative.[20]

By 2008, CALFED had accomplished little in terms of delaying species declines or even identifying why losses were increasing. The consortium was ultimately reduced to an agreement and a limited science program. Its demise was not so much due to problems of collaboration as to the failure of political will to acknowledge the scientific findings. The destructive consequences of conflicting water laws for surface, riparian, and groundwater rights, of the refusal to plan for and implement long-term efficiency and growth within available water supplies, and of ignoring signs of critical infrastructure and species collapse will affect all Californians.

Despite CALFED agreements, the reverse flows caused by pumping still trap significant numbers of fish, particularly the Delta smelt, which is listed as threatened under the Endangered Species Act. Despite CALFED recommendations, annual water exports also continued to increase until 2007, when state and federal court cases resulted in restrictions at the pumps.[21] Not only are Delta smelt at risk, but also "numerous species and populations dependent upon the estuary and the Central Valley watershed are on the verge of extinction, including winter- and spring-run Chinook salmon, Delta smelt, longfin smelt, and Sacramento splittail."[22] Because of a court order and drought, mandatory water export restrictions were implemented at the pumps in 2008 and 2009, requiring San Joaquin Valley farmers to leave land fallow, with ripple effects throughout California's economy. Pain is also felt in both the recreational and commercial fishing sectors, with salmon fishing essentially shut down off the coasts of California and Oregon.

Under pressure from environmental and fishing groups, the federal fish agencies have added further restrictions to operation of the projects based on biological opinions under the Endangered Species Act. State fish and water management agencies also continue to struggle with permit and planning processes in the Delta, sometimes working at cross-purposes. All agency actions affecting the Delta are controversial and most are subject to litigation.

Continued Subsidization of Unsustainable Water Use

Despite the grim outlook for species in the Delta, use of exported Delta water continues to be subsidized. The SWP provides startling examples of subsidies of clearly unsustainable water use. Remarkable for its design and engineering innovations, and presented as a necessary conduit of water for Southern California's ever-expanding households, the SWP was sold to voters with threats of another water famine and doctored cost estimates. But today, as we saw, 80 percent of SWP water actually goes to agriculture.

Although many are unaware of it, SWP pricing structures also provide large subsidies. In 1973, Robert Fellmeth reported that because SWP pricing structures undercharged for the base cost of SWP water, which was discounted further by large amounts of surplus water, state and county governments were paying $41 an acre-foot to deliver water that was sold to farmers for only about $12.50 an acre-foot. Multiply that per-acre subsidy by Tenneco's 350,000 acres, and if those farmers had all their acreage under cultivation they would get $10 million worth of corporate welfare a year for just one acre-foot per acre.[23] These are large beasts to be drinking at the public trough. Today, the average cost of agricultural water throughout the state is $30 per acre-foot, and it is still heavily subsidized.[24]

Compare these costs to Newlands Act (i.e., federal water) projects extending from eastern California to Nevada along the Truckee River watershed. The same problems of regional over-allocation of water, subsidies meant for small farmers largely going to land speculators, and imperiled native fish species occurred there—but were managed over twenty years ago through a series of court decrees and ensuing market responses. Water rights are now being sold in the Truckee watershed at approximately $40,000 to $50,000 an acre-foot, essentially the free-market cost for water in arid lands.[25]

Besides conferring inequitable subsidies, artificially cheap water has other ramifications throughout the food industry and for the average water consumer, because production and pricing decisions are based on an inaccurate measure of real costs. These costs include not only those of water storage and delivery, which might be measured by the market, but also the long-term environmental costs (often called "externalities") that are not measured. Were these externalities included in water pricing, agribusiness and the state might decide to make other plans—for example, to substitute drip for flood irrigation, to promote conservation, or to change crops. Moreover, water consumers, if forced to pay the true cost of water delivered to their faucets and hoses, might reduce their demand.

The BDCP—Another Attempt to Solve the Delta Puzzle

In 2006, a new approach to the problems of the Delta began in order to meet state and federal endangered species requirements associated with pumping water out of the Delta. Spearheaded by water agencies dependent on Delta water exports, the Department of Water Resources and the Bureau of Reclamation created the Bay Delta Conservation Plan (BDCP), a project that promotes a peripheral canal (or other conveyance around the Delta) and also includes a Habitat Conservation Plan under federal law, and a Natural Community Conservation Plan under state law. If approved, the BDCP would allow some level of "taking" or harm to species such as the Delta smelt, in exchange for commitments to avoid or minimize the impacts of the projects on other special-status species in the Delta.[26] The BDCP proposes a number of conservation measures to theoretically improve conditions for fish and other species in the Delta, and to restore and create marshes that could provide habitat and food supply for listed fish.

BDCP applicants are seeking "take" authorizations to last for fifty years, with only limited opportunities to amend those authorizations in light of new developments, except for prescribed "re-openers" if an ecosystem starts to crash after the authorizations are approved.[27] This length of time would provide a high degree of certainty for water purchasers. But it would also institutionalize existing agricultural and urban water uses, including their inefficiencies. Once the permits are issued, the water commitments would be essentially guaranteed, even if the species were not in fact conserved and regardless of the other project impacts to the Delta. Fifty years sounds like a long time, especially in light of the changes the state has seen over the last half-century.

A key part of the BDCP, in order to avoid the dangers to the Delta smelt posed by the projects' pumps, acquire higher-quality water, and stabilize or even increase water deliveries, is the proposal to construct new diversion points on the Sacramento River for a peripheral canal. Proponents of the canal claim that there would be environmental benefits to taking higher-quality water out of the watershed in an upstream location for their own use. The new upstream diversion points would do nothing, however, to address the fundamental problem—most of the state's water is not near the majority of its population. "A peripheral canal, first and foremost will not make more water. The present problem with California's water system is that it is short 5 million acre-feet of water annually to meet current state needs. Rerouting water will not solve that problem."[28] Many scientists doubt that diverting large amounts of water farther upstream, before it reaches the Delta, is likely to improve the ecology of an impaired system, and many believe such a diversion could actually further impair water quality and worsen conditions for fish in the rivers and sloughs of the Delta.[29]

A further concern of canal opponents is the enormous cost, which still has not been determined. Government estimates range from $6 billion to over $15 billion.[30] Thus the next massive public water expenditures could well benefit the few at the expense of the public, as large state water projects unfortunately have in the past.

Core Problems Illuminated by the Delta Experience

The travails of water and resource management in the Delta reveal several deficiencies of water management throughout the state. As a result, a sustainable balance between the needs of the natural and human environments with respect to water resources is not being attained. These deficiencies can be summarized as follows:

- The state's water infrastructure was designed and built with no overall plan for the future of affected natural and human communities, and no sustainability criteria have been applied to water projects, past or proposed.

- Unsustainable and wasteful water use is still promoted by direct and indirect subsidization.

- The state's legal and planning framework incorrectly assumes that more water will always be available to accommodate growth.

- The current water rights system does not ensure complete implementation of the existing constitutional requirement for reasonable uses of all water, including groundwater.

- Public trust uses—including water for environmental purposes— are not recognized as being on an equal footing with water used for cities and commercial purposes.

- The lack of reliable data about existing water uses prevents informed management decisions.

- The authority for protection of ecosystems is fragmented, and environmental protections are invoked only after harm has been done or when major crises arise.

Despite its leadership on some environmental fronts, the state is failing in its responsibility to protect its environmental resources while also providing sustainable high-quality water. Political and economic considerations have overridden enforcement of water quantity and quality requirements. Judicial remedies do continue to be available for those who can afford them, but fundamental changes are needed in the state's approach to natural resources, and experience suggests these are unlikely to occur through existing processes.

The Need for a Dramatically Different Approach

How might a constitutional convention address the problems of water management in California? Water is so central to the life of the state, and conflicts about it such a constant element of its politics, that it's fitting for the constitution to contain provisions about it. While Article X, Section 2 is a good beginning, additional provisions within Article X should be considered, specifically to:

- Incorporate sustainability criteria in all new infrastructure projects.

- Require water pricing that takes into account the true value and cost of water.

- Plan for drought conditions and limit automatic water exports to new development.

- Eliminate distinctions between different water types in favor of a system that creates certainty and facilitates proper management of water resources.

- Facilitate collection of data about all water uses.

- Clarify that ecosystem/natural community uses of water are beneficial uses requiring protection.

We now turn to these points:

Incorporate sustainability criteria in all new infrastructure projects. Sustainability in the ecological context refers to the ability of biological systems to remain diverse and productive over time. For humans, sustainability

Courtesy of the *San Francisco Examiner*

could be framed as the potential for long-term maintenance of beneficial life conditions, which depend on the sustainability of the natural world and the responsible use of natural resources.

The lack of consistent application of any sustainability criteria will lead to irreversible environmental damage. Existing environmental protections are resorted to now only after major failures occur, often when it is too late to prevent major harm to the environment. In the context of the Delta, for instance, scientists are not sure that extinction of the tiny Delta smelt can be prevented, no matter what we do.

To prevent future unexpected and negative impacts on our already strained resources, a sustainability requirement should be enforced as a prior condition for any new projects. Any new water infrastructure, for example, should be proven sustainable for at least several generations. A constitutional amendment would provide guidance that could then be incorporated into the relevant statutes. While this concept already appears in some existing legal requirements applicable to natural resources, a provision in the constitution could facilitate consistent and timely application of sustainability principles. This will also require adaptive management as conditions change and as information is gathered through experience.

What constitutes a sustainable project is obviously subject to argument. But without effort to clarify it the state will continue repeating its past mistakes. By planning ahead for several generations (e.g., at least fifty to a hundred years), the state can better manage water supplies for future generations. This requirement should also be applied to other natural resources.

Some business and utility interests may question the need for imposing a new sustainability requirement, but that requirement would generate a greater certainty for businesses too into the future. The drive for sustainability would increase the likelihood that resources will be available to support future economic activities. Without such a requirement, businesses will be subject to unexpected and draconian orders for change, as occurred recently with restrictions on water from the Delta.

Require water pricing that takes into account the true value and cost of water. Much of the water delivered out of the Delta and elsewhere is greatly underpriced, as we have seen. Artificially low water costs skewed by subsidies burden the public coffers and local watersheds by supplying water for export at reduced expense, often for purposes of unmanaged growth. Beyond direct capital and operational costs associated with the delivery of water to areas far from its origins, there are "ripple costs" throughout the affected ecosystems, as well as for the communities from which the water is taken. Resource economics can provide the tools to assign monetary values to these costs. And the state has the tools to more accurately determine the costs of water delivery and use. The free-market solution to these complex subsidies and unintended consequences of water contracted through publicly funded projects would be to remove the subsidies.

The constitution should specify that new water delivery projects should be paid for in full (infrastructure, mitigation, and maintenance) by the beneficiaries of those projects. And existing projects might be fully funded by the recipients of water and infrastructure costs paid without reliance on public funding of debt. SWP charges today, for example, do not include such mitigation of any kind.[31] If these reforms were adopted, water pricing would begin to reflect the true cost of delivering that water, encouraging thoughtful planning and incentives for greater conservation.

Fees should also be authorized for uses or diversions of water that degrade water quality. A new constitutional provision could clarify that reasonable fees, based on actual impacts of use, would be imposed on water users in order to fund necessary mitigation and ensure state maintenance of water quality.

Plan for drought conditions and limit automatic water exports to new development. It is incorrect to assume that more water will always be available to serve population growth. As laws have been passed to require more long-term planning with respect to water supplies, the ability to continue artificially rearranging the distribution of water throughout the state has been increasingly questioned. These engineering rearrangements impose large costs on the watersheds of origin and on the species that rely on them.

Drought is a predictable occurrence in California. That has to be taken into consideration in water management and contracting. In two recent below-normal but not critically dry years, for example, the SWP pumps still delivered massive amounts of water south with apparent disregard for the fact that Northern California reservoirs would be drawn down to dangerously low levels.

To change this destructive course, a constitutional amendment might require regional self-sufficiency for future water demands by specifying that new growth rely on water within the same region, or on water that is conserved from water already being imported from other regions. Moreover, water supplies for new growth should be based on the amount of water available in dry years, since such years occur so frequently.

Eliminate distinctions between different water types in favor of a system that creates certainty and facilitates proper management of water resources. Reliance on a hybrid appropriative and riparian rights system that does not regulate groundwater at the state level has proven unsuitable for California and led to severe depletion of groundwater resources. All water is hydrologically connected through the water cycle, regardless of its source. Groundwater is not separate from surface water. The theories under which percolating groundwater was exempted from state regulation over one hundred years ago are no longer credible, and California needs to come to terms with the hydrologic connection of surface water and groundwater, or risk complete depletion of a key component of its water budget. Most western states have recognized these facts and do regulate groundwater.

Other western states—Kansas, for example—have adopted purely appropriative systems for all their water users. Elimination of distinctions between types of water rights could allow for more evenhanded regulation and management decisions. California's current Article X, Section 2 goes part of the way by subjecting all water usage to reasonable use. Although groundwater is not specifically mentioned, case law even dating before 1928 applied the reasonable use doctrine to groundwater.[32] Section 2's effectiveness could be bolstered, however, by adding a specific reference to groundwater. Moreover, groundwater basin management plans should be required, not simply allowed, as at present. And the State Water Resources Control Board should possess direct regulatory authority over groundwater to ensure these plans are implemented and these resources conserved for future generations. Elimination of the legal distinctions between riparian and appropriative water rights might also be considered by the constitutional convention, to provide greater certainty in future water resources management.

Facilitate collection of data about all water uses. In the information age one might expect that we would have a good idea of how water is used in the state. But we do not. Some water users perceive the state's collection of this information as a threat, and its efforts to manage water resources are therefore thwarted by lack of information. The Department of Water Resources is left to focus mainly on delivering water. There appears to be little political will at present to get more accurate data. Proposed legislation in the regular 2009 session would have required the filing of statements of diversion for all water users but it lacked the votes to progress beyond the senate floor.[33] In a later and highly publicized special session, however, the legislature adopted a bill that requires groundwater elevations to be monitored by local governments, though other provisions with broader reporting requirements for surface water were ultimately jettisoned from the package.[34]

The lack of accurate information about all water use—regardless of type—hinders the state's ability to make informed management decisions. Much more water exists on paper than actually exists in the state's water systems. With a baseline based on real data, available resources could be identified for the various types of water years, and reallocation could occur if necessary. A constitutional amendment requiring mandatory reporting of all water uses to facilitate better water management would be welcome.

Clarify that ecosystem/natural community uses of water are beneficial uses requiring protection. Under existing legal principles, use of instream flows of water for wildlife and recreation are "beneficial uses." But domestic use, sanitation, and fire protection generally take priority over instream uses. (See, e.g., California Water Code sections 354 and 1243.) The public trust doctrine, affirmed in the important Mono Lake court decision of 1983, is a common law doctrine establishing the government's legal duty to maintain certain lands and waters as a trust in the public interest.[35] The doctrine also provides that the state has a duty to protect the public use of navigable waters and their tributaries, as well as to provide for environmental resources, recreation, and aesthetic purposes. Protection of public trust resources has, however, often been subordinated to meeting immediate demands for water, to the long-term detriment of all.

It is now estimated that environmental preservation accounts for at most 36 percent of the state's surface water supply, and that may not even be enough to sustain important natural communities, considering the Delta example. As the population grows, even more water is likely to be routed to human consumption. The need therefore emerges to specifically allocate a portion of our water supply to future environmental uses. A constitutional amendment could address this problem by specifying that beneficial uses of water for the environment are at least equal in importance to consumptive uses. Specifically, public trust uses should be included among the reasonable uses of water already required under Article X, Section 2 of the California constitution. Such a change would ensure, for example, that the goals of the Endangered Species Act to conserve species would be better supported by water law. Better stewardship of the environment would lead to greater long-term certainty for water users and for the business community too.

This change would also help streamline authority which is now fragmented between many different agencies with conflicting mandates. Myriad statutes provide conflicting goals and considerations for making decisions in the permit and planning processes. The merging, at least in principle, of water management, species protection, and other environmental protection uses of the state's water by constitutional mandate would provide more consistent policy making and implementation than exists today. Public trust principles could be directly incorporated into the Reasonable Use requirements of Article X, Section 2, or added as a separate amendment within Article X.[36] This approach could lead to formal allocation of specific amounts of water for species protection, as was done in Australia in the Murray-Darling Basin.[37]

Conclusion

It is time for California to learn from its own history and from mistakes made elsewhere. If our water resources are allowed to become completely exploited and commodified and we fail to protect areas of origin and beneficial uses, including the environment, damage may become irreparable. Adoption of more comprehensive water resource protections at the constitutional level would help lead California toward a sustainable future for generations to come. While any changes to the constitution involving water will be controversial, continued reliance on the current system governing its use is not a viable option. Adequate, fair, and environmentally sound protections for this most precious natural resource must be part of a new California constitution.

PART IV

Remedies
for the Crisis:
Overhauling
State Government

TEN

Remapping the California Electorate

Mark Paul and Micah Weinberg

HAVING SURVEYED CALIFORNIA'S political crisis and its effects, we turn to possible solutions in the next two chapters and epilogue. Severe as these problems have been shown to be, promising and effective remedies are readily conceivable. Some have been proposed in the chapters of this book. Few reform proposals are as comprehensive in their scope and as exciting and original as the one that Mark Paul and Micah Weinberg present here. Their ideas for changing how the state votes are particularly important because they aim not only at changing institutions but at revitalizing popular political life and activity.

Paul and Weinberg propose a modified form of the proportional representation proposed in chapter six, decentralized into electoral regions of the state and charged with electing representatives to a unicameral legislature in Sacramento. They call it a FAIR representative system: Full, Accurate, Individualized, and Regional. Besides the benefits of these attributes, their proposal also promises to give greater voice to minorities and to reduce the role of money in campaigns. It is a truly constitutional proposal because it would shake up the fundamental way the state's politics are constituted.

Mark Paul, senior scholar and deputy director of the California program at the New America Foundation, has also been an editor at the *Sacramento Bee* and deputy treasurer of the state of California. He is the coauthor, with Joe Mathews, of *California Crackup: How Reform Broke the Golden State and How We Can Fix It*, forthcoming from University of California Press.

Micah Weinberg is a senior research fellow in the California program of the New America Foundation, with research focuses on political reform and health-care policy.

ALIFORNIANS ARE NOT happy with their legislature. They berate it on talk radio, mock it in letters to the editor, and disapprove of it when the pollsters call. As state government hurtled toward insolvency in mid-2009, voter approval of the legislature's performance fell to 14 percent, the low-water mark in the nearly three decades the Field Poll has been taking such soundings. Although voter regard for public institutions and public officials tends to track the health of the economy, there is more to the current dissatisfaction with the California legislature than unhappiness over IOUs. The 2009 approval rating for the legislature, in which Democrats, Republicans, and independents showed striking agreement, was lower by half than during any previous state fiscal crisis. The last time a majority of voters expressed approval of the legislature was in 1988—just two years before they imposed term limits on lawmakers.[1]

At the heart of this discontent is an inescapable fact: California has outgrown its government. Its current legislative and electoral systems were established in 1879 at California's last constitutional convention, when the state had fewer than a million residents. These institutions no longer adequately provide representation for a state whose population has grown forty-fold and whose complexity—as a society, economy, and political community—is unrivaled across the nation. California's huge legislative districts, comprising nearly a half-million residents apiece in the assembly and nearly a million in the senate, distance voters from those they elect and elevate the importance of money in politics. Its winner-take-all district elections, when combined with Californians' new habit of bunching themselves in communities of the politically like-minded, eliminate most political competition and leave large segments of the electorate with no voice in legislative elections. Its exclusive use of geographic election districts ignores the fact that today's Californians live in a "nation" without states—a nation comprising more than a half-dozen distinct regions, each with its own economy, ecology, and political culture. California voters understand—and are often unhappy—that the legislature does not work, but are only dimly aware that, given how the state has changed over the last 140 years, it is never likely to work well again in its current configuration.

Incremental reforms like term limits or scaling back the legislature to a part-time body do not get to the heart of these problems. If California is to reinvigorate representative state government, it must start over by tailoring the legislature and electoral system to fit twenty-first-century realities, changes that can be accomplished only through a constitutional revision or constitutional convention.

To that end, we propose that California adopt a system we call FAIR Representation (Full, Accurate, Individualized, and Regional): a unicameral legislature elected in regional contests using a mixed-member system of representation that will allow California's citizens to set the agenda for their regions and for the state as a whole. FAIR would create a powerful mechanism for holding the legislature accountable, break the partisan stranglehold on legislative outcomes, and put California at the forefront of political and policy innovation.

The 360 seats in our proposed unicameral legislature would be apportioned among California's eight regions according to their respective populations (see Table 1). For example, the Central Coast would have 11 legislators, the San Diego Border region 36. (While it would be possible to implement this system and maintain the current number of chambers in the legislature [2] and legislators [40 in the senate and 80 in the assembly], for the reasons we spell out below we believe that it is important to sharply reduce the population of California's legislative districts.) Within each region, half the seats would be elected by district, the other half by proportional representation.[2] Californians in this system would cast two votes on Election Day. They would choose 1) an individual to represent their district, and 2) a party to represent their region.[3]

As under the current system, the candidate who won the plurality of votes in each district would be elected to the legislature. The remaining regional seats would be filled in order from ranked party lists of candidates made available to the public. Within each region, parties would win seats in proportion

TABLE 1. **Regional Representatives**

Region	Population	Regional Seats
Northern California	1,057,153	10
Gold Country	3,531,141	34
San Joaquin Valley	2,873,191	27
Bay Area	7,244,855	69
Central Coast	1,440,896	14
Greater Los Angeles	14,219,013	136
Inland Empire	4,109,782	39
San Diego Border	3,294,410	31

SOURCE: Current Population Survey, 2006.
NOTE: Assumes 360-seat unicameral legislature; half elected from single-member districts.

to the number of "party list" votes they received.[4] Party lists help maximize ethnic and gender representation as well as increase skills and knowledge within the legislature. A party would need to reach a threshold of 5 percent in a region to win seats under this system.[5] Individual district candidates could be included on the regional party lists. If they won their districts, party list apportionment would skip to the next candidate on the list.

The accompanying map (Figure 1) presents one way of dividing California into political regions. The regions we propose are generally coterminous

FIGURE 1. California's Political Regions

with the boundaries of media markets. Deliberation is at the heart of the democratic process, and public political communication generally occurs in California by means of the broadcast media. Our proposed regional setup draws on analyses of economic, cultural, and ecological criteria developed by others.[6] By necessity, we have split or combined some regions. For example, although we recognize the economic, cultural, and ecological distinctiveness of the Central Sierra counties, they are too sparsely populated to stand alone as a political region. Therefore, we split the Central Sierra counties between Gold Country and the San Joaquin Valley.[7] To understand how this system would work, let's look at how representation would be established in two hypothetical regional elections.

Under FAIR, Northern California, the least populous region, would have ten seats, five chosen by means of single-member district elections. Let's assume that party-list votes mirror current party registration,[8] with third party and "decline to state" registrants splitting their party-list votes evenly between the Republican list and a third party such as the Libertarians. This would result in:

- 51 percent of party-list votes for the Republicans

- 37 percent for the Democrats

- 12 percent for the Libertarians

Let's further assume that Republicans win four of the five single-member districts in this region and the Democrats win one seat, roughly in line with past electoral outcomes. Each of these winning candidates is elected. To apportion the regional seats so that each party's share of regional representation matches the proportion of party-list votes it receives, we need to step through those seats one by one, applying the following equation to each party's vote: Number of Votes the Party Received / (Number of Seats Party Holds +1). Table 2 shows the results of this calculation for Northern California using percentages to represent total votes. The Democrats win seats six and seven, the Libertarians win seat eight, and the Republicans win seats nine and ten.

The apportionment of seats for this region, therefore, is:

- 5 for the Republicans (4 elected by district, 1 representing region, or 50 percent of the total number of seats)

- 4 for the Democrats (1 elected by district, 3 representing region, or 40 percent of the total number of seats)

TABLE 2: **Apportioning Remaining Seats for Northern California**

Seat	Seats			Greatest Quotient		
	Republican	Democrat	Libertarian	Republican	Democrat	Libertarian
5th	4	1	0	51	37	12
6th	4	**2**	0	10.2	18.5	12
7th	4	**3**	0	10.2	12.3	12
8th	4	3	**1**	10.2	9.25	12
9th	**5**	3	1	10.2	9.25	6
10th	5	**4**	1	8.5	9.25	6

NOTE: Greatest quotient numbers listed in 5th seat row are percentage of party-list votes; other rows calculate Votes / (Seats +1); party with greatest quotient receives next seat.

- 1 for the Libertarians (1 representing region, or 10 percent of the total number of seats)

This roughly matches the party-list percentages. As the number of seats in a region grows, these approximations become more precise.

FAIR is likely to increase Democratic and third-party representation in Northern California, as it may for the San Joaquin Valley and the San Diego Border Region, but it would also likely increase Republican and third-party representation in the Bay Area and the Greater Los Angeles region. To show how it might work for a region currently dominated by the Democratic Party, here is a scenario to apportion the 69 seats for the Bay Area, 34 of which would be selected by single-member districts:

We assume that Democrats win 30 of those single-member seats and Republicans win 4, in line with past elections. Let's assume that party-list voting reflects current party registration status with half of "decline to state" and third-party voters in this region (28 percent of registrants) supporting the Democratic Party and the other half split roughly between the Green Party and the Libertarian Party. This would result in:

- 65 percent of party-list votes for the Democrats

- 21 percent for the Republicans

- 8 percent for the Greens

- 6 percent for the Libertarians

The apportionment calculation would result in:

- 46 Democratic legislators (30 elected by district, 16 representing the region, or 67 percent of the total number of seats)

- 14 Republican legislators (4 elected by district, 10 representing the region, or 20 percent of the total number of seats)

- 5 Green Party legislators (7 percent of the total number of seats)

- 4 Libertarian Party legislators (6 percent of the total number of seats)

This is a substantially more ideologically diverse representation for the Bay Area than at present, though Republicans elected from this region may have more in common with Bay Area Democrats than with San Joaquin Valley region Republicans.

The full representation system we propose is similar in its design to those used to elect members of Germany's Bundestag (lower house), Mexico's Cámara de Senadores and Cámara de Diputados, and New Zealand's uni-cameral House of Representatives.[9] The plan honors the political salience of regions that is already a part of California's governing documents and practices. The requirement that legislative districts respect regional boundaries is written into the state constitution.[10] (A court-appointed expert rejected the senate's proposed redistricting plan for the 1990s because it did not respect regional boundaries.[11])

Proportional and mixed electoral systems are more common worldwide than systems that rely exclusively on single-member districts. It is telling that when American experts advise fledgling democracies, they propose electoral systems with multimember districts and proportional representation, and innovations such as the "single non-transferable vote" (SNTV) system used to elect the members of the Wolesi Jirga, Afghanistan's lower house.[12] Indeed, Woodrow Wilson, political science professor turned president, argued passionately for the adoption of a parliamentary system of government for the United States,[13] and the Proportional Representation League of the United States actively promoted the implementation of parliamentary systems on the municipal level from 1893 to 1932.[14]

Full representation systems are more democratic than our current system, which effectively shuts out the voices and preferences of millions of Californians. The clustering of Democrats and Republicans into communities of the like-minded makes it inevitable that large numbers of districts will be uncompetitive in general elections, often for long stretches of time, even under "fair" redistricting plans. In such areas, there is little reason for the candidate of the majority party to pay any attention to the views and concerns of voters in the minority. For purposes of representation, it is as if those on the losing side had not even voted. This is similar to the effect of the Electoral College in presidential elections, where candidates can safely ignore tens of millions of citizens in California, New York, and Texas because their votes can have no effect on the outcome. Under full representation, every voter counts. Because each extra vote for a party increases its chances of winning an additional seat, no voter's concerns can be safely ignored. Due to the lower threshold for winning seats, a full representation system gives a voice to those whose interests are not reflected by the agendas of the major parties as well as to those who identify with a major party but who are in the permanent minority in their district. The current system overlooks these people and hence actively cultivates apathy and suppresses civic engagement.

In addition to making statewide election outcomes more reflective of the concerns of all voters, full representation increases political diversity, and hence deliberation, at the regional level. Illinois used a form of proportional representation involving multimember districts and cumulative voting from 1870 to 1980. This system "gave a voice to a critical minority so that Democrats in the suburbs had a spokesperson for their district," writes Abner Mikva, a retired federal judge, congressman, and Illinois legislator. "Similarly in Chicago you had Republican representatives and these Republican outcomes in a city that was dominated by the Democratic Party."[15] Under FAIR, each region of the state would have both Democrats and Republicans representing it in the State Capitol, and most likely third-party legislators as well.

How FAIR Will Improve Governance

For more than three decades, there have been two major indictments of the California State Legislature. First, citizens and political observers alike complain that the "politicians" in the legislature do not well represent the interests of the voters. The widespread sense that lawmakers had become a separate political class, out of touch with ordinary citizens, propelled the successful campaign to enact term limits in 1990. By limiting the length of legislative careers, term-limits proponents argued, California would create a "citizen legislature" more representative of the electorate. In certain important respects, they have been proven right. Term limits cleaned out the old hands and speeded the arrival of Latino, Asian, and female lawmakers, with the result that the demographics of the legislature more closely mirror those of a rapidly changing state. But they have not eased the basic complaint: Californians remain as unsatisfied as ever with the quality of representation they receive in Sacramento.

Second, according to its critics, the current legislature is not just out of touch; it is also incompetent, slow to deal with many major state issues, often careless and sloppy when it does act, and neglectful of its duty to oversee state operations and programs. On a whole range of issues, from fiscal policy to education to infrastructure, voters are dissatisfied with the quality of the policy made in the State Capitol.

By reconfiguring legislative elections along regional lines, FAIR would reshape the political playing field and, along with it, the nature of the state's political conversation. Within each region, there would be a separate legislative campaign, and voter choice among the parties and the ideas they offer. For the first time, there would be a way to talk about regional issues, debate different approaches to dealing with them, and chose a policy direction to advance in the legislature.

Today, such discussions rarely occur in state legislative campaigns. Most Californians get their political information through news reporting and political advertising in commercial media—television, radio, and newspapers—that operate across whole regions. But legislative politics is generally conducted on a much smaller scale. Except in the least populated regions, where one legislative district or two might take in the entire region, most urban regions have numerous assembly and senate districts, too many for these electoral contests to be judged newsworthy by media outlets seeking large audiences. For the commercial media to devote air time or column inches to follow the assembly election in California's 54th Assembly District may please some prospective voters in San Pedro, but it invites many more viewers and readers in Whittier, Santa Clarita, and Pasadena to change the channel or turn the page. Covering legislative elections often makes no economic sense.

The same economic realities that keep legislative races largely out of the news also discourage the use of regional media in campaign advertising. In heavily populated regions, it is inefficient and prohibitively expensive for legislative campaigns to buy advertising in regional broadcast and print media to reach voters; they would have to buy the whole expensive media pie to reach a small slice of the electorate. Unable to reach voters through the channel by which most Californians get most of their political information—broadcast television—campaigns and special interest groups rely heavily on direct mail. Most legislative races typically play out in obscurity and often degenerate into "gotcha" attacks on candidates based on small personal foibles; voters learn which candidate took how much in per diem payments, but nothing about how the candidates would reduce traffic congestion on the regional freeways. This is particularly true for primary election campaigns, where the great majority of legislative elections are settled.

Under FAIR, the key legislative elections that award power in the State Capitol would be more about policy and party, less about individual candidates. In the San Joaquin Valley, the parties could debate how to raise the region's lagging incomes, relieve its air pollution, and improve its level of educational attainment. Bay Area parties could debate how to prevent high housing prices from discouraging the growth of the region's high-tech industry. In the Sacramento region, the contending parties could debate their proposals to manage growth while protecting the region's quality of life. Because these debates would be conducted and their outcomes decided at a regional level, touching the interests of the entire regional electorate, they would likely receive coverage in the commercial news media, and the campaigns would likely use paid advertising in regional media to make their case to voters, increasing the amount of information available to all voters.

A Better Statewide Discussion

This reconfigured system would also sharpen the debate on statewide issues and make it easier for voters to hold the legislature accountable and to shift the direction of the state. Issues that take center stage in Sacramento—reducing emissions of global warming gases, reforming health care, providing adequate water supply—barely register in legislative races. This is partly because there are so few real contests and partly because there is so little news coverage that requires candidates to address these issues in any breadth or depth. While legislative elections potentially can, and sometimes do, shift the balance of power between Democrats and Republicans, the results can rarely be said to be "about" some statewide policy issue or another.

FAIR would bring statewide issues to the fore in legislative elections, alongside regional issues. The division of legislative seats in California would be determined by the success of each party in the regional elections, in which the electorate would be choosing among the party agendas offered to them. These agendas would get the kind of public scrutiny and discussion, in the commercial news media and online, that is now reserved for gubernatorial elections. Since every vote would count in the outcome of the election, the contending parties would find it necessary to reach out to all parts of the electorate with policies to meet their needs and values, and to build and sustain coalitions with grassroots organizations concerned about particular issues. Were the majority party in the State Capitol to fail to meet its responsibilities (for example, in the management of state finances) or its promises (for example, to improve the quality of schools), the minority parties would be able to offer an alternative and ask voters to hold the majority party accountable for its failures.

More Political Competition

In addition to changing the nature of California's political conversation, FAIR would reshape legislative politics, creating more political competition. Over much of the last half-century, one-party control of the legislature has been largely baked into the system. As Bruce E. Cain, professor of political science at the University of California, Berkeley, has pointed out, there are two electorates in California, one statewide, the other legislative, which often yield different results.[16] The statewide electorate, in elections for governor and ballot measures, swings between Democrats and Republicans, and between conservative and liberal positions on initiative measures. The same electorate, voting in legislative races, has produced Democratic control of both houses of the legislature for the last forty years, except for one cycle in the mid-1990s when Democrats briefly lost control of the assembly. The difference in outcomes is largely due to unequal distribution of the electorate across legislative districts. Districts have equal populations, but Democratic-leaning areas of the state tend to have larger populations of noncitizens and children who cannot vote. As a result, Democrats win a greater share of seats than of overall votes cast in legislative elections. FAIR would assure that the party balance in the legislature reflected the actual party preferences of the voters in each election.

More Electoral Opportunities for Third or Fourth Parties

In the past, in California and across the United States, third parties have occasionally challenged the major-party duopoly, pushing new ideas and invigorating political competition. However, California's current method of electing legislators reinforces a two-party system,[17] which is increasingly out of line with the preferences of the citizens of this state. The absence of third-party legislators does not signal voter satisfaction with the two major parties. A recent Public Policy Institute of California poll reported that 52 percent of Californians believe that a third major political party is needed because the two major parties are not doing an adequate job of governing.[18] About one-fifth of California voters are now registered as political independents: some of them to the left of the Democrats, some of them moderates, others libertarians.[19] Yet third-party or independent candidates rarely win, except in unusual circumstances, such as the extraordinarily low-turnout special election that propelled a Green Party candidate into an Oakland assembly seat in 1999. These voices are not often heard in the legislature because the threshold for entry in terms of votes and dollars in California's huge legislative districts is so high.

One important effect of FAIR would be to lower the barriers to political success for minor or new parties. Minor parties with the support of 5 percent or more of the electorate within a region would be able to win a place, and have a voice, in the legislature. Even the possibility that disaffected voters could band together to win a slice of the seats in the legislature would be reason for the major parties to be more attentive and responsive to voter concerns.

A Greater Voice for Minorities

Some observers have raised Voting Rights Act objections to full representation voting systems like FAIR. Their objections fall primarily into two categories: 1) legal concerns that districting schema other than single-member districts are unconstitutional, and 2) worries that full representation systems will muffle the voices of racial and ethnic minorities in legislative contests.

For two decades following the passage of the Voting Rights Act in 1965, the courts were hostile to districting plans, particularly in the South, that did not seek to maximize the representation of racial minorities through "majority-minority" districts. This jurisprudence has slowly been replaced by a more flexible interpretation of the requirements of the law.[20] In the words of a recent U.S. Supreme Court majority opinion, "The decision to rely on single-member geographic districts as a mechanism for conducting elections is merely a political choice—and one that we might reconsider in the future."[21]

Although constitutional jurisprudence in the area of voting rights will continue to evolve, the practical advantages of systems of full representation for different ethnic communities could not be clearer. In fact, such systems have long been vehicles for maximizing ethnic diversity in governing bodies without resorting to techniques such as the creation of majority-minority districts. A review of the history of full representation on the municipal level in Ohio by Kathleen Barber, retired professor of political science at John Carroll University, underscores the advantages of these systems for ethnic minorities: proportional representation encouraged fairer racial and ethnic representation. It produced the first Irish Catholics elected in Ashtabula, and the first Polish Americans elected in Toledo. In Cincinnati, Hamilton, and Toledo, African Americans had never been able to win city office until the coming of PR. Significantly, after these cities abandoned PR, African Americans again found it almost impossible to get elected.[22] Barber also points out that the ultimately successful campaigns to eliminate these systems were based explicitly on opposition to the minority representation they had created. Far from being a challenge to regional-level minority representation in California and diversity in the state legislature, personalized full representation is the system that best guarantees it, particularly as regional ethnic diversity continues to grow. [23] Further, it helps to create ideological as well as ethnic diversity for those members of ethnic communities who have different political preferences than do the majorities of their communities.

A Less Dominant Role for Money

FAIR would also change the role of money in politics. Today, money is critical in legislative elections—and bolsters the influence of the statewide interest groups that can provide it. Because legislative races do not receive much attention in the commercial news media, it falls to the candidates themselves to communicate directly with voters. Elsewhere in America, where the median lower-house district has about forty thousand residents, candidates can do much of that work through face-to-face contact, local organizing, and events. In California, however, districts are too big for retail politics; candidates must seek votes wholesale, largely through paid advertising, an expensive proposition in districts that range from almost a half-million residents (for the assembly) to nearly a million (for the senate). It is now typical, in a competitive election contest for an assembly seat, for the two candidates to raise and spend, between them, a total of more than $4 million—a sum difficult to raise but still relatively small when measured by the expense of communicating with the many voters in each district. But even where legislative candidates succeed in raising all the funds needed for paid advertising, their voices are often drowned out by independent expenditure committees funded by economic interest groups like gaming tribes, unions, real estate brokers, and trial lawyers. It is not unusual for such committees to spend more than the candidates themselves. Increasingly, the interest groups set the agenda and frame the messages of legislative elections.[24]

Under FAIR, districts would have fewer residents and candidates would need to raise fewer dollars to communicate with them. Money would remain important, but in these smaller districts political assets acquired through direct contact with voters—candidates' prior service and performance in local government, their reputations in their careers, their neighborhoods, and in civic society, their ability to harness local grassroots organizations—would have greater relative weight than they do now. Major statewide interest groups may still inject independent expenditure dollars into certain campaigns to help friendly candidates win election. But since district elections would no longer determine the partisan balance of the legislature, special-interest groups with deep war chests would be more likely to focus their dollars and efforts on the regional party contests. And on that larger stage, big-dollar campaigns would be more visible both to the news media and the electorate, making it easier for voters to judge their motives and impact.

Improved Representation

The advantages of FAIR extend beyond the political effects of sharpening the debate over issues and increasing legislative accountability by means of the ballot. Under FAIR, the legislature would be stronger, both as a representative institution and as a policy-making body.

The combination of California's relentless population growth and its small legislature has produced the nation's most populous legislative districts. California's assembly districts each contain about 471,000 persons, requiring members to represent about three times as many people as do members of the Texas House of Representatives, which has the next largest lower-house districts, and about ten times as many people as the average lower-house lawmaker in other states.[25] As James Madison wrote in the Federalist Papers, "No political problem is less susceptible of a precise solution than that which relates to the number most convenient for a representative legislature."[26] There is no disputing, however, that, in Madison's words, "by enlarging too much the number of electors, you render the representatives too little acquainted with all their local circumstances and lesser interests."[27]

By reducing the number of residents of legislative districts by nearly 60 percent, FAIR would improve the acquaintance of voters and those they elect—not to the levels of other state legislatures but at least to the levels California enjoyed in the early 1960s, a time of greater trust in the legislature. It would send to the State Capitol a larger group of legislators with a greater variety of ethnic backgrounds, occupations, educational training, and life experiences, the variety needed to represent the most complex society and economy in the nation. Because these legislators would be elected under rules that make it possible for the voters to change party control of the legislature at any election, they would have greater reason to listen not just to the lobbying corps in Sacramento but also to the views of the broader electorate in their regions.

Strengthening the Legislature as a Policy-making Institution

FAIR also directly confronts a flaw in the current legislature that has not been widely addressed because the solution runs against the cheap and easy cynicism that blames all our ills on "politicians." Representation and lawmaking are work and, as in any other institution, the amount and quality of the work done by a legislature depends on the number of workers, the skills they bring to the job, and the system used to organize the effort. Much of the media and popular commentary about the legislature charges or implies that the reason the legislature does not do good work is the quality of the members themselves. But there is no evidence that the legislators Californians elect are less capable, on average, than those in states where the legislatures are more highly regarded. The major difference between California and other states is the small number of lawmakers in relation to the size of the state. Just as newspapers serving large and diverse urban regions need large news staffs to cover those regions adequately—and are having to reduce the amount and quality of news reporting as declining revenues force them to lay off hundreds of reporters—legislatures in heavily populated states are unlikely to work well if they are too small.

FAIR would both increase the number of members in the legislature and expand the skills and experiences that lawmakers can bring to bear on complex issues. The use of party lists would allow each party to present expert candidates experienced in such areas as public finance, health care, criminal justice, and the environment, the kind of prospective members who can improve the quality of lawmaking but are not likely to run for, or get elected to, district seats under the current system. Today, legislators typically sit on a half-dozen or more standing or select committees; few ever master, in the short time they are in Sacramento, all the issues those committees deal with. By contrast, a legislature under FAIR would permit policy specialization by members on committees, allowing them to explore one or two areas more deeply.

In addition, FAIR would allow—and indeed, because of the larger membership, would force—the legislature to develop a more robust committee system. Unlike today's system, where committees do little real policy development and serve mostly as speed bumps or dark corners where lobbyists and special interests strangle bills, the committee system under FAIR could do the kind of lawmaking that the electorate expects: hold hearings, screen rival approaches, write comprehensive legislation, consider amendments, and report the results to the legislature as a whole and to the public. A larger legislature and its committees and subcommittees would have the time and manpower to conduct serious oversight of state government, a function badly neglected under the current system.

Creating a more representative legislature in this way need not add to the public expense of running the legislative branch. A unicameral legislature would eliminate the cost of maintaining separate committee and leadership staffs in each chamber. It would also simplify and shorten the legislative process. If California were to adopt FAIR and a two-year budgeting cycle, it would become feasible to return, as some have suggested, to a part-time legislature in which most members would be paid only a fraction of their current salaries and employ only a fraction of their current staffs. There is no practical reason why the legislature created by this proposal should not be able to live under the existing constitutional cap on appropriations for legislative operations.[28]

Small Ideas Are Not Equal to California's Big Challenges

FAIR would represent a major change for California, and a bold departure for the nation as a whole. Only one other state, Nebraska, has a unicameral legislature. Although proportional representation is common in electoral systems around the world and was adopted in many U.S. cities in the early twentieth century, it is currently not used for legislative elections in any state. FAIR is a big idea. It would require a constitutional revision (the first since the 1960s), possibly a constitutional convention (the first since 1879).

Big ideas are hard to bring to fruition. However, given the recent history of reform efforts in California, it is clear that incremental change is not adequate to the tasks of reinvigorating the legislature, improving governance, and reviving public confidence in the state's republican institutions. For the first time in decades there is a growing interest from groups across the political spectrum in fundamental constitutional reform.[29] Whatever their merits, term limits on lawmakers have not improved the public's regard for their elected representatives. Redistricting reform will keep incumbents from drawing their own district lines, but it will have little or no effect, most experts believe, on who gets elected to the legislature or how they behave in office.

A state so large, with so many people and such distinct regions, which operates at the leading edge of a fast-paced and increasingly competitive global economy, has outgrown government institutions tailored in the nineteenth century. After years of mending and trimming, California needs to be refitted with a legislature that is equal to the challenges ahead. FAIR Representation can do the job.

ELEVEN

A People's Convention for California

R. Jeffrey Lustig

THE PREVIOUS CHAPTERS show that it is time to begin remaking California's constitution. Further piecemeal tinkering with its dysfunctional institutions will not make state government more effective and representative. There are a few different ways of going about making the deeper changes needed. In this chapter we will review those ways and explain why some people have recently called for a third constitutional convention in California. And we will get a sense of the difficult questions entailed in picking delegates who will be charged with representing "the entire sovereignty of the people" as a constitutional convention does.[1]

It has been many years since Californians attended to the fundamentals of their politics. There is much work to be done, and many communities to be heard from. Part of this work will also be to recognize that parts of the original federal design have been thrown into question by the special character of California society and politics, and that new means are needed for achieving some of the ends the national framers sought.

This chapter concludes by proposing a set of reforms that would reestablish California as a genuine republic—a system that not only protects private interests but also helps people discover their common interests and fulfill the public good.

*[A] government is republican in proportion as every member compos-
ing it has equal voice in the direction of its concerns....Try by this as a
tally, every provision of our constitution, and see if it hangs directly on
the will of the people.* —THOMAS JEFFERSON, 1816[2]

ALIFORNIA'S PREDICAMENT IS broad and deep. Its problems
range from procedural obstacles like the two-thirds rule to structural flaws like a stunted electorate, and from a fissured executive
to a deadlocked legislature easily circumvented by unchecked initiatives.
These derangements affect not only legislators in Sacramento but millions of
people in the communities of the state—families whose CalWORKS benefits are cut, workers who are laid off and lose medical insurance, mothers
and children deprived of health care, college students charged half again
as much in tuition for fewer classes, and cities and towns denied control
over their own affairs.

But political systems are not set in stone. They can be changed and
have been changed in the past. From the time of the Declaration of Independence to the California constitution of 1879, Americans have exercised
their right and duty, in the words of the Declaration, to "alter or to abolish
[their government] and to institute a new government" when circumstances
required. Only a generation after their first constitution, Californians exercised that right when they called their second convention in 1879. Thirty
years later the Progressive reformers enacted a program to strengthen public
authority against the private power of the Southern Pacific Railroad. Since
that time, however, the reform spirit has faltered on the Pacific Coast. It has
been a century since Californians sought to remedy the growing problems of
their fundamental law and their democracy. It is time to take up that neglected
right and obligation again. And it is necessary for citizens to become active if
they are not only to restore government operations in Sacramento, but also
improve the conditions of their own lives.

Methods of Constitutional Reform

The delegates who descended on Sacramento in September of 1878 for the
state's second convention included veterans of numerous battles fought to
right the wrongs of the times. Angered by the speculative monopolies which
by 1870 had enclosed a third of the state's area and most of its arable land,
they had staged protests that resulted in a report by the 1871-72 legislature's Committee on Land Monopoly that condemned those holdings as

usurpations of the opportunities of new settlers. Burdened by mortgage practices that forced borrowers to pay taxes on the mortgaged part of their property as well as the unmortgaged while the state's great speculators paid little, they had launched a campaign to outlaw such "double taxation." Infuriated by the railroad's monopoly on transportation and the power it wielded over the lives of individuals and entire communities, they had voted an Independent Party into the governorship and major state offices in 1873, which by 1876 had created a state railroad regulatory commission. Less admirably, the reformers had launched what would become a long state tradition of racializing and scapegoating outsiders, the Chinese having the bitter honor of being the first to fall subject to such treatment.

But the mortgage law was repealed. Land engrossment continued. The Independent Party lost office after a term. Railroad-subsidized legislators killed the regulatory commission in 1878.[3] And the state supreme court continued to quash ordinances meant to harass and exclude the Chinese. Finally, in the midst of the depression of the 1870s, the Workingman's Association from the sandlots of San Francisco and farmers from local Grange chapters renewed the call, which had sounded since the 1860s, for a new constitutional convention. This time they succeeded.

In this, the workingmen and farmers availed themselves of one route to constitutional reform. A second route, amendment, attracted few devotees in 1879, given the above-noted record of partial efforts. Two more routes were added in the early twentieth century: those of popular initiative and constitutional revision commission. The first has been discussed in previous chapters. The second was initially used by Governor C. C. Young in 1930 and subsequently authorized in 1947, 1962, and 1993.[4] The 1962 commission (which met until 1976) confronted a document that had ballooned to seventy-five thousand words. It eliminated twenty thousand of them, but by 2000 more than that number had been added again.

By the first and most thorough of these routes, California recognizes a right to alter or reform the government when "the public good may require it" (Article II, Section 1). This clause is clearly modeled on the Declaration's and reserves a broad and plenary right to the people, and a collective right to be exercised when the public good necessitates it.[5]

Each of these methods of reform has its advantages and disadvantages. The legislative route to constitutional amendments is the most difficult in California. The 1879 convention raised the bar for initiating amendments from the previous constitution's 50 percent of the state assembly and senate to two-thirds. That made the passage of new amendments, as Henry George noted at the time, nearly impossible. The initiative, whereby legislation and constitutional amendments can be placed on the ballot via petitions signed by voters, emerged during the Progressive Era as an alternative. With the amount of signatures needed to qualify for the ballot amounting to only 8 percent of the number of votes cast in the last gubernatorial election, initiatives have proven far easier to pass. But in their narrow, single-shot focus and insulation from information about their possible consequences at the drafting stage, initiatives are also most conducive to incoherence and disorganization in the political system as a whole. In 1930 Governor Young was already complaining that initiative amendments had produced a constitution "bad in form, inconstant in particulars, loaded with unnecessary detail, encumbered with provisions of no permanent value, and replete with matter which might more properly be contained in the statute law of the state."[6]

And he hadn't seen the half of it.

The idea of revision by a commission is broader in its implications than simple amendment, which is limited to a single subject. But the courts have been reluctant to enforce the distinction between amendment and revision. Despite the fact that Proposition 140 in 1990 (for term limits) altered nine articles in six sections of the constitution, the courts held it was a simple amendment. Revision commission operations are also more susceptible to intervention by interest groups and to eventual veto than amendments. The intrusion may occur, Bruce Cain notes, at any of three points: when the commission is meeting and deliberating, when they attempt to gain two-thirds of the legislature's support, and when they go to the voters for ratification. The second of these steps is the most perilous, as amendments have to pass muster with "the powerful interest groups that lobby and deal with the legislature regularly." Such interests smothered the high hopes of 1949, according to jurist and scholar Joseph Grodin. The recommendations of the California Constitution Revision Commission in 1996 never got a vote in the legislature, let alone a chance at ratification by the public.[7]

A constitutional convention is the most logical and most "representative and democratic means" to enact comprehensive reform, the League of Women Voters notes.[8] But it is also the most difficult politically. The constitution's current requirement that at least two-thirds of the assembly and the senate issue the call for a convention assumes the unlikely prospect that the bulk of state politicians would, at a point when it counted, agree to cede their power and change a system of which they were primary beneficiaries. The process, moreover, is susceptible to obstruction by powerful interests. Californians tried unsuccessfully to call a third convention in 1897, 1914, 1919, 1930,

1934, and 1947. (The 1934 effort actually authorized a convention, but it was never convened.) This contrasts with the practices of other American states that regularly provide citizens with the means for periodic review of their fundamental law. Fourteen states ask voters every ten to twenty years whether they want a constitutional convention, and a quarter of the time their voters approve. Seven other states permit a convention to be called by a simple legislative majority. Illinois's constitutional convention in 1968 was its sixth. In fact, there have been sixty-three state constitutional conventions since 1900, most consisting of between eighty and one hundred and fifty elected delegates.[9]

Even effectively calling a convention does not guarantee that successful revision will occur. The potential barriers to success are formidable. Those who make the call for a convention must establish with voters how a convention differs from normal politics. They must also withstand the opposition of interests with a stake in current arrangements.[10] They must decide upon a method of picking delegates that represents the different peoples and major problems of the state. The delegates must then determine methods for informing themselves about the issues and deliberating successfully about their differences. And their eventual proposals must be capable of generating organized and effective mobilization in their support if they antagonize powerful interests.

Faced with these obstacles some groups have opted for a non-convention route to solve the state's formidable problems. California Forward, for example, seeks to prepare initiative amendments on a few specific issues, from the budget process and removal of the two-thirds rule to a measure to devolve powers back to local government to revive the connection between local responsibilities and local powers. California Forward's caution is easy to understand. Yet in addressing single issues separately, it risks contributing to the incoherence of the system as a whole. California's political system, after one hundred and thirty years, deserves a more comprehensive overhaul.

Despite the difficulties of this convention route, it is therefore the one that has received a groundswell of support in early twenty-first-century California. By September 2009, one poll by convention proponents put support for a convention at 70 percent of the population. A month later the more rigorous Field Poll put it at 51 percent—still a bipartisan majority—with Republicans favoring it over a revision commission more than two to one.[11] The reasons are not hard to see. The state's budget morass was growing, the legislature stalemated, and people suffering the greatest loss of their homes, jobs, and medical coverage since the Great Depression. Even businesses were unable to count on a stable climate, though all the while, the state's productivity continued to rise. People were aware that reformers had tried partial remedies, as they had on the eve of the second convention—campaign reform laws, tax reform laws, term limits, recommendations for budgetary reform, and more—without success. Now they agreed with Jim Wunderman of the Bay Area Council (BAC) that "Drastic times call for drastic measures."[12]

The BAC emerged as an unlikely vanguard for this movement, made up as it was of CEOs from businesses like Bank of America, Chevron, Google, United Airlines, and McKinsey & Co. It had not only raised the call for a convention, but also found a way around the serious obstacles placed on this route by the constitution of 1879. Taking up the idea proposed by the League of Women Voters in 1964, the council turned to the initiative to alter the way a constitutional convention is called.[13] Forming an organization called "Repair California," the BAC framed two initiatives for the November 2010 ballot—the first, a constitutional amendment to let voters bypass the legislature and call a convention directly themselves; the second, to issue that call and specify the convention agenda. These initiatives held the potential for unleashing the most sweeping reforms of California's fundamental law in over a century.

By the end of 2009 other groups joined the BAC and California Forward in promoting structural reform. The state legislature had also established a Joint Select Committee on Constitutional Reform to consider and propose changes to California's governance structure. It began by considering the hundreds of reform constitutional amendments already languishing in both houses.[14] Early in 2010 the BAC initiatives were cancelled, however, because of the lack at the time of popular support.

Limits of the Federalist Constitutional Model

If a convention were actually to be called, what would it do? What sort of reforms should it consider? Among other things, given the systemic character of the state's problems, it would have to reconsider the adequacy of the original federal model for handling the problems of a grizzly bear of a state, ten times the population of the original thirteen states combined. Columnists Peter Schrag and Dan Walters have noted this, as have the BAC and Governor Schwarzenegger, among others.[15] Three points in particular about the original model deserve attention in light of the conclusions of the previous chapters: its basic checks-and-balances design, its lack of controls for minority faction, and the weakness of its provision for effective representation.

Checks and balances. The original reason the United States adopted three branches of government, two houses of Congress, and the division of national and state powers, we remember from chapter one, was to block and fragment majority factions. Whatever its virtues, the debilities of this arrangement had become clear by the end of the Constitution's first century. The Progressives pilloried the original design because it was rooted in a mechanistic mindset ill-suited to how politics really worked. "Government is not a machine," Woodrow Wilson wrote, "but a living thing. It falls...under the theory of organic life....It is accountable to Darwin not to Newton." This was one of the reasons that he supported parliamentarianism and partial unification of the executive and the legislature, as Paul and Weinberg noted in chapter ten.[16] An even greater collection of checks and obstacles has been added to the scheme in California: two-thirds rules, tax limits, dedicated portions of the budget. These have made coherent legislation on complex topics nearly impossible and multiplied the points open to interference by private interests.

Charles H. McIlwain, the noted constitutional historian, located the root failing of the theory underlying the checks-and-balances approach in its assumption that a government of limited powers had to be one of internally divided and conflicted powers. "Feebleness is no guarantee of constitutionalism," he observed about this approach, and usually opens the way to "government for private interests." Government must have "full political responsibility to the people and to the *whole* people" for its proper actions, he explained. But to achieve that, the government needs to have powers equal to its assigned responsibility.

The checks-and-balances approach, Walters adds, is "essentially a negative one, making policy change difficult....It works fairly well when there is a broad civic consensus, but when that consensus evaporates, as it has in California due to deep-seated socioeconomic change, the checks and balances become seemingly insurmountable hurdles."[17]

The setup eventually adds to the state's social balkanization by proliferating initiatives, hobbling the majority will, as Witko described in chapter four, and fostering campaign methods that no longer aggregate interests but fragment them further, exaggerate private differences, and thereby keep people apart. What California needs is a system in which legislators and executive officers can act capably and be held responsible, but which also helps people see their common interests and develop shared purposes in pursuit of which they can work together.

Minority faction. The main problem in contemporary California is not majority faction, as we saw in previous chapters, but minority faction—special interests "adverse to the rights of other citizens, or to the permanent and aggregate interests of the community."[18] The framers' model lacks adequate controls for minority faction, and this has led to a crisis in the social context of Pacific Coast republicanism. The vote, as powerless as it has become, is inadequate to solve this problem. But minority factions do not have to hold elective office to work their effects in any case. The Southern Pacific did not hold elective office; Artie Samish did not; and when General Motors, Standard Oil, and Firestone Rubber bought up and scuttled the Los Angeles Red Car system in the 1940s, preempting public transit, shaping urban growth, and indirectly imposing air pollution and rising cancer rates for years to come—activities that were clearly "adverse to the permanent and aggregate interests of the community"—they could not be voted out of public office because no one had ever voted them in.

To assume that voters can deal with such an issue also requires that information about the minority factions' activities first be known. Without farsighted leadership to monitor events, however, Los Angelenos had no way of knowing what was happening to their trolley system in the forties. And few Californians in the midst of the 2008-09 budget negotiations knew that a few top corporations had won billions of dollars of tax cuts while the state was furloughing state employees, firing teachers, and shutting down home care programs.[19] Such factions typically work their effects before the vote even occurs, as we saw in chapter six, shaping the options from which voters will choose.

Democracies and republics require the active participation of their citizens. Any acts or policies, private or public, which discourage the involvement of broad sectors of the population are adverse to the permanent and aggregate interest of the community. These systems also require a neutral rule of law. They cannot survive what the pro-capitalist William Graham Sumner at the end of the nineteenth century called "plutocratic" (i.e., monied) subversion of the political process.[20] California tried a hundred years ago to remedy this defect in the federal plan and it would do well to return to that effort today.

Inadequate representation. The third weakness of the federal model is that it makes no mention of how representation is to be organized and conducted, aside from the mention, at a few places, of elections. And the federalists operated with a quite restricted franchise—less than two thousand people voted on the Constitution in 1787-88. Over the years, suffrage has been extended to new groups of people. But if California teaches one thing, it is that legal extension will not automatically lead to everyone's inclusion if that legal right is offset by the lack of access to a job, to education, and to the regular participation which teaches people, as Tocqueville noted, "the habits of self-government."

Real representation requires that the people are involved. But a vote by itself is insufficient to keep them involved. Representation is supposed to keep those they have elected accountable. But districts of a half-million people and a capital five hundred miles away do not permit that. Picking representatives well presumes a knowledge of public affairs, but most California voters know little about such affairs. And "a people that has not been accustomed to self-government," Machiavelli predicted, will soon lose its liberty if it is "ignorant of all public affairs."[21]

The federalists turned to their checks-and-balances institutions to block disruptive impulses, not to cultivate constructive ones, nor to engage people in a participatory political education. Their effort to "supply by opposite and rival interests the defect [or absence] of better motives" has given rise over the years to the American tendency to think of democracy as a thing primarily *of* institutional mechanics—three branches of government, a two-party system, regular elections, etc.—instead of a product of people's actions. This has bred the Newtonian desire Peter Schrag sees expressed in Californians' adoption of measures mandating term limits, balanced budgets, and three-strikes-you're-out sentencing to establish "government by autopilot." Schrag also sees this as revealing an antipolitical impulse that has been part of the national orientation from the first.[22]

Unresolved school, water, and prison problems, budget deadlocks, and counties bankrupted by sometimes venal officials all attest to the fact that this approach to representation ultimately doesn't work. And the term-limits decision to put up a rotating team of rookies against the seasoned pros of the third house weakens the system further.

The need for a better system of representation is especially important in California because citizens of the Golden State have tasks those of the early thirteen states did not. Learning about new immigrants from other parts of the world is one of them. Creating a common culture out of disparate groups is a second. The public space of participation is not only a place for decision making, but also for people's creation of this cultural and continual recommitment to each other. Enabling citizens to come to an understanding of their place in the natural world and of the means for preserving its richness and fecundity is a third.

California needs a form of representation, in sum, in which people are motivated to vote because they have real power over the decisions that affect their lives, because they have acquired habits of self-government that teach them how to vote intelligently, and because they have learned how to think about their common interests and the long-term public good.

Supreme Court Justice Louis Brandeis once referred to the states as laboratories for testing new arrangements. That being the case, why shouldn't Californians come up with new experiments to remedy these three weaknesses of the framers' government design?

Who Will Fix California?

To make the sort of revisions suggested by these reflections, California will need a third constitutional convention, open to new ideas and to letting its citizens' concerns shape the convention agenda. Solving the state's problems will require that the delegates canvass other states' and nations' experiences as well as the ideas of past thinkers and current democratic theorists.

But who is to do this? Who will those members of a new constitutional convention be?

A constitutional convention is distinguished from other assemblages not only by the breadth of what it attempts to do but by the authority under which it does it. "The entire sovereignty of the people rests in a constitutional convention," as the League of Women Voters put it. That means that such a convention is not a creature of the executive nor the legislature. It is not an assembly of the constituted powers, to use an older formulation, but of the constituent power. It provides the clearest demonstration of Thomas Paine's insight that "a constitution is not the act of a government, but of a people constituting a government."[23]

But actually convening a body of people that can do this and represent the "entire sovereignty of the people" presents a host of problems. The body that meets to erect a new order operates under the habits, outlooks, and interests of the old. Lest anyone think that is unimportant, they need only remember the convention of 1879, where thirty-two at-large delegates added to the original plan by a temporary Non-partisan Party of pro-business Democrats and Republicans wound up tipping the scales.

The state's voters selected Workingmen for 51 of the 152 seats and farmer Grangers to many of the others, but the "fusion" forces, swelled by the thirty-two delegates who had the money and backing to win the statewide contests, were able to elect, by a single vote, their candidate for convention president. With him, they secured the power and patronage to control much of the convention proceedings.[24]

The ancient Greeks and Romans avoided this predicament by calling on the services of a great lawgiver, a Solon, Lycurgus, or Numa, to deliver new laws from outside the melee of existing parties and interests. But no Lycurgus or Solon is expected to arrive at LAX or from over the Sierra. Who then will do the constitution-building? How are the convention delegates to be chosen?

Theoretically speaking, delegates might be selected in one of three ways. They could be appointed, elected, or selected randomly, the way we pick juries or respondents for scientific polling. None of these methods is perfect. In the first, the independence and legitimacy of the delegates could be compromised by the character of the people that appointed them. Appointees also might lack the larger authority necessary to persuade the electorate to ratify their final proposals, as happened with the 1993 California Constitution Revision Commission.

The second method, permitting broad public participation, is the one most consistent with democratic traditions and the desire to call a "people's convention" (a phrase used in the BAC's first convention calls). It is also the method prescribed by the current constitution, which states, "Delegates to a constitutional convention shall be voters elected from districts as nearly equal in population as may be practicable."[25] If delegates were to be picked by assembly districts today, however, in jurisdictions of a half-million people each, it might turn out—as in 1879—that only those with the money or backing to run an at-large campaign could win.

Some constitutional reformers therefore favor the third option. Picking delegates in a way similar to how juries are selected would yield a group of average citizens not chosen on the basis of their wealth, fame, or special-interest connections. The delegates could also be chosen to reflect the state's demographic characteristics. Celebrating the virtues of the average citizen, one proponent of this method admits that delegates chosen in this way might nevertheless know little to qualify them for such a significant and difficult task, and suggests they be given a course in the state's problems and potential solutions. Other citizens would accept their status and eventual recommendations, he urges, because the selectees would be "people just like us."[26]

This proposal has some real advantages compared to local district elections or political appointments. The jury method is quick, efficient, and free of special-interest influence, at least at its initial step. But it also has some serious drawbacks, a consideration of which will help to clarify the special character and responsibilities of a constitutional convention.

First and most seriously, the jury selection method denies people the right to pick their own representatives. It bypasses the process by which we citizens can pick who we want and who we think best voices our and our districts' concerns. We would remain in this plan passive bystanders of state politics, given the choice at the end of the process to merely accept or reject proposals others have devised. Usually, furthermore, when we participate in nominations and elections in our schools, cities, unions, or other local associations, we do not seek someone average for office. We want someone special. We back the man or woman who expresses our views best, or analyzes problems more logically than others, or simply knows more about the issues than the rest of us. The jury method would prevent us from doing this.

Not having been chosen by their constituents, this randomly selected mix of people would not, properly speaking, really be delegates at all. No one would have delegated them or entrusted them to do anything. They would not be representatives in the political sense of the word, though they might be a "representative sample." And that is a very different thing. Political representatives are chosen by their constituents and authorized to act for them. That authorization is what binds the voters, in turn, by their representatives' acts. The relationship between constituent and representative is a rich and complex one. Statistical representatives, by contrast, are chosen by someone else through a mechanical process and not authorized by, or accountable to, anyone.

Random selection according to demographic categories adds another wrinkle to these questions of representation. The demographic categories would also be determined by someone else, though such determinations are always open to political debate. This aspect of the plan would only generalize identity politics. And even if that were desirable, being typical of a particular segment of the population does not make one its political representative.[27]

A constitutional convention is a representative body, not a substitute for the larger population, or an extended focus group, or a jury (from which lawyers can peremptorily dismiss the unqualified). It is an assembly that aspires through its debates and deliberations to represent the sovereignty of the people. And its need for people who are well informed about public affairs raises questions whether recent leaders and officeholders should be excluded from the delegate pool as some constitutional proponents suggest.

Second, proponents of the jury plan are overly optimistic about the ability of recruited experts to provide randomly selected delegates with the education they need. Who would do the educating? The experts themselves do not always agree on the issues. The debates over the future of the Sacramento–San Joaquin Delta show that, as does the national colloquy on health care. Nor would the selection of such experts be free of bias. One might say that specialists would be recruited from all points of view. But that is not really possible. Choices have to be made, and those choices would reflect the outlooks of those implementing this plan, not those back in the local communities from which the convention members came. Would the delegates' education include experts on the need for public works programs to combat unemployment? On the continued impact of institutionalized racism in the state? On the benefits of publicly owned, as opposed to private, utilities? Would business groups sponsor experts on the dangers that the increased concentration of wealth poses to democracy, or the need to close the loophole on commercial property taxes opened by Proposition 13? One must be skeptical of the ability of specially tutored juries to address the range of problems that need to be solved.

Third, the jury selection method would pass up the greatest opportunity for civic education California has had in a century. It would do that by omitting any role for the people as a whole in the new convention. Four to five hundred people might participate in designing the state's new constitutional framework; the rest of California's thirty-eight million citizens would do nothing. They would be excluded from the very beginning, just when the public should be identifying the items for the convention agenda and new leaders might be recruited. The delegates to the 1879 convention were nominated at lively meetings throughout the state in the midst of arguments over public affairs in places like Marysville, Benicia, Vallejo, Weaverville, San Jose, and Los Angeles. Meetings like that today would enable people to learn more about the issues that concern them, about neighborhoods beyond their own, and about the needs of the state as a whole.

Groups like this created to nominate local delegates might also remain in operation for the duration of the convention, educating citizens on the topics addressed in debates and keeping their delegates accountable. The delegates might even contribute to the larger educational process by, for example, setting up district task forces on topics, such as water or K-12 education or legislative reform, that could advise them over the course of convention deliberations. The state might become connected by webs of these local committees, corresponding with each other and focused on the statewide convention. Part of the burden of the previous chapters has been to show that California's problem is not only one of political institutions but also a lack of underlying community and of widespread shared purposes. One goal of a constitutional convention process must therefore be to help, in its very methods of operation, to build community and elicit shared purposes. Picking delegates either by jury or appointment would forgo the possibility for doing either.

Some propose that the weaknesses of the jury selection method can be overcome with high-tech processes and corporate training techniques.[28] But technology provides no silicon bullet. It offers a supplement, not a replacement, for the face-to-face politics through which alone we can debate, and learn what we need to know, and undergo the tension which changes outlooks and produces new ideas.[29] Taken as a whole, the random selection method may, in fact, reveal an aversion to the real give-and-take of politics, perhaps a loss of confidence in what we can potentially accomplish as citizens. But if its proponents truly admire the average citizen, the best sign of it would be to trust them to choose their own representatives.

Democracy may be messy. And given the deterioration of California's public life and rise of the sham democracy of talk radio and stage-managed "town hall meetings," many Californians may have become erratic in their political views and susceptible to the blandishments of well-briefed demagogues. But then so have the elite Californians. And the experts. (The energy deregulation of 1996 and subsequent Enron windfalls show that, as do the bankers' pre-2008 confidence in derivatives and subprime mortgage practices.) Political sagacity is rare in all the precincts. All things considered, local elections remain the best, most democratic and educational means for picking convention delegates. Ways do have to be found to control the effects of wealth and special interests in local, district elections. The critics are right about that. And because districts are so large, it will be necessary to start with smaller assemblages and build up to district meetings (in a "graduation of authorities, standing each on the basis" of the other, as Jefferson suggested).[30] And it would be advisable to elect more than one representative per district. But a new constitutional convention should develop a new politics in the very way it is organized and conducted, and not sustain the old politics in its very foundations.

Once delegates to the convention are selected, what will they do? What sorts of reforms would make California's governance more responsive and effective, and its people more politically active?

Proposals for Constitutional Reform

The previous chapters of this book have proposed a number of valuable reforms. Here I will present a summary program selecting from some of these proposals and adding a few new ones. Those that have been discussed earlier in the book I will only note briefly. The point here, as mentioned in chapter one, is not to present a program that as yet has popular support or that conforms to current nostrums. It is to note what would be necessary to reestablish government in California and to fulfill the public good. [31]

A. Increase Governing Capacity and Effectiveness

Budget and taxation. An effective government needs clear lines of authority, focused leadership, and sufficient resources. To get these and remedy the effects of the nation's federalist model as further confused by decades of haphazard reforms the convention should:

- *Eliminate the two-thirds rule* for passing the annual budget and raising taxes. The two-thirds rule means that two yes votes are required for every no vote, and a legislative minority can hold the majority captive. In 1996 the California Constitution Revision Commission reported that the two-thirds rule also "permit[s] those who have specific interests, which may or may not be related to the budget, to delay passage of the budget by leveraging their issue into the budget debate." Cities and counties should also be permitted raise taxes and pass bonds by a simple majority.[32]

- *Revise Proposition 13's tax provisions* to establish a rational fiscal system, restore local authority, and make state taxes less volatile. The proposition's proponents sought to protect the value of their homes; and that can be done without introducing the irrationalities and inequities Goldberg explained in chapter three. The place to start is to take businesses off the homeowners' tax roll and require them to pay taxes on the full market value of their properties.

- *Tax resources taken from the public domain.* This pertains mainly now to oil revenues made from the state's common-wealth. California is the third-largest oil producer in the nation, but the only major oil state that does not impose a severance tax on each barrel of oil removed from the state's lands, despite Big Oil's enormous profits in recent years. When oil sells at seventy dollars per barrel, the 240 million barrels the state produced in 2008, taxed at the rate of 6 percent, would bring in more than one billion dollars a year.[33]

The legislative process:

- **Restrict initiative use.** By their nature, initiatives are drafted without consideration of the trade-offs they will require or their effects on other parts of the political system. It is unwise to use them as a means for making policy. Nor is it wise in a democracy to permit individual interests to alter the rules to their own advantage. To amend the U.S. Constitution 75 percent of the state legislatures must agree, and legislative amendments to the California constitution require a two-thirds vote. A California ballot measure can change the rules with only a majority of a low-turnout election.

  The legislature should be authorized to hold hearings on the probable impacts of a proposed initiative and offer technical and clarifying changes to its language. A two-stage approval process for initiatives should also be adopted, with a year interval between them.[34] Lastly, a supermajority should be required to pass constitutional (not statutory) initiatives.

- **Annul term limits.** Term limits have failed in their original objectives. The terms provided are too short, as the California Constitution Revision Commission reported, for legislators to develop the expertise they need about the "processes and operations of the legislature" or the expertise in specific subject areas necessary to perform their responsibilities.[35] Nor can short-time legislators build up the acquaintance with and trust in each other necessary to deliberate and compromise effectively. California has the most severe term limits in the nation. The fact that from a third to a half of the assembly are always freshmen hobbles that body, and the entire branch is weakened vis-à-vis the executive branch and lobbyists. The latter fact means the public interest is weakened relative to private interests.

  Some propose simply to extend term limits. A more fundamental question is why the state should have them at all. They deprive people of the right to vote for who they think is best for the job.

If legislators have overstayed their usefulness, it is their districts' democratic duty to vote them out of office, not to tie everyone else's hands. California's first constitutional delegates at Monterey rejected a similar proposal. They had "no right," delegate William Shannon of Monterey declared in 1849, "to dictate to the people the...character of their representatives." His reasoning on the point was unassailable. Term limits are fundamentally unrepublican and should, in fact, be eliminated.[36]

- *Divided government.* It is time to reconsider the effects of the deep divide between the executive and legislative branches established by the federalist model. Many nations, including the United Kingdom, use parliamentary government, gaining the efficiency that the Golden State lacks. Parliamentary governments have a single legislative chamber and select the state's chief executive from among its members. He or she then becomes the prime ("first") minister. The legislature remains in constant contact with the prime minister and can recall him or her as well. Such an organization provides for unity in policy making and dispatch in implementation. It also strengthens the majority will.[37]

Even short of this, Syer's proposals in chapter five would promote unity and a clearer focus of responsibilities than the state currently possesses. He, like the 1993 revision commission, advises that reducing the number of independently elected executive offices would help release California from its present confusion.

B. Protect the Social Bases of Republicanism

The quickest way to control minority faction and halt California's tendencies to class polarization, rising poverty, and private-interest power would be to limit the amount of special-interest monies that can be contributed to campaigns or to sitting representatives. This should be a primary goal of a new constitutional convention, and it is consistent with the efforts of the 1879 convention to control corporate power as represented by the Southern Pacific Railroad.

California's current laws leave a crucial step in the chain of public representation—the campaign—subject to capture by private wealth. New laws are needed to set limits on what can be given and spent for both campaigning and lobbying, and to establish public campaign funding. Those committed to rehabilitating democratic social conditions will also have to work to overturn or regulate the free speech rights the U.S. Supreme Court has extended to corporate campaign contributions.[38] The people who fought for free speech through the ages had no intention of allowing the powers of the artificial individual called the corporation to dominate real individuals.

C. Strengthen the Process of Representation

The causes of the underrepresentation and misrepresentation of minorities, immigrants, and the working poor who "can't vote, don't vote, and are confused about the vote," as Xiuy Velo put it in chapter eight, need to be addressed directly by a new convention. It is not possible to get government working again democratically without getting it to work for all the people.

If large parts of the electorate do not vote, we saw, they remain unrepresented, and the formulation of the public good—the representative process for the whole society—becomes skewed. But their nonparticipation, we also saw, is a product of institutional arrangements. It is a product, first, of the atrophy of the state's old party system. Large parts of the population are effectively disenfranchised because the issues that count for them—jobs, housing, medical care, and more—are not on the menu of choices offered during elections. Second, this nonparticipation is a product of the loss of forums for active political participation. And third, it is a product of spreading poverty and economic instability. The Jacksonian democrats who settled California originally looked to a bountiful land and economic boom to provide the material preconditions for citizenship. The new structure of California's economy denies those preconditions to millions of its people. Underpaid seamstresses in El Monte sweatshops, unemployed old-age-home nurses, and laid-off Nummi-Fremont autoworkers, health-care, and high-tech workers have a hard enough time making ends meet, let alone leaving time to participate meaningfully in politics. In addition to controlling the power of money in elections, three major constitutional reforms could remedy California's crisis of representation.

- *Change the party and electoral systems*. A fuller set of electoral choices is needed in the Golden State. Instead of reducing the range of choices by moving to an open primary, the state needs to multiply its parties. A Green Party, American Independent Party, or New Majority Party in California which started out with even 10 to 15 percent of the vote could not, in the state's current system, gain recognition, political experience, or influence. In the current system a minority governs in the name of the people.

It is time for the state to experiment with some form of the proportional representation system, like Paul's and Weinberg's proposal in chapter ten. Adopting this and also increasing the size of the state legislature would greatly expand the possibilities for real representation and participation in California. The legislature's current size, 120 assembly members and senators, was set in 1862 when the state had four hundred thousand people. This remains a fundamental impediment to genuine democratic governance, in which people are citizens and not just subjects.

A proportional representation system would also restore party platforms to central significance in elections, currently dominated by celebrity-oriented campaigning. With substantive issues to work with, campaigns could educate voters rather than having to subject them to a stream of sound bites and buzzwords in the attempt to manipulate their choices.

- *Halt California's transformation into a two-tier society.* The state needs to find ways to shore up the material preconditions for citizenship, as the federal government did with policies like the Homestead Act in the 1860s, the Works Progress Administration in the 1930s, the GI Bill in the forties, and large defense budgets up through the early nineties. Adam Smith, who conservatives are fond of quoting, recognized that:

> The property which every man has in his own labour, as it is the original foundation of all other property, so it is the most sacred and inviolable. The patrimony of a poor man lies in the strength and dexterity of his hands; and to hinder him from employing this strength and dexterity...is a plain violation of this most sacred property.[39]

The great economic thinker recognized that part of the right to property was a right to labor—a right to *acquire* property as well as possessing and protecting it. And the state constitution since 1849 has recognized a right of "acquiring property" in its very first section. The legislature should be entrusted with the duty to enforce this provision and create public jobs programs when unemployment in a region or community rises above a certain level—say, the 4 percent set in the nation's Full Employment Act of 1946. The schools, roads, and other infrastructure of the state could use the work.

In the wake of the economic blows of the last twenty years, the state needs an industrial policy. In a wealthy state, business practices should not be permitted to reduce the living standard of those who produce that wealth to that of people just emerging from pre-industrial conditions around the world. There are costs for doing business in a democracy. One of them is that employers cannot reduce their fellow citizens and local communities to penury.[40]

- **Restore powers to local government.** Consistent with the classical republican insight about the necessity of political education, people will only learn how to vote intelligently if they have first learned about public affairs and how to participate in them. But they will only participate and acquire that education if their cities and counties have the ability to make real decisions, decisions that count. The California Constitution Revision Commission noted in 1996 that "over the last 20 years...California has lost its long tradition of home rule" and went on to recommend a revival of that tradition by giving communities "power to exercise all authority with respect to local matters."[41] Political thinkers as diverse as John Dewey, Hannah Arendt, C. Wright Mills, and Jürgen Habermas have agreed that only local forums of public activity can prevent a democratic community from deteriorating into a mass society, with the general powerlessness and potential for a tyrannical form of politics that reside in such a society.

Taken together, these proposals make up a broad and daunting program. But different measures promoting variants of them can be expected in California in the next few years given the seriousness of its problems. A number of them were submitted along with a call for a constitutional convention for the November 2010 election. Some of the initial measures may not succeed if their drafters are out of touch with voter sentiment, or the voters themselves with the real character of their problems. But that is just as well at present. Californians need time to educate themselves beyond buzzwords and talk-show slogans about the state's systemic political problems. They need to think through the consequences of specific reforms better than they have done over the last thirty years. That self-education is the first order of the day.

Conclusion

This book has shown that the debilitating budget battles that have emerged in recent years are the surface signs of deeper institutional problems and social conflict in California. And the state's current politics are working to exacerbate rather than resolve those problems and that conflict.

But California is a wealthy state. There is no reason for its people and public realm to be poor. Its people are imaginative and creative. There is no reason for them to feel trapped and discouraged.

The reforms that might remedy their problems, however, cannot enact themselves. Nor, if the past is any guide, will most of the state's leaders eagerly promote them—benefiting as those officials do from the existing arrangements. To achieve real improvements, to provide public goods and for the public good, Californians in the past have had to prod and push the politicians. That was the case with the calling of the second constitutional convention, Progressive reforms, the social programs of the New Deal, and the civil rights movement of the 1960s. Californians have understood the need for popular action and been capable of mobilizing energetically around new political ideas. They will have to show those same skills again if a constitutional convention is to move the state in a desirable direction. It is time to call that convention and find that direction. Ultimately institutions don't run a democratic republic. People do. But Californians need political institutions that enable them to do it and teach them how to run it well. In that sense the best constitution for their state would be one that establishes ways to constitute active, capable citizens. Providing that would be a fitting goal for a third state constitutional convention.

"If I Ran the Zoo"

Proposals for
Constitutional Reform

"What's the one thing you would do if you ran a California constitutional convention today?" That question was posed to a number of California leaders, former leaders, writers, and citizens. This epilogue presents their responses.

How California Can Solve Its Budget Crisis: Form a Bank

Ellen Hodgson Brown

"AS GOES CALIFORNIA," says the adage, "so goes the nation." All eyes were therefore on the Golden State as it struggled in 2008-09 to solve its $26 billion budget deficit. The world's eighth-largest economy was not going to go quietly into that pit of debt and devastation that had devoured Third World countries whole. State legislators were deadlocked, caught between the rock of tax ceilings and the hard place of debt limits. The situation was so desperate that Governor Arnold Schwarzenegger began paying the state's bills with IOUs.

At least he tried, but most banks refused to honor them. Had the state accepted them in the payment of taxes, they could have served to supplement its currency; but the legislature could not agree on that step either. What to do?

The situation requires original thinking. The constitution prohibits states from issuing "bills of credit," but they can create another form of money called "checkbook" money. *They just have to form their own bank.* Chartered banks are allowed to create credit on their books, limited only by the "reserve requirement" and the "capital requirement." Today, the reserve requirement is virtually obsolete. What limits bank lending is chiefly the capital requirement, and California has a huge capital base. Besides its wealth of tax revenues, it owns property up and down the state. At an 8 percent capital requirement, this base could generate hundreds of billions of dollars in credit.

That's what the state of North Dakota has done for nearly a century. North Dakota is one of only two states (along with Montana) that are not facing budget shortfalls. North Dakota has beaten the Wall Street credit freeze by generating its own credit. Ever since 1919, the state's revenues have been deposited in its own state-owned bank, the Bank of North Dakota (BND). Other banks in the state do not see the BND as a threat, because it partners with them and backstops them, serving as a sort of central bank for

North Dakota. BND's loans are not insured by the Federal Deposit Insurance Corporation (FDIC) but are guaranteed by the state.

Virtually all of our money today comes from bank loans, and bank lending has dried up. Since neither the federal government nor the Federal Reserve has stepped in to fill the void, the states need to do it themselves. If banks can create credit on their books, and if North Dakota has done it for ninety years with its own state-owned bank, the world's eighth-largest economy can solve its credit problems in the same way. The state could deposit its revenues in the state bank and pay its payroll through it, generating an enormous deposit base for making new loans. Enough credit could be generated to allow the state not only to meet its short-term budget needs but to buy back its outstanding bonds (or debt). Bond interest and redemption costs on California's General Fund for the current year are estimated at nearly $5 billion—about 20 percent of the budget shortfall. All of that money could be saved in interest, since the state would be paying interest to itself.

The state could do more than just chase the wolf from its door. It could generate enough credit to engage in the sort of economic stimulus being undertaken by the federal government. It could create jobs for the 11.5 percent of the state's population that are currently unemployed, augmenting the tax base and supplying the incomes necessary to prop up the languishing housing market. An even better model than the U.S. government's is that of China, the world's fastest-growing economy. China is putting its stimulus money into domestic development rather than into bailing out a failed banking system. The Chinese government can do this because it actually *owns* its banks, rather than the banks effectively owning the government.

We the people did not precipitate this credit crisis; the banks did. We should not have to pay for the damage with increased taxes, or with decreased services, or with our public parks and parking meters. If California legislators act quickly, they can have a state-owned bank up and running before the next annual budget battle. Weary legislators trying to agree on a budget could all shake hands and go home.

Ellen Hodgson Brown is an attorney practicing civil litigation and is the author of *Web of Debt*, a critique of the Federal Reserve, "money trust," and the current U.S. banking system, and of ten other books including studies of the pharmaceutical cartel and Nature's Pharmacy. She can be reached at www.ellenbrown.com.

Education and the State Constitution

John F. Burns

CONSTITUTIONAL CHANGE is born of crisis. In 1849 the demand for a settled system of law and order in the aftermath of the Mexican-American War and conquest of California produced the first constitution. The financial panic and depression of the 1870s provided the backdrop for the second California constitution which, heavily modified, remains the law of the land today.

Today, as in 1878, a growing sense of constitutional crisis emerges, as the political establishment operates within a governmental structure that virtually precludes effective response to an economic crisis. This situation has generated a call for constitutional revamp. But will a new constitution result in civic improvement, or merely move the pieces around on a playing field that remains dominated by giant narrow interests that resist real change? As constitutional change in California again looms on the horizon, one area that demands critical attention is education.

Education is one of the truly vital responsibilities left by the federal government to the states, and the one most demanding of California's resources. Education receives roughly half of the state's allocations, a much larger proportion than any other sector of state government. It is arguably also the most important function of state government in terms of its long-term impact, since a well-educated citizenry is essential to economic growth and to an effective political process.

For many years California has been in educational decline. Test scores are low compared to those of other states and nations, and the amount spent on education per capita often lags alarmingly behind the national average. Of course, education is an enormously complex endeavor, as teacher quality, population demographics, parental involvement, individual student needs, and a host of other factors beyond state funding impinge on educational outcomes.

Constitutional fixes can have only limited impact on these complexities. Despite the state's large commitment to education, provisions pertaining to it make up only a relatively small part of the state constitution and focus mainly on funding and educational governance. They also treat miscellaneous topics ranging from free textbooks to setting an archaic minimum of $2400 for teacher salaries.

While some governmental policies can be substantively altered by changing state institutions—increasing the size of the legislature, for example—teaching the state's children to read, write, compute, and be prepared to assume adult civic responsibilities is primarily a local activity. Or, in higher education, it is one that is handled by each college or university as an individual entity.

There are two public policy areas, however, where the constitution does have a significant impact on education, where change might be useful. One is in governance. Ask someone, "Who's in charge of education?" Responses will range from the governor and his education secretary to the state superintendent of public instruction, to the legislature, to the State Board of Education, and to county or district superintendents and boards. All answers are partially correct. The result is that no one can be held accountable at the policy level for educational successes or failures.

Any constitutional revision must effectively address this matter. Perhaps all of these officials and boards are not necessary, and perhaps the current mixed division of responsibility between state and local entities can be improved. The effects of current practices of fragmented control need to be reexamined. The sheer size of the state's allocations for education speaks strongly for methods of accountability that permit identification of the officials who should be praised or blamed for educational outcomes, in both the K-12 and university systems.

This issue of governance is affected by the second area where the constitution has a powerful effect: funding. When the state's voters enacted Proposition 98 in 1988 (amended in 1990) they guaranteed minimum funding levels for the state's schools based on complex formulae that take into account revenues, the previous year's spending, per capita personal income, and more. But does this allocation, which was meant to serve as a protective floor, now operate as an impermeable ceiling? And when it is impossible to determine who is accountable for the results of state education spending, is there willingness to expend funds much higher than that floor?

Such constitutional budget limitations tie the hands of those elected to balance state revenues and expenditures. They also create erratic spending priorities that prevent allocation of resources based on availability and need. Ending these limitations and providing for transparent accountability for educational results would enable policy makers to tie educational funding to educational needs and positive outcomes with a view toward what advances the state as a whole. That would be real constitutional progress.

John F. Burns was California State Archivist for sixteen years and has been the state education administrator responsible for California's alternative schools and overseeing development of California's history–social science academic content standards. He was coeditor of and a contributor to *Taming the Elephant: Politics, Government, and Law in Pioneer California*.

Publicly Funded Elections for Public-Interest Government

Ernest Callenbach

A CONSTITUTIONAL CONVENTION allows us to reconsider the *structures* of California government. Structures determine function, and unless we change structures we will be condemned to a continuation of the status quo: paralyzing partisanship, domination by corporate interests, reckless neglect of both short-term and long-term public welfare.

Of all state structures, that for selecting our representatives is the most fundamental. At present, as on the national scene, we have a pay-to-play system. Even the most idealistic new assembly or senate member soon understands—and probably has already grasped it or wouldn't have been elected—that on any significant issue, campaign funders call the tune. From representatives in Arizona's or Maine's publicly funded "Fair Elections" system, used successfully in several election cycles, we learn that getting funders off their backs is an immense relief to representatives. When considering a bill or policy, they no longer have to look over their shoulder at the personal financial consequences of their votes; they can (and indeed should) talk with lobbyists of all kinds, but they no longer need fear them. They can vote as they see best—without having to spend 80 percent of their time raising money, which is common now. As the *Arizona Daily Star* put it, "Public financing is the best thing that has happened to politics and public-policy making in this state in decades."

How does a Fair Elections system (sometimes called Clean Elections) work?

If you decided to "run clean" for an office, you would first gather a prescribed number of backer signatures (large enough to show you have significant citizen support) and something like five dollars from each signer. You would proceed to the secretary of state's office. You would then be offered about 75 percent in public money of what has been spent in private funds in campaigns for that post in previous election cycles. If your privately funded opponent(s) spend more, you get matching funds up to a set maximum. In return, you must promise not to accept other funds—from corporations, individuals, unions, or any other interest groups. You are then in a position to argue for your ideas in open competition with other candidates (some of whom will *not* run clean, but will in many cases lose anyway). In states where this system has been adopted, large proportions of both Democrats and Republicans often choose to run clean, and win.

States finance clean elections in different ways, but as state moneys go it is a trivial expense. In 2010, California voters will have the chance to enact AB 583, the California Fair Elections Act, which sets up trial Fair Elections for a sole office, secretary of state, in 2014 and 2018 (financed mainly by increased state fees on lobbyists). This bill, limited as it is, was finally signed by the governor, unlike previous attempts the legislature had passed. A constitutional convention could go further and faster.

Oddly enough, naive opponents of public election financing swear that they don't want a nickel of their money going to any politician. In reality, of course, they fail to notice that allowing politicians to be bought by big money costs the public enormously more than public funding would. Huge benefits routinely get channeled to special interests whose money has gained them "access" to our representatives, while public interests are sidetracked. The leverage of investing in candidates or elected representatives can run to a hundred to one: spending $100,000 on legislators routinely secures many millions of dollars in benefits to funders. Even in budgetary crisis times, lobbyists are busy in the Capitol corridors, attempting to shape the budget to their liking, sacrificing the public good in the process.

So what should a constitutional convention do? It should remove the monopoly of the pay-to-play electoral campaign system by establishing a Fair Elections alternative for *all* state offices, not just the secretary of state. This will greatly extend the pool of political talent we can draw on, since entering the political arena will no longer depend on securing financing from the rich and powerful. It should greatly improve the quality of political ideas and discourse in California: considerations of what is best for the state, rather than best for its big financial players, could be honestly argued. On health, education, taxation, environment, crime, water, and other fundamental state governance issues, we could look forward to rational debate and responsible decisions.

Electoral reform is like a prerequisite in college. Without it our legislature and officials will remain stuck in their present failing grade. To move on to advanced studies and a healthy future, we must clean up our elections.

Ernest Callenbach is the author of *Ecotopia* and *Ecotopia Emerging* and coauthor of *A Citizen Legislature* and was for many years the editor of *Film Quarterly*.

There's No Time to Waste: An Educator's Approach to California Governance Reform

Sheila Jordan

A NEW BUDGET was adopted by California legislators in late 2009 to make up for the $26 billion budget gap. Their "solution" relied on heavy borrowing from counties and accounting tricks, and makes deep cuts to social services and education. Although it is heartening to know that the state has stopped issuing IOUs, the new budget is hardly a cause for celebration.

As superintendent of Alameda County Schools, in charge of budget oversight for eighteen school districts, I understand the difficult process of budgeting. I know that challenging times call for difficult choices, but the staggering cuts to education are unacceptable. Federal stimulus funds have temporarily blunted the impact of cuts for some counties; however, many predict that half of all districts will be underwater in three years when stimulus funds run out. The emerging truth is that the budget process is deeply flawed, or worse, broken.

Responses to this failure of state government include efforts by groups like the Bay Area Council to call a constitutional convention to rewrite the state's charter. Efforts by Repair California and California Forward are encouraging, but we must provide immediate action even while this lengthy debate takes shape.

Appropriate short-term solutions to stabilize the state budget and support adequate funding of education and public services include:

- The development of a system of county/regional taxes to support local services—placing a portion of the growth of the region's tax base in a pool to allow all communities to capture the benefits, leaving school funding, for example, neither the obligation of a single cash-starved city nor of the distant state;

- A requirement for the legislature to pass fiscally sound multi-year budgets, as school districts are required to do; and

- A change to requiring a majority vote to pass the state budget and to raise local revenues.

Benefits of the strategy proposed above include:

- Tax dollars in the hands of local citizens. At a county or regional level, people are more willing to engage in the political process in support of their own communities. Also, equitable distribution of funds on the regional level provides more stable support for all children in all schools.

- Compensation for the volatile swings of the economy, providing for sensible, gradual budget growth. This means that when the economy is booming, we would save money for leaner times.
- Release from the two-thirds majority for passing a budget. In recent years, a militant minority has consistently stalemated the budget process. The ensuing gridlock prevents efficient budget planning necessary for safe and effective schools.

Even in the current economic downturn, our state is rich in intellectual and financial capital—but our current system makes the state ungovernable. This grim moment in our state's history holds significance in its potential to educate our citizens and engage them in democratic action. Can we turn some of the work by constitutional convention advocates into a lesson in building and sustaining a democratic state, while also meeting the needs of our vulnerable populations?

It is my hope that we can combine a healthy discussion about revision of the constitution with immediate efforts to relieve the suffering of millions of Californians in a complementary way. Let us not lose this learning opportunity. There is no time to waste.

Alameda County Superintendent of Schools **Sheila Jordan** was a teacher for more than twenty years working with special-needs students and has also initiated programs for school dropouts. She has been a teaching consultant of the Bay Area Writing Project and the president of the Oakland School Board and has also served on the Oakland City Council.

State Constitutional Reform: A Primer

Barry Keene

NEARLY TWO DECADES AGO I wrote a paper for the Center for California Studies at California State University, Sacramento entitled "The Dangers of Government Gridlock and the Need for a Constitutional Convention." It predicted the governmental disaster of 2009-10.

Why a convention rather than a constitution revision commission? Because I had served as an associate counsel for the successful Constitution Revision Commission in the mid-1960s, and I perceived that the reforms needed in 1992 were of a dimension too challenging for any group appointed and controlled by beneficiaries of the political status quo.

That paper identified six major causes of government paralysis. Its analysis remains fundamentally sound today. But then, when the prospects for imminent constitutional reform were nonexistent, I had the luxury of thinking about what would be *perfect.* Today, with constitutional reform on the horizon, I must think instead of what's *possible.*

Today's electorate is fractured and alienated. There is far more need than before to craft reforms that will build consensus and bring people together. I propose three principles to guide Californians toward those goals: reverence for the founders of the country; respect for the will of the people; and opposition to reforms made only by political "insiders."

Reverence for the founders of the country. Fidelity to the first of these dictates a new state constitution that closely resembles the federal constitution, despite the desire of many to improve upon it. In my earlier paper I pushed for a one-house legislature and consideration of a parliamentary system to reduce policy-making divisions. Today, in the interests of practicality, I would recommend retaining James Madison's separation of the powers of the three branches. There should be a unified executive instead of California's multiplicity of state-level offices. The unicameral issue can be decided upon later, after public deliberation. There would be a Bill of Rights resembling the federal, with the addition of rights adopted by Californians but not found in the U.S. Constitution. Obviously, there would need to be a skillful translation of the federal system to suit state conditions. I would remind detractors that the federal system has worked for more than two centuries.

Respect for the will of the people. The will of the people may or may not permit a taming of the initiative process. To tie the hands of legislative representatives by initiatives, then complain that legislators are acting as if their hands are tied, then punish them by tying their hands tighter makes no sense. But the power of public education, the inevitable product of a constitutional convention, should never be underestimated. The public is already aware that the current governmental system is gridlocked. The next step would be to desanctify measures like Propositions 13 and 98 by subjecting them to a current vote of our present population. Does today's will of the people, informed by the lessons of disastrous ballot-box budgeting, still favor keeping our policy makers in a constitutional straitjacket? This is a fair question for those who pay homage to the will of the people. That will can be informed and strengthened by new alternatives—by policy proposals and procedural reforms that can renew confidence in the political system.

I believe, for example, that we can devise a property tax system in lieu of the existing Proposition 13 that can potentially satisfy even that measure's most faithful adherents. Like the reformed tax on timber (a yield tax), it would postpone the collection of property taxes until the property changes hands in a way that results in actual, realizable profits from any increase in value. No one would be "taxed out of their home"—as senior homeowners complained when Proposition 13 was enacted. Similarly, Proposition 98 adherents might, at first blush, be unwilling to let go of their perceived advantage. Nevertheless, most are educators or involved parents who have the civic awareness to understand that decisions made in a legislative body that actually works would give them ample opportunity to make their case effectively. It would also free support for education from the ties that currently bind it.

Opposition to reforms made only by political "insiders." The power to change rests on the credentials of, and confidence in the integrity of, the change agents. No one could argue that randomly selected members of a constitutional convention are in anyone's pocket. Far from being "insiders," they are the consummate outsiders. If they determine the best antidotes to gridlock; if they untie the hands of policy makers while holding them accountable; if they eliminate some of the self-inflicted barriers to government action, we will have ourselves a new and productive California. Still, restoring trust and confidence in policy making is ultimately the responsibility of the governor and legislature. It will be an uphill battle. As the 1992 paper said, "Government failure feeds on itself." Today, this sense of failure is exacerbated by the public's attraction to the simplicity of talk radio and its proclivity to see corruption and stupidity in every facet of public decisions and undertakings. This also prevents people from seeing, as the 1992 paper maintained, that California's problems are chiefly structural, not personal.

Institutional structure matters. We can, and must, do better.

Senator Barry Keene served for twenty years in both houses of the California legislature, retiring in 1992 after authoring major legislation in environment, health care, and government openness. In 1992 he authored SCA 84, calling for a constitutional convention. He has taught at California State University, Sacramento and Stanford and authored two casebooks in government and public administration. He is chair of the California Student Aid Commission.

Change How We Appoint Judges

Rodney F. Kingsnorth

CALIFORNIA GOVERNORS possess powers of judicial appointment that U.S. presidents might envy. Over the last thirty years they have used their authority to redistribute power in California's criminal courts in a manner inimical to judicial impartiality and the public interest. In addition, the ability to manipulate fear of crime for political and economic gain has advantaged certain groups at the expense of others within the court system. Specifically, the power of the prosecution to control procedures and shape sentencing outcomes has expanded at the expense of judicial authority by fulfilling the agenda of the California District Attorneys Association (CDAA), the political arm of California prosecutors.

The means to accomplish this shift has been provided by the California constitution itself, through its conferral on the electorate of the authority to recall judges and create law by means of ballot initiatives. The recall spearheaded by CDAA in 1987 of three California Supreme Court judges stands as a nationally unique assault on the independence of the judiciary. Another initiative removed from judges and granted to prosecutors the power to determine which juveniles shall be tried in adult court. Mandatory minimum sentences such as California's Three Strikes law (also passed by popular vote and aggressively promoted by prosecutors) have reduced the discretionary authority of judges to set sentences. Once signature-gathering requirements are met, initiative constitutional amendments can overturn California State Supreme Court decisions. The message from the prosecution to the state's judges is clear: if your decisions are contrary to our interests we can recall you, diminish your decision-making authority, and overturn your decisions.

In addition to these high-profile events, a less noted development has been the transformation of California judges into an increasingly homogeneous group dominated by former prosecutors. Sacramento County serves as a typical example. Of the sixty-three trial court judges in the county, twenty-seven were deputy district attorneys prior to ascending the bench. Thirteen were promoted from within the state attorney general's office. Thus almost two-thirds of the bench in Sacramento County were prosecutors before they became judges. Sixteen more worked in private practice before their elevation. Only four had dedicated their careers exclusively to a public defender's office or legal aid. In brief, lawyers who have committed to criminal defense work have been almost completely excluded from serving on the bench. Evidence from other counties confirms that this is a statewide phenomenon. Nor is this situation likely to change soon, since only 4 percent of Governor Schwarzenegger's statewide appointments have come from the ranks of criminal defense lawyers.

All appeals court judges are appointed, and governors are constrained only by the Judicial Appointment Commission, which in the seventy-five years of its existence has rejected only one nominee. These judges must be confirmed by popular vote in the election following their appointment and serve twelve-year renewable terms. Though trial court judges can achieve their positions by election (five of the sixty-three Sacramento judges have done so), most ascend to the bench by gubernatorial appointment. For these, not even the fig leaf of commission approval is required. These appointees serve for only six years and then must be reelected. If unchallenged, their names do not appear on the ballot. Since judges are seldom challenged and rarely defeated, most enjoy continuous service to retirement.

The dominance among judges of ex-prosecutors is explained by the fact that in the twenty-seven years since 1982, California has experienced twenty-two years of Republican gubernatorial rule. One Republican governor appointed only two trial judges in Sacramento with prior defense experience. The sole Democratic governor included only two people with defense or legal aid backgrounds among his eighteen currently serving appointees, revealing that he favored criminal defense lawyers no more than his Republican colleagues.

This exclusion of defense lawyers from the bench undermines the appearance of judicial impartiality and public confidence as well. No doubt the judicial role works substantively to limit bias, and most judges attempt to set aside the values they spent the previous twenty years of their careers implementing. That they fully succeed in this endeavor is doubtful, and data from the California jurisdictions that have been studied empirically suggest strongly that they do not. In any event, in a democratic society committed to the value of diversity, a judicial culture that emerges from a blend of perspectives is surely to be preferred over a narrow and punitive vision of the law. The remedy is simple. The California constitution should be changed to mirror the United States Constitution and require California governors to secure the consent of the California senate to any judicial appointment.

Rodney F. Kingsnorth is a professor of sociology at California State University, Sacramento. His research interests focus on case processing in the criminal courts with particular emphasis on policy evaluation and the impact of race and gender on official decision making. Recent coauthored publications have appeared in *Criminology, Justice Quarterly,* and *Violence against Women.*

Two Asymmetries

David W. Lyon

THERE ARE TWO asymmetries in California governance that should be addressed by a constitutional convention. The first is the requirement of a majority vote to approve a constitutional initiative, but a supermajority vote to modify the constitution once it has been amended. There is logic to making it difficult to modify the constitution, given the mischief that might arise from targeted attacks on the common interest clauses of the document. However, there is not a strong case for requiring only a majority popular vote on constitutional amendments. Raising the bar to 55 or 60 percent would make it harder to approve amendments and more closely align additions to and modifications of the constitution.

Second, California continues to have a mismatch between the distribution of the population by age, income, race, and geography as against those who choose to register and/or choose to vote. The likely voter in California is older, richer, whiter, and less likely to be from Los Angeles than the voter-eligible population at large. A 2002 Public Policy Institute of California (PPIC) study by Jack Citrin and Benjamin Highton, *How Race, Ethnicity, and Immigration Shape the California Electorate,* concluded that "by 2040, whites are projected to be little more than one-third of the adult population in California. However, if the citizenship and turnout rates of Asians and Latinos remain at their 2000 levels, whites will continue to make up a majority (53 percent) of the voting population."

A more recent report from PPIC, "California's Likely Voters" (Sept. 2009), concluded that "Although whites represent less than half (47%) of California's adult population, they constitute 68% of likely voters. Despite the fact that Latinos represent about one-third of California's adult population, they constitute only 17% of likely voters and 66% of those not registered to vote."

There are of course various reasons why many people don't register to vote and many choose not to vote when the time comes. Numerous suggestions have been made for "get out the vote" campaigns and some implemented. Nevertheless, the asymmetry between those registered and voting and the population at large is striking and raises the question of whether outcomes for elected officials and initiatives truly reflect the preferences of the majority of Californians. Perhaps it is one reason that the state legislature has such low approval ratings.

Delegates at a constitutional convention should seriously consider linking state benefits and program participation to voting behavior. It need not be a matter of yes or no, but perhaps a record of being registered to vote and actually voting would create an incentive to vote that is lacking among many eligible citizens—both long-term and more recent arrivals. In any event, this is one governance asymmetry in California that threatens to make distrust of the political process a permanent condition.

David W. Lyon was the founding president of the Public Policy Institute of California from 1994 to 2007, having served as a vice president and head of the Domestic Research Division of RAND from 1975 to 1994. He was a regional economist at the Federal Reserve Bank of Philadelphia from 1969 to 1971.

Change Needed, Convention Not Necessarily the Answer

Jean M. Ross

CALIFORNIA, FACING severe economic hard times, plummeting tax revenues, an outdated tax system, and a dysfunctional political process that requires a two-thirds vote for both budget and tax increases, is in dire straights. The depth of the current crisis has prompted more and more far-reaching calls for reform of the rules that govern California's budget and its system of governance. While there is widespread agreement on the need for change, there is little agreement about what that change should entail or the process that should be used to achieve it.

Recent calls for a constitutional convention are intriguing. Convention proponents argue that only a comprehensive review can achieve the magnitude of change necessary to set the state on a path to fiscal and political vitality. Calls for far-reaching reform are persuasive. Perhaps it is time to wipe the slate clean and start anew. But as with all complex and important problems, the devil is in the details. And it is hard to imagine a "start anew" proposal that would not engender sufficient opposition to ensure its eventual defeat at the ballot box. Perhaps more importantly, designing a process that is appropriately representative of the diversity that is California's strength would be a daunting challenge. Even more formidable would be the challenge of ensuring that delegates grasp the facts and history underlying the current relationship between the state and local governments, the structure and process of the budget and state and local tax systems, and the demands on the state's governance and fiscal systems—all of which are sufficiently complex to test even longtime students of California government.

Last but not least, there is a significant risk that such a convening could make California's problems worse, not better. While proponents argue that a convention call could be limited to fiscal and governance reform, it is unclear how such limits could be imposed or how they would work in practice. Moreover, voters' decisions through the ballot box have caused many of the problems that a convention would seek to change, and there are solid grounds to question whether voters would safeguard the interests of the vulnerable and less powerful Californians. As one longtime observer of California's policy landscape reminds me, the state's last constitutional convention resulted in the enactment of the Chinese exclusion laws. More recently, it was the voters themselves who imposed limitations on the state's budgeting and taxing powers and curtailed the basic rights of large numbers of the state's residents.

An incremental approach to fiscal and governance reform could achieve more limited goals, at least in the short run, and with lower risk. The first and more important step would be to eliminate the supermajority vote requirements that leave the state facing recurring budget crises and impose a stranglehold on lawmakers' ability to respond to economic and demographic demands. California, the nation's largest and most diverse state, is the only one saddled with a "double supermajority" requirement. Three states—California, Arkansas, and Rhode Island—require more than a majority of lawmakers to pass a spending plan under any circumstance. Twelve states require more than a majority of lawmakers to pass any state tax increase. California alone requires both.

This double supermajority vote requirement, coupled with a deeply polarized legislature, makes it difficult and often impossible to raise revenues and has resulted in budgets balanced through deep reductions to nearly all areas of public spending—with the notable absence of prisons and infrastructure bond debt—as well as accounting gimmicks, questionable assumptions, and borrowing. These one-sided budget solutions have left California ill prepared for the future and facing ever greater budget gaps.

The supermajority vote requirement for any measure that increases state tax revenues—even those that would close tax "loopholes" shown to have little or no impact on their intended policy objective—reduces the effectiveness and accountability of the state's tax code. Take, for example, the state's enterprise zone program. The authors of the most exhaustive evaluation of the program concluded that "the safest conclusion is that California's enterprise zone program is ineffective." Yet, because a two-thirds vote of each house of the legislature would be required to scale back tax credits offered through the program, it remains intact while college funding is slashed and children lose health coverage.

During California's rare "good budget" years, the double supermajority vote produced budget agreements that increased spending, on the one hand, and cut taxes, on the other, a mathematical recipe for disaster during economic downturns. Last, but not least, California's supermajority vote requirements reduce the accountability of the legislature and, by letting a small minority determine the outcome of critical policy debates, result in outcomes that may be at odds with the positions of the vast majority of lawmakers.

Other changes that would improve California's governability include restricting the ability of voters to approve new costs and program responsibilities through the ballot box, and limiting voters' ability to permanently earmark revenues. The state can and should modernize its tax system without sacrificing growth and progressivity. Within the sphere of governance, lengthening or eliminating the limits on the number of terms legislators can remain in office would go a long way toward restoring a balance of power between the executive and legislative branches of government. It would also give lawmakers the time to acquire the knowledge and experience needed to address complex policy issues, from water to the budget. In addition, abolishing term limits would discourage the use of short-term budget "fixes" that leave larger problems on the doorsteps of future legislators.

It is clear that bold action is needed to bring reform to a state hobbled by a tough economy, dysfunctional budget rules, and an outdated tax system. But the best way to heal California's wounds, without adding more to its already long list of ailments, remains anything but certain.

Jean M. Ross is founding executive director of the California Budget Project. She was principal consultant to the Assembly Revenue and Taxation Committee, senior consultant to the Assembly Human Services Committee, and assistant research director of the Service Employees International Union in Washington, DC, coordinating its research on tax, budget, and employment issues. She serves on the Advisory Committee of California's Franchise Tax Board and on the board of the California Tax Reform Association.

Towards a Politics of Place

Gary Snyder

WHAT IS "CALIFORNIA?" It is, after all, a recent human invention with many hasty straight-line boundaries that were drawn with a ruler on a map and rushed off to an office in Sacramento. But landscapes have their own shapes and structures, centers and edges, which must be respected. California is made up of what I take to be about six regions. There is the central coast, the great Central Valley, the long mountain ranges of the Sierra Nevada, the Modoc plateau and volcano country, the northern coast with its deep interior mountains, and the coastal valley and mountains south of the Tehachapis, running on into Baja. Almost all of core California has a summer-dry Mediterranean climate with fairly abundant winter rain. More than anything else, this climate is what gives our place its fragrance of oily aromatic herbs, its olive-green drought-resistant shrubs, and its patterns of rolling grasses and dark forest.

I do not propose that we instantly redraw the boundaries of the social construction called California, although that will happen someday. But we are becoming aware of certain long-term realities, and this is leading toward the next step in the evolution of human citizenship on the North American continent. For the present, however, and for most people, the land we all live on is simply taken for granted—and the proper relation to it is not considered part of "citizenship."

If we look at land ownership categories in California beyond private land, we get the Bureau of Land Management, national forest, national park, state park, military reserves, and a host of other public holdings. This is the public domain, a practice coming down from the historic institution of the commons in Europe. Conservationists have worked since the 1930s for the preservation of key blocks of public land as wilderness. But we have become aware that this exclusive emphasis on disparate parcels of land ignores the insouciant freeness of wild creatures. Individual islands of wild land cannot by themselves guarantee the maintenance of natural variety. Habitat flows across both private and public land. We must find a way to work with wild ecosystems that respects both the rights of landowners and the rights of bears.

One name for the ecosystems within the state's larger regions is "bioregion." California-based federal and state land managers trying to work together on biodiversity problems in the early 1990s identified eleven or so working regions within California. People in some of those bioregions had already formed "watershed councils" as building blocks for a long-range strategy for social and environmental sustainability. For the watershed, cities and dams are ephemeral and of no more account than a landslide that temporarily alters the channel. The water will always be there and always find its way down. As constrained and polluted as the Los Angeles River is at the moment, in the larger picture it is also alive and well under the city streets, running in giant culverts. Watershed councils start their work in a modest way, like saying, "Let's try and rehabilitate our river to the point that wild salmon can successfully spawn here again."

All land ownership is ultimately written in sand. The only jurisdiction that will last in the world of nature is the watershed. Dan Kemmis, former mayor of Missoula, reminds us that the word "republican" in the eighteenth century meant a politics of community engagement. He adds that "what holds people together long enough to discover their power as citizens is their common inhabiting of a single place." Being so placed, people will volunteer for community projects, join school boards, and accept nominations and appointments. A bioregional perspective gives us the imagination of a citizenship in something beyond politically designated space. It gives us the imagination of a citizenship in a place called, for example, the Great Central Valley, which has valley oaks and migratory waterfowl as well as humans among its members. Urban bioregionalism ("green cities") has developed a sense of this citizenship too.

The great Central Valley does not prefer English over Spanish or Japanese over Hmong. It will welcome whoever chooses to observe its etiquette. Watershed consciousness and bioregionalism are not just a form of environmentalism or just a political program, but a move toward resolving both nature and society with the practice of a profound citizenship in both worlds. If the ground can be our common ground, we can begin to talk to each other (human and nonhuman) once again. A new constitution for California might well acknowledge the need for this more profound citizenship, provide for it, respect it, develop arrangements to encourage it, and provide representation for all the members of the larger community in its assemblies.

Gary Snyder is a poet, author, scholar, cultural critic, and professor emeritus of the University of California at Davis. He has been a Guggenheim Fellow and is a member of the American Academy of Arts and Letters and the American Academy of Arts and Sciences. His *Turtle Island* won the Pulitzer Prize for poetry in 1975, and his book-length poem *Mountains and Rivers Without End* won the Bollingen Prize in poetry in 1997. In 2008 he was awarded the Ruth Lilly Poetry Prize for lifetime achievement.

Reestablish Cross-Filing

Kevin Starr

THE CENTRAL PROBLEM of California politics on the state level has been the collapse of the center. That collapse can be dated to the gubernatorial election of 1958, which in turn precipitated the end of cross-filing in 1959. If I had my druthers, I would reestablish cross-filing. Every primary for every election would be open to every candidate, no matter what his or her party might be. Democrats could enter Republican primaries, and vice versa. Independents could enter both primaries simultaneously. Thus we would eliminate control from the margin of left and right that has destroyed the center and has thereby made politics—defined by Aristotle as the art of the possible—impossible to pursue, as the current impasse in Sacramento so egregiously underscores.

In contemplating this proposal to restore cross-filing, ask yourself the following questions. What has happened? How has a state that for so long has prided itself on being a cutting-edge American commonwealth in terms of its public programs and services, a nation-state even, global in importance, by turns the seventh- or eighth-largest economy on the planet—how has such a state brought itself with such swiftness to such banana republic status?

The causes are multiple and conjoined. They include term limits; the professionalization of the legislature; the disappearance of centrism and the rise of red and blue enclaves; and a confused and spoiled electorate, incapable of properly wielding the powers of a direct democracy.

Now let's flash back for a moment. If you happened to have found yourself in Sacramento, California, a half-century and more ago when the legislature was in session, you would have encountered an assembly and a state senate dominated by good old boys, a few good old girls, and a number of pink-cheeked portly Masons in rimless glasses and double-breasted suits. The good old boys could be found of an evening boozing at the Torch Club near the Capitol, or chowing down on Chinese food at Frank Fat's, the legislative eatery of choice. Or, if the hour were late, you would find them knocking back a glass or two or even three of bourbon at a late-night party, thrown by a lobbyist most likely, in the Hotel Senator across the street from the Capitol. Even a couple of the Masonic Republican suits might be on hand, yukking it up with their Democratic colleagues. It was, I suppose, a disreputable scene, dominated by part-time politicians who repaired to Sacramento every other year for six months to pass laws, while remaining the rest of the time in their communities earning a living.

Yet these good old boys, Babbitt businessmen, and a smaller cadre of female solons—in the days preceding their late-night carousals, indeed amidst the give-and-take of the good times at the Torch Club or Frank Fat's—managed not only to balance the budget but to lay down for California the social and infrastructural foundations of a developing megastate en route to nation-state status. Democrats and Republicans alike, playing politics, cutting deals, managed the creation of a world-class freeway system, a statewide water project that would become the single largest public works effort of its sort in American history, and a program of higher education offering to each Californian, at minimal cost, instruction at a local community college, a state college campus, or, for the top 12 percent of academic performers, admission to a great public university, the University of California, a distinguished institution that the legislators, high school graduates included, had played a major role in creating. Not bad for part-time work by men and women proud to call themselves citizen politicians, willing to earn their livings in their own communities and to engage in the give-and-take of negotiations which, two and a half millennia ago, Aristotle in his *Politics* defined as politics, the art of the possible, the art of getting done what could get done.

The abortive candidacy for governor, in 1958, of United States Senator William Knowland, the ultra-right anti-Communist "senator from Formosa," as he was called, not only cost moderate Goodwin J. Knight the governorship and moderate Republican San Francisco mayor George Christopher a seat in the United States Senate, it obliterated the centrism which, along with cross-filing (rescinded in 1959), had enabled a centrist Republican Party to remain in power in the postwar era. Even Ronald Reagan, as is now being recognized, although he was a product of the post-Goldwater migration of the Republican Party to the right, seems in retrospect to have been a governor capable of cutting deals with Democrats when necessary.

A growing divide, Red State California versus Blue State California, soon reduced legislative politics to a condition of Manichean conflict, each side seeing in itself the absolute embodiment of good and demonizing the opposition. Localized in such places as Los Angeles (with the exception of the San Fernando Valley), Santa Monica, Oakland, Berkeley, Palo Alto, San Francisco, and Marin, Blue State California opposed itself to Red State California, localized in greater San Diego, portions of Orange County, the Inland Empire, the Central Valley, and the Far North.

When cross-filing was in effect, Republicans gravitated to the center because they realized that Democrats outnumbered them by one million voters at the polls. Hence, they would have to get along with Democrats to stay in power. Democrats, meanwhile, depended upon Republican support to achieve the two-thirds majority necessary to finance their programs. Reestablishing cross-filing would reestablish this enforced détente. It would also foster the growing Independent movement, and this in turn would further marginalize the extreme left and the extreme right by bolstering still more the sea anchor of a dominant center.

Kevin Starr, National Humanities Medalist for 2006, is University Professor and Professor of History at the University of Southern California. He recently published the eighth volume of his prizewinning series on the history of California, *Golden Dreams: California in an Age of Abundance, 1950–1963.* He was California State Librarian from 1994 to 2004.

California: The Perfect Storm

John Vasconcellos

I WANT TO SHARE ideas gained from my thirty-eight-year odyssey representing the heart of Silicon Valley in the California legislature (including fifteen years as chair of the Assembly Ways and Means Committee, responsible for our annual state budget), and also following the principles of humanistic psychology in the attempt to become a whole and more fulfilled person.

Based on these two backgrounds I see the causes of our fiscal and constitutional crisis as the dysfunctional interaction between our political structures, our roles within those structures, and our basic needs and potentials as human beings.

A good deal has been written about the current disarray of the first two of these, and steps are being taken to set them right. But no matter how much we change any organizational chart, if the same persons occupy the positions of power we will get the same results. It is that third realm, the human dimension, which holds the key to both the cause and cure of our fiscal crisis. That third realm exists within and between us as people, not above or below us.

We have had major revolutions over the past fifty years. They affect gender and race, economy and technology. But the most important of them has been what Willis Harman calls the New Copernican Revolution, which puts us back at the center of our universe—our vision of ourselves, our human nature and potential, and taken together, our self-esteem.

What does this perspective suggest about the divisions and dysfunction of our state legislature?

One part of the human dimension is the relational. Relationally, what California needs to resolve the budget crisis is for our legislators and governor to develop more trusting relationships in fulfillment of their common mission, the wise governance of our state.

To develop this trust I propose an orientation program for new legislators to give them shared experiences in learning how to become effective legislators—not only how to develop policy proposals but also in such things as the psychology of survival in a highly charged bipartisan setting, how to recognize each other as unique persons, and how to think about the kind of California they will jointly govern and want their children to grow up in. Providing such an orientation program ought to be one of our first reforms.

The other, deeper part of the human realm is the personal dimension where we form our basic vision of ourselves, which informs and determines our expectations, choices, and actions. A conflict of these visions divides people in America and California today. One of these visions sees us humans mainly as economic beings without any innate sense of self-worth, whose sense of freedom is almost entirely associated with rights to amass property and wealth, and who see others' value as determined by how much they possess. The alternative vision sees humans as having innate worth, their sense of freedom associated with their self-fulfillment as life-affirming, constructive, and trustworthy people, as humanistic psychologist Carl Rogers taught. This view values self-realization, identity, and autonomy, and it sees humans not only as economic beings, but as psychological and moral beings.

These visions lead to contrary views about the appropriate role of government. One sees government as limited almost solely to providing for public safety and security, or protection of persons and property. The other recognizes a larger role for government: advancing human beings beyond security needs, upholding equity and compassion, and assuring basic food and shelter, health, and educational opportunity for all.

This is the conflict at issue in California's budget gridlock. It is a conflict between more faithful and more cynical views of human nature. The one recognizes government's responsibility to provide the preconditions for people's self-realization and all-round development. The other thinks people should shift for themselves and are on their own.

The most troubling aspect of it all is a "rule of eight" which informally operates in the fifteen-person Republican caucus. Considering that Democrats from currently apportioned districts get about twenty-five senate seats, this converts what began with a two-thirds constitutional threshold for a budget or tax increase into an 83 percent requirement—a vote of thirty-three (twenty-five plus those eight) out of forty. And stopping the senate stops the whole political process. The two-thirds rule thus winds up letting eight conservative senators grasp the aspirations of thirty-eight million Californians in their hands.

This conflict of visions goes beyond specific policies to the core of our identities. Our beloved state of California is of course a political entity. And it is an economic entity. But more basically it is a moral entity. If we are to work beyond our current crises, all of us have to self-consciously decide about our visions of human nature. Do we believe that people have innate worth as human beings or that they don't? Let us honor our deepest aspirations, recognize that our ship of state has the most diverse, talented, and creative group of humans ever aboard it, and redirect it from today's perfect storm towards a once again Golden State.

> **Senator John Vasconcellos** served thirty-eight years in the California State Legislature and was chair of the Assembly Ways and Means Committee, the committee responsible for the state budget, for fifteen years. He chaired the Senate Public Safety, Education, and Economic Development committees. He is cofounder of the Vasconcellos Legacy Project and its Politics of Trust Network, which works to restore functionality to the legislature and transform state culture from cynicism to faithfulness.

Needed: An Education in Governance

William T. Vollmann

ONE REASON THAT the special interests win so much of the time is that the people have not consistently educated themselves and interjected themselves. I would like to see a lottery system at the high school level which would be equivalent to the process of jury summonses. Students called up would be required to go to Sacramento, all expenses paid, live commonly with their peers, and attend sessions of the legislative committee of their choice as fully briefed, nonvoting members. Students who obstructed or skipped their obligations would be assigned to useful community service (for instance, picking up trash). At the end of their tenure, a press conference would be held for the students, who would say what they liked. Hopefully this would make the political system less distant and alien. It might also (who knows?) reduce corruption and cronyism.

William T. Vollmann is the author of many volumes of both fiction and nonfiction, including the recent *Imperial*, the series *Seven Dreams: A Book of North American Landscapes, An Afghanistan Picture Show, Europe Central,* which received a National Book Award for fiction in 2005, and *Rising Up and Rising Down*, a seven-volume treatise on violence. His work has also been published in *The New Yorker, Esquire, Spin, Gear,* and *Granta*.

Notes

ONE California at the Edge

1. "Rethinking California's Public Life" forum, Center for California Studies and California Council for the Humanities, May 16, 1991, CSU Sacramento.
2. Dan Walters, *Sacramento Bee*, 1 Sept. 1991, and 5 May 1994. Barry Keene, "The Dangers of Government Gridlock and Need for a Constitutional Convention," Center for California Studies Occasional Paper No. 1, CSU Sacramento, 1992.
3. Dan Walters, *Sacramento Bee*, 4 July 2004. George Skelton, *Los Angeles Times*, 23 Feb. 2009.
4. Gloria Duffy, *San Francisco Chronicle*, 5 Oct. 2003. J. Rakove, *San Francisco Chronicle*, 21 Sept. 2003. Jim Wunderman, *San Francisco Chronicle*, 21 Aug. 2008. Mendonca comments, Convention Summit, Sheraton Grand Hotel, Sacramento, 14 Feb. 2009. The "alter or abolish" phrase is from the Declaration of Independence.
5. Peter Barnes, *Capitalism 3.0: A Guide to Reclaiming the Commons* (San Francisco: Barrett-Koehler, 2006), 4–5.
6. California's Gross Domestic Product grew 2 to 3 percent a year in 2004 to 2007, and even .4 percent in the downturn of 2008. California Department of Finance, Table D-2, 2008; and U.S. Bureau of Economic Analysis: www.bea.gov, accessed January 2010.
7. Machiavelli, "Discourses on Livy," in *The Prince and the Discourses* (New York: Modern Library, 1950). And "It is not individual prosperity, but the general good, that makes cities great." (282, 161)
8. Hans P. Johnson, "A State of Diversity: Demographic Trends in California's Regions," Public Policy Institute of California *California Counts: Population Trends and Profiles* 3(5): 3 (May 2002). Raymond Dasmann, "Environmental Quality" (California Studies Conference, Sacramento, 11 Feb. 1989). Gary Snyder, "Coming into the Watershed," in *A Place in Space* (Washington DC: Counterpoint, 1995), 222–223. Gerald Haslam, "Literary California: The Ultimate Frontier of the Western World," *California History* 68: 188 (1982).
9. Tomás Almaguer, *Racial Fault Lines* (Berkeley: Univ: of California, 1994), 54–55.
10. T. George Harris, "California's New Politics: Big Daddy's Big Drive," *Look* (25 Sept. 1962), 80.

11. Joan Didion, *Where I Was From* (New York: Alfred Knopf, 2003), 66.

12. Josiah Royce, *California* (1886; reprint Santa Barbara, Calif.: Peregrine Press, 1970), 216, 182, 28. Royce also noted the racial expression of the careless brutality.

13. The public trust doctrine goes back to Rome's Justinian code: "By the law of nature these things are common to mankind—the air, running water, the sea and consequently the shores of the sea." *National Audubon Society et al. v. Superior Court of Alpine County, Department of Water and Power of the City of Los Angeles et al.,* 33 Cal.3d 419, S.F. No. 24368. California Supreme Court, 1983.

14. Letter to James Madison, 6 Sept. 1789, in *Jefferson: Political Writings,* ed. Joyce Appleby and Terence Ball (Cambridge: Cambridge Univ. Press, 1999), 593.

15. Leon Bouvier and Philip Martin, *Population Change and California's Future* (Washington DC: Population Reference Bureau, 1985), i. Dan Walters, in "More Poverty a New Reality," *Sacramento Bee,* 22 Sept. 1991, reporting on Robert Mogull's finding that Californians in poverty grew from 11.6 percent to 17.6 percent of the population in the 1980s.

16. Poverty among people in single-mother families was 37 percent two years before the mortgage crisis. Deborah Reed, "Poverty in California: Moving Beyond the Federal Measure," Public Policy Institute of California *California Counts* 7(4), 11.

17. Susan Burkhardt, *San Francisco Examiner,* 28 Oct. 1990. Peter Schrag, *Sacramento Bee,* 2 Sept. 1992. "California Failing," *The Economist* (Aug. 8, 1992), 19. Robert Reinhold, *New York Times,* 17 Nov. 1991. Also see *Los Angeles Times* editorial, 12 Sept. 1992.

18. Alissa Garcia, David Carroll, and Jean Ross, "A Generation of Widening Inequality: The State of Working California, 1979 to 2006" (California Budget Project, August 2007), 4. Martha Groves, "The California Puzzle: Hard-Pressed by Recession...[and] New Realities," *Los Angeles Times,* 31 Jan. 1993.

19. L. Stein, "State Income Disparity Tops Industrialized World, Nation," *Sacramento Bee,* 17 Nov. 1996. Groves, "California Puzzle." Deborah Reed, "California's Rising Income Inequality: Causes and Concern," *PPIC Research Brief* 17, viii-ix (Feb. 1999). Even at the median, male weekly real wages declined from $720 in 1969 to $554 in 1997 (p. 14). At the 90th percentile, however, income actually grew between 1969 and 1989 by 31 percent. Deborah Reed, Melissa Glenn Haber, and Laura Mameesh, *The Distribution of Income in California* (San Francisco: Public Policy Institute of California, 1996), xi.

20. That 13 percent would be at least 16 percent by the adjusted measure appropriate to California's high cost of living. Reed, "Poverty: Moving Beyond." Deborah Reed and Richard Van Swearingen, "Poverty in California," Public Policy Institute of California *California Counts* 3(3): 3-4, 10 (Nov. 2001). Southeast Asian American figure from Deborah Reed, "Recent Trends in Income and Poverty," Public Policy Institute of California *California Counts* 5(3): 2 (Feb. 2004). Also, "Making Ends Meet: How Much Does It Cost to Raise a Family in California?," California Budget Project, Nov. 2005.

21. Garcia et al., "Widening Inequality," 1.

22. Edward Yellin, "Working Families in California Face Greater Demands: Single Parents Falling Behind (San Francisco: UCSF Institute for Health Policy Studies, 1998), 2. Income data from Reed, "Recent Trends," 9. Peter Schrag, "California's Curious Comeback," *Sacramento Bee,* 23 April 1997.

23. Stein, "State Income Disparity." Reed, "California's Rising...", 14. Reed, "Recent Trends," 3, 5-6. Also, Garcia et al., "Widening Inequality," 4.

24. Reed and Van Swearingen, "Poverty," 1-12. Illustrative of the jobless character of the new recoveries, "Following the 2001 recession, poverty in California increased from 12.6 percent in 2001 to 13.1 percent in 2002." Reed, "Poverty: Moving Beyond," 12.

25. Peter Gosselin, "The Poor Have More Things Today—Including Wild Income Swings," *Los Angeles Times*, 12 Dec. 2004, and *High Wire: The Precarious Financial Lives of American Families* (New York: Basic Books, 2008).

26. Edward Luttwak, *Turbo-Capitalism* (New York: Harper Collins, 1999), 46.

27. John Dewey, *The Public and Its Problems* (1927; reprint Athens, OH: Swallow Press, 1954), 143.

28. Gosselin, *High Wire*, 310, 322, 138.

29. Charles Howard McIlwain, *Constitutionalism, Ancient and Modern* (Ithaca: Cornell University Press, 1947), 142–144 (his italics).

30. Alexander Hamilton, James Madison, John Jay, "Federalist No. 10" in *The Federalist Papers* (New York: Mentor Books, 1961) 78, 80.

31. Ibid., 78.

32. Gary Snyder, *The Practice of the Wild* (San Francisco: North Point Press, 1990), 39, 40.

33. George Mowry, *The California Progressives* (Chicago: Quadrangle Books, 1951), 101, 104.

34. Alexis de Tocqueville, *Democracy in America*, ed. T. Bender (New York: Modern Library, 1981), 4, 587. He also saw participatory local involvement as the only means capable of teaching a person "the extent of his rights" and "the nature of his duties" (55).

35. California Budget Project, "New Data Show That California's Income Gaps Continue to Widen," *Policy Points* (June 2009), 3. Stein, "State Income Disparity."

36. California Budget Project, "New Data," 2.

37. California Budget Project, "To Have and To Have Not," *Budget Brief* (June 2009), 2–3. R. Bayne, "Budget Includes Billions in Tax Breaks," *California Progress Report* (June 4, 2009).The tax cuts were made in the September 2008 and February 2009 budget agreements without public hearings.

38. Reed, "Poverty: Moving Beyond," 13, 15–16. High levels of social inequality correlate with poor health, poor quality of life, and declining life expectancy. Richard Wilkinson and Kate Pickett, *The Spirit Level: Why Equal Societies Almost Always Do Better* (London: Allen Lane, Penguin Books, 2009)

39. Peter Schrag, "Our Growing Income Gap: Is Education the Fix?," *Sacramento Bee*, 8 March 2006.

40. Luttwak, *Turbo-Capitalism*, 187.

41. Winthrop, "A Model of Christian Charity." And "The wellfare of the whole is [not] to be put to apparent hazard for the advantage of any particular members." "A Defense of an Order of Court,…1637," Perry Miller and Thomas H. Johnson, *The Puritans, A Sourcebook of Their Writings* (New York: Harper and Row, 1963), 197, 200.

42. Madison, "Federalist No. 10," 78, 80.

43. Mowry, *California Progressives*, 9.

44. Delegates Clitus Barbour and Thomas Laine both used this phrase. E. B. Willis and P. K. Stockton, *Debates and Proceedings of the Constitutional Convention of the State of California* (Sacramento: State Office, 1880), 16.

45. I am indebted to Frank Bardacke for this formulation.

THREE **Proposition 13**

1. Abel Maldonado, a moderate Republican, got a measure placed on the ballot for an open primary.

2. A lawsuit brought by Macy's after the company was purchased and reassessed was accepted by the U.S Supreme Court for hearing, before the *Nordlinger* case. However, anti-tax groups threatened to boycott Macy's, and the department store chain dropped its lawsuit.

FOUR **The California Legislature and the Decline of Majority Rule**

1. Peverill Squire, "Legislative Institutionalization and the California Assembly," *The Journal of Politics* 54(4): 1026–1054 (1992).
2. Ibid.
3. Jay Michaels and Dan Walters, *The Third House: Lobbyists, Power and Money in Sacramento* (Berkeley: Berkeley Public Policy Press, 2002).
4. Peverill Squire, "Legislative Professionalization and Membership Diversity in State Legislatures," *Legislative Studies Quarterly* 17(1): 69–79 (1992).
5. Seth E. Masket, "It Takes an Outsider: Extralegislative Organization and Partisanship in the California Assembly, 1849–2006," *American Journal of Political Science* 51(3): 482–497 (2007).
6. E. E. Schattschneider, *Party Government* (New York: Rhinehart and Company, 1941) and E. E. Schattschneider, "Political Parties and the Public Interest," *Annals of the American Academy of Political and Social Science*, 280: 18–26 (March 1952).
7. Masket, "It Takes an Outsider."
8. Jack L. Walker, "Diffusion of Innovations among the American States," *American Political Science Review* 63(3): 880–899 (1969).
9. Robert Greenstein, "The Constitutional Amendment to Require a Two-Thirds Super-majority to Raise Taxes," The Center on Budget and Policy Priorities: www.cbpp.org/4-24-01tax.htm, accessed Nov. 2009.
10. U.S. Department of Education, "National Assessment of Educational Progress: The Nation's Report Card," National Center for Educational Statistics: http://nces.ed.gov/nationsreportcard, accessed Nov. 2009.
11. *Education Week*, "Quality Counts 2008": www.edweek.org/ew/toc/2008/01/10/index.html, accessed Nov. 2009.
12. Susanna Loeb, Anthony Bryk, and Eric Hanushek, "Getting Down to Facts: School Finance and Governance in California (Summary)." Stanford University, Institute for Research on Education Policy and Practice: http://irepp.stanford.edu/documents/GDF/summary-paper-final.pdf, accessed Nov. 2009.
13. Katherine Bishop, "Political Giants Deflated in California," *New York Times*, 24 Jan. 1991.
14. Ibid.
15. Todd Donovan and Joseph R. Snipp, "Support for Legislative Term Limits in California: Group Representation, Partisanship and Campaign Information," *The Journal of Politics* 56(2): 492–501 (1994).
16. Thad Kousser, *Term Limits and the Dismantling of Legislative Professionalism* (New York: Cambridge University Press, 2005).
17. Lawrence H. Goulder, "California's Bold New Climate Policy," *The Economist's Voice* 4(3) (2007). Chapter nine explains AB 32.
18. Environmental Defense Fund, "California's Landmark Global Warming Legislation Poised for Passage," press release, 30 Aug. 2006: www.edf.org/pressrelease.cfm?ContentID=5419, accessed Jan. 2010.
19. John W. Ellwood and Mary Sprague, "Options for Reforming the California State Budget Process," in *Constitutional Reform in California*, ed. Bruce E. Cain and Roger E. Noll (Berkeley: Univ. of California Institute of Governmental Studies, 1995).
20. Schattschneider, *Party Government* and "Political Parties."

21. Schattschneider, "Political Parties," 24.
22. Ibid., 26.
23. Michael Hiltzik, "Wanted: Profiles in Courage," *Los Angeles Times*, 1 June 2009, online edition.
24. Gary C. Jacobson, "Partisan and Ideological Polarization in the California Electorate," *State Politics and Policy Quarterly* 4(2): 113–139 (2004); Masket, "It Takes an Outsider."
25. Dan Walters, "Legislature Seems to Get Less Work Done," *Sacramento Bee*, 14 Oct. 2005.
26. Richard C. Paddock, "Less to Bank on at State Universities," *Los Angeles Times*, 7 Oct. 2007, online edition.
27. Seem Mehta and Gale Holland, "California Lawmakers Hear Pleas Not to Further Slash Education," *Los Angeles Times*, 2 June 2009, online edition.
28. Peter Schrag, *Paradise Lost: California's Experience, America's Future* (Berkeley: Univ. of California Press, 1999), 62, 139.
29. Stephanie Zou, "Students Mourn California Dream," *California Aggie*, 22 April 2005, online edition.
30. Jacobson, "Partisan and Ideological."

Additional References, Chapter 4

Sam Aanestad, "Gut and Amend Legislation Shortchanges Our Constituents." Press Release, Oct. 1, 2004.

Bill Ainsworth, "Universal Insurance Proposal Flounders," *San Diego Union Tribune*, 31 Oct. 2007, online edition.

Mark Baldassare, Dean Bonner, Jennifer Baluch, and Sonja Petek, "Californians and the Environment," Public Policy Institute of California Statewide Survey: www.ppic.org/content/pubs/survey/S_707MBS.pdf, accessed Nov. 2009

———, "Californians and their Government," Public Policy Institute of California Statewide Survey: www.ppic.org/content/pubs/survey/S_507MBS.pdf, accessed Nov. 2009.

Bill Boyarsky, *Big Daddy: Jesse Unruh and the Art of Power Politics* (Berkeley: Univ. of California Press, 2007).

California Budget Project, "How Is Transportation Funded in California?" *Budget Backgrounder* (Sept. 2006): www.cbp.org/pdfs/2006/0609_transportationprimer.pdf, accessed Nov. 2009.

California Postsecondary Education Commission, "Public Higher Education Performance Accountability Framework Report: Commission Report 07-11": www.cpec.ca.gov/completereports/2007reports/07-11.pdf, accessed Nov. 2009.

The California State Constitution: www.leginfo.ca.gov/const-toc.html, accessed Nov. 2009.

Tom Chorneau, "New California Laws: Smoking Drivers, Minimum Wage, Celebrity News," *San Francisco Chronicle*, 2 Jan. 2008.

Richard A. Clucas, *The Speaker's Electoral Connection: Willie Brown and the California Assembly* (Berkeley: Institute of Governmental Studies Press, 1995).

Ken Debow and John C. Syer. *Power and Politics in California*, 7th ed. (San Francisco: Pearson Education, 2003).

Lynda Gledhill "Sizable Deficits Ahead for State, Analyst Warns," *San Francisco Chronicle*, 16 Nov. 2006.

Ian J. Goldsmith, "Gut and Amend Process Has Its Place," *San Diego Union Tribune*, 20 Aug. 2006, online edition.

Evan Halper, "Gov. Finds Himself in a Bigger Budget Bind," *Los Angeles Times*, 24. Nov. 2007, online edition.

Leroy C. Hardy and Charles P. Sohner, "Constitutional Challenge and Political Response: California Reapportionment, 1965," *Western Political Quarterly* 23(4): 733–751 (1970).

D. Kenyon and K. Benker, "Fiscal Discipline: Lessons from the State Experience," *National Tax Journal* 37, 433–446 (1984).

Brian G. Knight, "Supermajority Voting Requirements for Tax Increases: Evidence from the States," *Journal of Public Economics* 76, 41–67 (2000).

Judy Lin, "Budget Brawl Boosts Lure of Majority Vote," *Sacramento Bee*, 26 Aug. 2007, online edition.

———, "Budget Battle Gets Greener," *Sacramento Bee*, 9 Aug. 2007, online edition.

Greg Lucas, "2003's Turmoil Yields New Laws," *San Francisco Chronicle*, 1 Jan. 2004.

———, "Infrastructure Bonds: Voters Backing Governor's Public Works Spending," *San Francisco Chronicle*, 8 Nov. 2006.

Mark Martin, "A Global Warming Moment," *San Francisco Chronicle*, 28 Sept. 2006.

Ed Mendel, "Governor Proposes 10% Cut in Spending across the Board," *San Diego Union Tribune*, 11 Jan. 2008, online edition.

National Conference of State Legislatures, "Supermajority Vote Requirements to Pass the Budget": www.ncsl.org/programs/fiscal/supmjbud.htm, accessed Nov. 2009.

Aurelio Rojas, "Health Plan Defeated," *Sacramento Bee*, 29 Jan. 2008.

Dan Schnur, "Getting Past the Extremes in California's Budget Battle," *Los Angeles Times*, 22 May 2009, online edition.

Peverill Squire, "Professionalization and Public Opinion of State Legislatures," *Journal of Politics* 55(2): 479–491 (1993).

Jesse M. Unruh, "Scientific Inputs to Legislative Decision-making," *Western Political Quarterly* 17(3): 53–60 (1964).

E. Dotson Wilson and Brian S. Ebbert, *The California Legislature*, 2006 ed. (Sacramento: Office of the Chief Clerk of the California State Assembly, 2006).

Gordon S. Wood, *The Creation of the American Republic, 1776–1787* (New York: Norton and Co., 1969).

Matthew Yi and Tom Chorneau, "California Facing $10 Billion Shortfall as Home Market Tanks," *San Francisco Chronicle*, 15 Nov. 2007.

FIVE **Reforming the Executive**

1. John F. Burns, "Introduction to California's Statehood and Constitutional Era," in *Taming the Elephant: Politics, Government, and Law in Pioneer California*, ed. John F. Burns and Richard J. Orsi (Berkeley: Univ. of California Press, 2003), 7.

2. James R. Bell and Thomas J. Ashley, *Executives in California Government* (Belmont, CA: Dickenson Publishing Co., 1967), 4.

3. E. Dotson Wilson and Brian S. Ebbert, *The California Legislature*, 2006 ed. (Sacramento: Office of the Chief Clerk of the California State Assembly, 2006), 253.

4. Peter Detwiler, "How Often Do Governors Say No?" California State Senate, Committee on Local Government, Oct. 15, 2007: http://sinet2.sen.ca.gov/locgov/governors-vetoes.htm.

5. California Constitutional Revision Commission, *Final Report and Recommendations to the Governor and Legislature* (Sacramento, 1996).

6. Deborah Solomon, "The Comeback Kid," *New York Times Magazine*, 26 Nov. 2006, 19.

SIX **Voting, Elections, and the Failure
of Representation in California**

1. Alexis de Tocqueville, *Democracy in America*, ed. T. Bender (New York: Modern Library, 1981), 86. Epigraph, 136.

2. Bruce E. Cain, "Constitutional Revision in California: The Triumph of Amendment over Revision: The Politics of State Constitutional Reform," in *State Constitutions for the 21st Century*, ed. G. A. Tarr, R. Williams, and F. Grad. (Albany: SUNY Press, 2006), 69.

3. "Over the last three decades the gap between the rich and the poor has grown faster in California than in the rest of the nation…" Deborah Reed, "Poverty in California: Moving beyond the Federal Measure," Public Policy Institute of California, *California Counts* 7(4), 11, 13, 15–16 (May 2006). Also California Budget Project, "Policy Points," June 2009: http://www.cbp.org/pdfs/2009/0906_pp_IncomeGaps.pdf (accessed Nov. 2009).

4. E. E. Schattschneider, *The Semi-Sovereign People* (New York: Holt, Rinehart and Winston, 1960), 20, 56.

5. William N. Chambers and Walter D. Burnham, *The American Party Systems: Stages of Political Development* (New York: Oxford University Press, 1975), 278.

6. Philip Ethington, *The Public City: The Political Construction of Urban Life in San Francisco, 1850–1900* (New York: Cambridge University Press, 1994), 67, 128, 250.

7. Walton Bean, *California, An Interpretive History* (New York: McGraw-Hill, 1973), 335. For Bean the Progressives aimed at "the virtual destruction" of the parties.

8. Carey McWilliams, *California: The Great Exception* (New York: A. A. Wyn, 1949), 202, 205.

9. *Reynolds v. Sims*, 377 U.S. 533, 1964, dismantled the "federal system" by which rural counties in California were greatly overrepresented in the senate and effectively controlled the legislature.

10. These percentages are for the electorate only. For the adult population as a whole, 57 percent is unaffiliated with either major party. Mark Baldassare, "California's Exclusive Electorate" (Public Policy Institute of California, 2006), 2. Field Poll, "The Changing California Electorate," Aug. 2009, p. 2.

11. Office of the California Secretary of State, "Statement of Vote: 2006 General Election" and "Historical Voter Registration and Participation in Statewide General Elections, 1910–2009": www.sos.ca.gov/elections/sov/historical-voter-reg/hist-voter-reg-and-part-general-elections-1910-2009.pdf (accessed Nov. 2009). Frank Russo, "California Progress Report," 14 Dec. 2006: www.californiaprogressreport.com/site/?q=archive/200612 (accessed Nov. 2009).

12. Sharon Kyle, "US and Local Voter Turnout: Nearly Lowest in World's Democracies," "California Progress Report," Feb. 19, 2007: www.californiaprogressreport.com/site/?q=node/4897, accessed Nov. 2009. Baldassare, "California's Exclusive Electorate," 5. David Carr, "States of Play:…Minnesota Politics Can Look Odd," *New York Times*, 5 July 2009.

13. John Jacobs, "The Skewed Electorate," *Sacramento Bee*, 18 Feb. 1997.

14. Baldassare, "California's Exclusive Electorate," 6. Jacobs, "Skewed Electorate."

15. Baldassare, "California's Exclusive Electorate," 5, 17. Field Poll, *California Opinion Index*, "Vote in the 2004 Presidential Election," Jan. 2005, 3.

16. Baldassare, "California's Exclusive Electorate," 2. Field Poll, "The Changing California Electorate," Aug. 2009, 3. For an early view of this see Schreiner, "Why a Minority Is Doing the Electing," *San Francisco Chronicle*, 7 Nov. 1986.

17. Baldassare, "California's Exclusive Electorate," 9, 14. Mark Baldassare and Jonathan Cohen, "Public Opinion: California's View of the Present, the Future, Governance and Policy Options," in *California 2025: Taking on the Future*, ed. E. Hanak and Mark Baldassare (San Francisco, Public Policy Institute of California, 2005), 236. The national study is Martin Gilens, "Preference Gaps and Inequality in Representation," *PS: Political Science & Politics*, 42(2), 335, 339–340 (April 2009).

18. J. Habermas, *The Structural Transformation of the Public Sphere* (Cambridge, Mass.: MIT Press, 1991), 85.

19. Leon Bouvier and Philip Martin, *Population Change and California's Future* (Washington, D.C.: Population Reference Bureau, 1985). The authors placed Asians in the top tier, but groups classified as Asian are in California's bottom voting and wage tier. Dan Walters, "Polling Reveals California's Fragmented Electorate," *Sacramento Bee*, 4 Aug. 2009. Gilens, "Preference Gaps," 335, 340.

20. H. Pitkin, *The Concept of Representation* (Berkeley: Univ. of California Press, 1972), 90. Lani Guinier, *The Tyranny of the Majority: Fundamental Fairness in Representative Democracy* (New York: The Free Press, 1994), 55, 62, and on "Black Electoral Success Theory," 43 ff.

21. *Garza v. County of Los Angeles*: 918 F.2d 763. R. Simon and F. Muir, "L.A. Supervisor Districts Illegal, *Los Angeles Times*, 5 June 1990. D. Ferrell, "Vote Marks New Era for 1st District," *Los Angeles Times*, 20 Feb. 1991. The *Garza* ruling was preceded by a similar ruling for the city of Los Angeles.

22. Bruce Cain, *The Reapportionment Puzzle* (Berkeley: Univ. of California Press, 1984 (147 and passim).

23. Frédérick Douzet and Kenneth P. Miller, "California's East-West Divide," in *The New Political Geography of California*, ed. Douzet, Thad Kousser, and Miller (Berkeley: Institute of Governmental Studies, 2008), 39. Frédérick Douzet, "Residential Segregation and Political Balkanization," in *New Political Georgraphy*, 54, 63.

24. Douzet, *New Political Georgraphy*, 65, 67. Douzet observes that the already advantaged locales have sometimes turned to initiatives to gain their objectives, to the detriment of "the most disadvantaged areas…whose interests are better represented by the legislature."

25. J. W. Endersby and K. B. Shaw, "Strategic Voting in Plurality Elections: A Simulation of Duverger's Law," *PS: Political Science & Politics*, 42(2), 393 (April 2009).

26. Burnham, "Party Systems and the Political Process," in Chambers and Burnham, *American Party Systems*, 287–304.

27. www.followthemoney.org, "California, 2008," Candidates, accessed Dec. 2009.

28. J. Sander, "Eyes on the Prize," *Sacramento Bee*, 11 Oct. 2004. D. Morain, "California Elections Private Gifts Boost Races," *Los Angeles Times*, 26 May 2006.

29. In 2007-08, the secretary of state's office reported total lobbyist expenditures of $558 million, or $764,000 a day. Shane Goldmacher, "Special Report: Top Spenders Win Most Policy Battles," *Sacramento Bee*, 29 March 2009. Robert Dorrell and Shane Goldmacher, "AT&T and the Influence Game," *Sacramento Bee*, 29 March 2009.

30. Jay Michael and Dan Walters, *The Third House: Lobbyists, Money and Power in Sacramento* (Berkeley: Institute of Governmental Studies, 2002), 2. "It would be fair to say that 200–300 of the 1,200 registered lobbyists…routinely and reliably call the shots on at least 80 percent of the issues coming before the Legislature" (p. 5).

31. Field Poll, Aug. 2009, 1–3; Douzet, *New Political Georgraphy*, 65–67.

32. www.followthemoney.org, "California, 2008," Table 3: Top Twenty Contributors. Union membership data from Barry Hirsch and David Macpherson, "Union Membership and

Coverage Database from the CPS," unionstats.com, "Union Membership Coverage, Density and Employment by State, 2008: California," 10 Aug. 2009.

33. "Without power and independence a town may contain good subjects, but it can have no active citizens": Tocqueville, *Democracy in America*, 53, 67.

34. Bertolt Brecht, "The Solution," *Bertolt Brecht, Poems 1913–1956*, ed. John Willett, Ralph Manheim (New York: Methuen, 1987), 440.

35. W. D. Burnham, "The Changing Shape of the American Political Universe," *American Political Science Review* 59(1), 23–26 (March 1965). Also, Chambers and Burnham, *American Party Systems*, 298–304.

36. Jefferson, Letters to Joseph Cabell, 2 Feb. 1816; John Adams, 28 Oct. 1813; and P. Cartwright, 5 June 1824. Tocqueville, *Democracy*, 587, 400–402.

37. The most well-known of these were Fountain Grove (1875–1900), Kaweah Colony (1885–1892), and Lomaland, Point Loma's Theosophical commune (1897–1943). Robert V. Hine, *California's Utopian Colonies* (Berkeley: Univ. of California Press, 1953).

38. Christopher Lasch, "The Lost Art of Political Argument," *Harper's Magazine* (Sept. 1990), 17.

39. "One of its certain and intended effects…is to weaken the ties between candidates and parties and between voters and parties." Ken DeBow and John C. Syer, *Power and Politics in California* (New York: Longman Publishing Group, 2008), 162, referring to the blanket primary, which includes names of all candidates from all parties on a single ballot, but the verdict applies to open primaries too.

40. Guinier, *Tyranny*, 121–122.

SEVEN **Immigration, Diversity, and the Challenge of Democratic Inclusion**

1. See Nathan Glazer, ed., *Clamor at the Gates: The New American Immigration* (San Francisco: Institute for Contemporary Studies Press, 1985).

2. U.S. Census Bureau, "Table 19. California—Race and Hispanic Origin: 1850 to 1990" (2002): www.census.gov/population/www/documentation/twps0056/tab19.xls, accessed Dec. 2009.

3. U.S. Census Bureau, "Selected Social Characteristics: California," 2005 American Community Survey (2006).

4. Elias Lopez, "Major Demographic Shifts Occurring in California," California State Library CRB Note 6(5): 7 (July 16, 1999).

5. Migration Information Source, "States Ranked by Foreign-Born, 1990, 2000, and 2005." Washington, DC: Migration Policy Institute, 2006.

6. U.S. Census Bureau, "Selected Social Characteristics."

7. Ibid.

8. California State Department of Education, 2006

9. Dan Walters, "California—A State of Change," in *California Political Almanac, 1991–1992*, ed. Stephen Green (Sacramento: California Journal Press, 1991).

10. U.S. Census Bureau, "Selected Social Characteristics."

11. See Wilson Carey McWilliams, "On Political Illegitimacy," *Public Policy* 19(3): 442–451 (Summer 1971).

12. As seen by this writer, the Progressive Movement's voter initiative process represents a political response from an earlier generation of middle-class voters worried, in part, about the political consequences of a large influx of newcomers.

13. It should be noted here that the elimination of California's state affirmative action programs did not remove the state's responsibility for complying with the U.S. government's affirmative action requirements, which remain in effect as of this writing.

14. Pew Hispanic Center, "The Foreign Born at Mid-Decade, Table 19: English Ability by Age and Region of Birth" (2006): http://pewhispanic.org/files/other/foreignborn/Table-19.pdf, accessed Dec. 2009.

15. See Hans P. Johnson, "At Issue: Illegal Immigration," Public Policy Institute of California, April 2006: www.ppic.org/main/publication.asp?i=676, accessed Dec. 2009.

16. See, e.g., Peter Brimelow, *Alien Nation: Common Sense about America's Immigration Disaster* (New York: Harper Perennial Books, 1996); Patrick J. Buchanan, *The Death of the West: How Dying Populations and Immigrant Invasions Imperil Our Country and Civilization* (New York: St. Martin's Griffin, 2002); Patrick J. Buchanan, *State of Emergency: The Third World Invasion and Conquest of America* (New York: Thomas Dunne Books, 2006); Victor Davis Hanson, *Mexifornia: A State of Becoming* (New York: Encounter Books, 2003); Samuel P. Huntington, *Who Are We: The Challenges to America's National Identity* (New York: Simon and Schuster, 2004).

17. Victor Davis Hanson, "Do We Want Mexifornia?," *City Journal* (Spring 2002): www.city-journal.org/html/12_2_do_we_want.html, accessed Dec. 2009.

18. Victor Davis Hanson, "Mexifornia, Five Years Later," *City Journal* (Winter 2007): www.city-journal.org/html/17_1_mexifornia.html, accessed Dec. 2009.

19. See, e.g., Latino National Survey, "Redefining America: Findings from the 2006 Latino National Survey," Power Point presentation to the Latino Issues Forum, San Francisco Foundation (February 23, 2007): http://depts.washington.edu/uwiser/documents/BayAreaD_2.23.07.ppt, slides 20, 23, accessed Dec. 2009.

20. See, e.g., Richard Alba, "Language Assimilation Today: Bilingualism Persists More Than in the Past, but English Still Dominates," Center for Comparative Immigration Studies, University of California, San Diego, Working Paper 111 (2004).

21. Rubén G. Rumbaut, Douglas S. Massey, and Frank D. Bean, "Linguistic Life Expectancies: Immigrant Language Retention in Southern California," *Population and Development Review* 32(3): 1–14 (Dec. 2006).

22. National Latino Survey, "Redefining America," slide 21.

23. For a fuller explanation of why this author finds these arguments more persuasive, see Ronald Schmidt, Sr., *Language Policy and Identity Politics in the United States* (Philadelphia: Temple Univ. Press, 2000); and Ronald Schmidt, Sr., "English Hegemony and the Politics of Ethno-Linguistic Justice in the United States" (paper presented at the International Sociolinguistics Symposium 16, Limerick, Ireland, 2006).

24. See, e.g., Janelle S. Wong, *Democracy's Promise: Immigrants and American Civic Institutions* (Ann Arbor: Univ. of Michigan Press, 2006).

25. See, e.g., Lisa Garcia Bedolla, "Rethinking Citizenship: Noncitizen Voting and Immigrant Political Engagement in the United States," in *Transforming Politics, Transforming America: The Political and Civic Incorporation of Immigrants in the United States*, ed. Taeku Lee, S. Karthick Ramakrishnan, and Ricardo Ramirez (Charlottesville: Univ. of Virginia Press, 2006), 51–70.

EIGHT **The View from East L.A.**

1. Luis Rodriguez, *Always Running* (New York: Simon and Schuster, 2005), 184–185.

2. All statistical data, unless otherwise indicated, is from "2000 Census Profile on General Demographic Characteristics for East Los Angeles," U.S. Census Bureau, *Profile*

  of General Demographic Characteristics: East Los Angeles,CA: http://censtats.census. gov/data/CA/1600620802.pdf (accessed July 1, 2009).

3. U.S. Census Bureau, *Income Stable, Poverty Up, Numbers of Americans With and Without Health Insurance Rise, Census Bureau Reports,* 2004: www.census.gov/ Press-Release/www/releases/archives/income_wealth/002484.html (accessed July 2009).

4. The California Budget Project figured that an adequate standard of living, including food and housing costs, day care, etc., for a two-parent household with one working adult in 2007 would have been, minimally, $50,383. California Budget Project, "Making Ends Meet: How Much Does It Cost to Raise a Family in California?", Oct. 2007.

5. Latinos, both native and foreign-born, experience the highest rates of fatal occupational injury in the country—4.6 fatalities per 100,000 workers, as compared to 3.9 for African Americans and 3.8 for white workers in 2007. C. Singley, *Fractures in the Foundation: The Latino Worker's Experience in an Era of Declining Job Quality* (Washington: National Council of La Raza, 2009), 17–23.

6. Gretchen Livingston and Joan R. Kahn, "An American Dream Unfulfilled: The Limited Mobility of Mexican Americans," *Social Science Quarterly* 83: 1003–1012 (2002).

7. Mario Barrera, *Race and Class in the Southwest: A Theory of Racial Inequality* (Notre Dame: Univ. of Notre Dame Press, 1979).

8. Los Illegals, "El Lay," on *Internal Exile,* A&M Records B000M1A9HQ. Rough translation by J. Arias: "Standing on the corner, without course without end / I am in L.A., with nowhere to go, / A man came close, My name? he asked / Not knowing his language, he took me with him / Is this the price we pay / When we end up on this side?/ We pull through and pay taxes / The Migra comes and hits us./ El Lay, L.A...."

9. For an informative and disturbing account of the Chicano Moratorium Riot, see Hunter S. Thompson's *Rolling Stone* article "Strange Rumblings in Aztlan," in H. S. Thompson, *The Great Shark Hunt: Strange Tales from a Strange Time* (New York: Simon and Schuster, 2003).

10. Laura Pulido, "Rethinking Environmental Racism: White Privilege and Urban Development in Southern California," *Annals of the Association of American Geographers* 90(1) (2000), 27.

11. Rodolfo F. Acuña, *A Community under Siege: A Chronicle of Chicanos East of the Los Angeles River, 1945–1975* (Los Angeles: Chicano Studies Research Center Publications, UCLA, 1984), 12.

12. Ibid., 88.

13. Ibid., 95–97.

14. United Way of Greater Los Angeles, *Latino Scorecard 2003: Grading the American Dream* (Los Angeles: The Center, 2003), 11.

15. Ricardo Romo, *East Los Angeles: History of a Barrio* (Austin: Univ. of Texas Press, 1983), 94.

16. For a well-researched discussion on this process and its impact on communities of color, see Andrew L. Barlow, *Between Fear and Hope: Globalization and Race in the United States* (Lanham, MD: Rowman and Littlefield, 2003).

17. Miguel León-Portilla, *Pre-Columbian Literatures of Mexico, Civilization of the American Indian,* vol. 92 (Norman: Univ. of Oklahoma Press, 1986), 86.

18. See David Geffner, "Inevitably, Renewal Leads to Gentrification (Who Owns Downtown?)," *Los Angeles Business Journal,* 28 March 2005.

19. C. M. DiMassa, "LAPD Skid Row Searches Found Unconstitutional," *Los Angeles Times,* 25 April 2007.

20. Jessica Hoffman, "LAPD Gentrifies Skid Row," *Colorlines,* Sept./Oct. 2007.

21. Howard Fine, "East Side Story: Rail Line Spurring Boom in Development Activity," *Los Angeles Business Journal*, 1 Aug. 2005. Hector Becerra, "Gold Line Extension to L.A. Eastside Stirs Hopes, Fears. *Los Angeles Times*, 30 Nov. 2008.

22. For a brief summary of Roybal's unwavering service to the Eastside community, see Rodolfo Acuña, *Anything but Mexican: Chicanos in Contemporary Los Angeles* (New York: Verso, 1996), 45–46, 69. Ken C. Burt offers a thorough treatment in *Search for a Civic Voice: California Latino Politics* (Claremont, CA: Regina Books, 2007), ch. 3 and passim.

23. Roger Vincent, "Towering Ambitions for Boyle Heights," *Los Angeles Times*, 11 Jan. 2008.

24. The nonprofit Economic Roundtable calculated that concentrated poverty neighborhoods, which include the Eastside neighborhood of Boyle Heights, have 86 percent more public safety problems and a 100 percent higher rate of violent crime than Los Angeles City as a whole. Michael Matsunaga, *Concentrated Poverty in Los Angeles: Prepared for the City of Los Angeles* (Los Angeles: Economic Roundtable, 2008), 9, and George Tita et al., *Reducing Gun Violence: Results from an Intervention in East Los Angeles* (Santa Monica, CA: RAND Public Safety and Justice, 2003), 5.

25. Pulido, "Rethinking Environmental Racism," 21.

26. Richard Toshiyuki Drury, et al., "Pollution Trading and Environmental Injustice: Los Angeles' Failed Experiment in Air Quality Policy," *Duke Environmental Law and Policy Forum* 9:254 (1999) and Los Angeles County, *Key Indicators of Health by Service Planning Area* (Los Angeles: Los Angeles County Dept. of Heath Services, 2009), 28. Such afflictions can serve as an insurmountable burden for children already struggling to achieve in the narrow ways now demanded by our state's obsession with high-stakes testing. See Sheniz A. Moonie, David A. Sterling, Larry W. Figgs, and Mario Castro, "The Relationship between School Absence, Academic Performance, and Asthma Status, *Journal of School Health* 78(3): 140–148 (2008).

27. The Los Angeles County Department of Public Health reported that in the largely Latino central service planning areas (SPA4, SPA6, and SPA7) an average 29.5 percent of all adults and 9.27 percent of all children lack proper health coverage. Los Angeles County, *Key Indicators*, 18.

28. Susannah Rosenblatt, "East L.A. Launches Cityhood Drive," *Los Angeles Times*, 15 June 2007.

29. Cityhood for East L.A.: It's Time: http://www.cityhoodforeastla.org (accessed Aug. 2009).

30. Pulido, "Rethinking Environmental Racism," 29–30.

31. George Lopez (producer), *Tall, Dark and Chicano* (motion picture). Home Box Office, 2009.

32. According to the Minnesota Pollution Control Agency, an urban green space, such as a park, "stimulates cleanup of contaminated property, improves adjacent water quality by halting polluted runoff and erosion, adds green plants that produce oxygen and *consume* carbon dioxide, a major contributor to global climate change," in addition to enhancing the quality of life in urban communities and residential property values. "Brownfields to Green Space," Minnesota Pollution Control Agency Fact Sheet, Aug. 2006.

33. Economic Roundtable, "California Under-employment Rate Reaches 17.1 Percent; 3.4 Million People," press release, 29 Aug. 2009.

34. Economic Roundtable, *Hopeful Workers, Marginal Jobs: LA's Off-the-Books Labor Force* (Los Angeles: Economic Roundtable, 2005).

NINE **California's Water Crisis**

1. *Herminghaus v. Southern California Edison Co.,* (1926) 200 Cal. 81.
2. Wells A. Hutchins, *The California Law of Water Rights,* U.S. Dept. of Agriculture Production Economics Research Branch, Agricultural Research Service, 1956.
3. Ibid.
4. David Carle, *Introduction to Water in California,* California Natural History Guides No. 76. (London: Univ. of California Press, 2009).
5. An acre-foot is the amount of water it takes to cover an acre roughly (a football field) to the depth of one foot: 43,560 cubic feet or 325,850 gallons.
6. Ellen Hanak, "Water Plan Update 2005: Implications for California Agriculture" (paper presented at the UC Water Resources Coordinating Conference, Woodland, Calif., April 26, 2006): http://groups.ucanr.org/waterquality/documents/2006_Water_Resources_Coordinating_Conference9046.pdf, accessed Dec. 2009.
7. Carle, *Introduction to Water.*
8. Barry Yeoman, "Delta Blues," *OnEarth* (Fall 2008).
9. The water infrastructure is one of the largest energy uses in the state, and the SWP's pumps are the single largest user of energy. In a modern Southern California home, imported water may be the single largest energy use. Robert Wilkinson, "Methodology for Analysis of the Energy Intensity of California's Water Systems, and an Assessment of Multiple Potential Benefits through Integrated Water-Energy Efficiency Measures" (Berkeley: Lawrence Berkeley Laboratory, California Institute for Energy Efficiency, 2000).
10. Documentation of water use is incomplete, with reporting by about two-thirds of water users. Actual use differs from documented water rights due to various factors, including: discrepancies between water actually utilized and the rights described in water entitlements—combined with the over-reporting of use to avoid losing rights from non-use; unreported legal uses not subject to reporting requirements; and unpermitted diversions. The most recent information compiled by SWRCB for Delta Vision stated that water rights on paper far exceeded estimated annual diversions, and exceeded the total volume of water known to flow through the Delta in even the wettest years. State Water Resources Control Board, "Water Rights within the Bay/Delta Watershed, prepared for Delta Vision Blue Ribbon Task Force: http://deltavision.ca.gov/BlueRibbonTaskForce/Oct2008/Respnose_from_SWRCB.pdf (Sept. 26, 2008), accessed Dec. 2009.
11. Governor's Delta Vision Blue Ribbon Task Force, *Our Vision for the California Delta:* http://deltavision.ca.gov/BlueRibbonTaskForce/FinalVision/Delta_Vision_Final.pdf (Jan. 29, 2008), accessed Dec. 2009.
12. Described by the U.S. Geological Survey as "one of the single largest human alterations of the Earth's surface topography." U.S. Geological Service, "Land Subsidence in the United States," USGS Fact Sheet-165-00: http://water.usgs.gov/ogw/pubs/fs00165 (Dec. 2000), accessed Dec. 2009.
13. Carle, *Introduction to Water.*
14. Andrew N. Cohen and James T. Carlton, "Accelerating Invasion Rate in a Highly Invaded Estuary," Science 23, 279(5350): 555–558 (January 1998); Alan D. Jassby, James E. Cloern, and Brian E. Cole, "Annual Primary Production: Patterns and Mechanisms of Change in a Nutrient-Rich Tidal Ecosystem," *Limnology and Oceanography* 47(3): 698–712 (May 2002).
15. CALFED Science Program, The State of Bay-Delta Science: www.science.calwater.ca.gov/pdf/publications/sbds/sbds_2008_final_report_101508.pdf: 2008, p. 114, accessed Dec. 2009.

16. Central Valley Project Improvement Act, Floor Debate, Bill S. 3365 ("Central Valley Project Fish and Wildlife Act of 1992"), *Senate Daily Digest* S17289, S17299 (CVPIA), 7 Oct. 1992.

17. CALFED stands for California Water Policy Council and Federal Ecosystem Directorate.

18. CALFED Bay-Delta Program, Programmatic Record of Decision: www.calwater. ca.gov/content/Documents/ROD.pdf (28 Aug. 2000), accessed Dec. 2009.

19. Public Policy Institute of California, "Voting Patterns on Proposition 9 (Peripheral Canal), June 1982": www.ppic.org/main/mapdetail.asp?i=855, accessed Dec. 2009.

20. Norris Hundley, Jr., *The Great Thirst: Californians and Water, A History,* rev. ed. (Berkeley and Los Angeles: Univ. of California Press, 2001).

21. *Watershed Enforcers v. DWR* (Alameda Sup. Ct. April 18, 2007) Case No. RG06292124; see also *NRDC v. Kempthorn* (C.D. Cal. May 25, 2007), Case No. 1:05-cv-1207 OWW GSA; *NRDC v. Kempthorn* (C.D. Cal. Dec. 14, 2007), Case No. 1:05-cv-1207 OWW GSA.

22. David Fullerton, "Summary and Analysis: Principles for Agreement on Bay/Delta Standards between the State of California and the Federal Government," *Hastings West-Northwest Journal of Environmental Law and Policy* 14(1), 179 (Winter 2008).

23. Robert C. Fellmeth, *Politics of Land: Ralph Nader's Study Group Report on Land Use in California* (New York: Grossman Publishers, 1973).

24. Juliet Christian-Smith, Heather Cooley, and Peter Gleick, *Sustaining California Agriculture in an Uncertain Future,* Pacific Institute: www.pacinst.org/reports/california_ agriculture (July 2009), accessed Dec. 2009.

25. William Joe Simonds, "The Newlands Project," U.S. Dept. of the Interior, Bureau of Reclamation History Program: www.usbr.gov/projects/Project.jsp?proj_Name= Newlands%20Project&pageType=ProjectHistoryPage (1996), accessed Dec. 2009. Douglas Cannon, Shawn Elicegui, William McKean, and Dan Reaser, "High and Dry in Nevada: When Water Rights Trump Development," *ABA Business Law Today* 15(4) (2006).

26. See 16 U.S.C. 1532(19). The activity resulting in "take" is already in place. Though pumping has been limited by recent court orders, the reliance by so many people makes unlikely the prospect of ending water exports altogether.

27. "No surprises" assurances are provided under the federal Endangered Species Act for qualifying landowners as a means to provide an incentive for landowners to participate in Habitat Conservation Plans (see www.fws.gov/endangered/HCP/NOSURPR.HTM).

28. Dan Bacher, "Restore the Delta Challenges Public Policy Institute's Report Supporting Peripheral Canal." *California Progress Report:* www.californiaprogressreport.com, accessed Dec. 2009.

29. Jay Lund, et al., *Comparing Futures for the Sacramento–San Joaquin Delta* (San Francisco: Public Policy Institute of California, 2008): www.ppic.org/main/publication. asp?i=810, accessed Dec. 2009.

30. Bay Delta Conservation Plan, Delta Habitat Conservation and Conveyance Program, meeting notes: www.ci.sacramento.ca.us/council/documents/files5318/BDCP%20 4-27-09%20Meeting%20Notes%20_Final%20for%20Distribution_6-19-09.doc (April 27, 2009), accessed Dec. 2009.

31. Dean Misczynski, "Fixing the Delta: How Will We Pay for It?" Public Policy Institute of California, Aug. 2009, p. 10: www.ppic.org/content/pubs/report/R_809DMR.pdf, accessed Dec. 2009.

32. *Katz v. Walkinshaw* (1902) 141 Cal. 116.

33. See Senate Bill 681 (2009-2010 session).

34. See Senate Bill X7 6 (2009-2010, 7th extraordinary session).
35. *National Audubon Society v. Superior Court* (1983) 33 Cal.3d 419.
36. Antonio Rossman, Letter re: 2009 Delta Water Bill Package (principally preprint SB 1) addressed to Senate Committee on Natural Resources and Water and to the Assembly Committee on Water, Parks, and Wildlife, 2009. Rossman, Outline of Written Testimony to California Senate Committee on Natural Resources and Water: "Issues and Perspectives on California Water Rights Laws," 2009.
37. J. Croegaert, "If the Cap Fits: Hard Lessons for California from the Australian Murray-Darling Basin," unpublished manuscript, 2009.

Additional References, Chapter Nine

Mark Arax and Rick Wartzman, *The King of California: J. G. Boswell and the Making of a Secret American Empire* (New York: Public Affairs, 2003).

David Carle, *Water and the California Dream: Choices for the New Millennium* (San Francisco: Sierra Club Books, 2003).

Delta Vision Blue Ribbon Task Force, Strategic Planning Documents and Public Comments: http://deltavision.ca.gov/StrategicPlanningDocumentsandComments.shtml (2008), accessed Dec. 2009.

Governor's Commission to Review California Water Rights Law, *Final Report* (Sacramento, Dec. 1978).

Little Hoover Commission, "Testimony of Lester A. Snow, Director, California Department of Water Resources, Hearing on State Water Governance," June 24, 2009.

Carey McWilliams, *California: The Great Exception* (Berkeley: Univ. of California Press, 1999).

M. Catherine Miller, *Flooding the Courtrooms: Law and Water in the Far West* (Lincoln: Univ. of Nebraska Press, 1993).

Natural Resources Defense Council, "Judge Throws Out Biological Opinion for Delta Smelt" (press release): www.nrdc.org/media/2007/070526.asp (2007), accessed Dec. 2009.

Frona M. Powell, "Defining Harm under the Endangered Species Act: Implications of *Babbitt v. Sweet Home.*" *American Business Law Journal* 33(1): 131–153 (Sept. 2, 1995).

State Water Contractors, "Bay Delta Conservation Plan Fact Sheet: Preserving the Delta and Our Water": www.swc.org/uploadfiles/swc%20bdcp%20facts%203.9.09.pdf (2009), accessed Dec. 2009.

State Water Resources Control Board, "Water Rights within the Bay/Delta Watershed, prepared for Delta Vision Blue Ribbon Task Force: http://deltavision.ca.gov/Blue RibbonTaskForce/Oct2008/Respnose_from_SWRCB.pdf (Sept. 26, 2008), accessed Dec. 2009.

United States v. Gerlach Live Stock Co. (Gerlach) (1950) 339 U.S. 725.

TEN Remapping the California Electorate

1. Mark DiCamillo and Mervin Field, "New Lows in Voter Approval of State Legislature and Schwarzenegger" (San Francisco: Field Research Corporation, May 2009).
2. If there are an odd number of legislators, the extra seat is an additional regional seat.
3. For a similar proposal, which does not use regional elections, see Kathleen Bawn, "Reforming Representation in California: Checks and Balances without Gridlock" in *Constitutional Reform in California*, ed. Bruce Cain and Roger Noll (Berkeley: Institute of Governmental Studies Press, 1995).

4. The apportionment would use the "D'Hondt method," a calculation that produces the same results as the method Thomas Jefferson developed in 1792 for assigning congressional seats to the states. This system is used in Argentina, Belgium, Chile, Colombia, Czech Republic, Denmark, Ecuador, Finland, Israel, Italy, Japan, the Netherlands, Paraguay, Poland, Romania, Scotland, Spain, Turkey, and Wales.

5. Because a party must receive sufficient votes to win a single seat in any given region, the "effective threshold" for regions with populations of less than 2 million would be higher than 5 percent. Under our proposal for a 360-seat unicameral legislature, the effective threshold for Northern California is 10 percent and for the Central Coast is 7.1 percent.

6. Jed David Kolko, David Neumark, Ingrid Lefebvre-Hoang, *Business Location Decisions and Employment Dynamics in California* (San Francisco: Public Policy Institute of California, 2007); California Economic Strategy Panel, *California Economic Strategy Panel Regions* (Sacramento: Workforce Development Agency, October 2006).

7. Following Public Policy Institute of California, we divide the fast-growing and culturally distinct "Inland Empire" region from the "Greater Los Angeles" region. We also acknowledge the important differences between the northern and southern parts of the San Joaquin Valley, and add San Joaquin and Stanislaus counties to the Gold Country region. These areas are a part of the Sacramento media market and are becoming increasingly intertwined with the economy of the state capital. Many regional schemas recognize the Northern Sacramento Valley as a distinct region. It also does not have adequate populations to function as an independent political region.

8. Office of the California Secretary of State, Report of Registration as of September 5, 2008: Registration by County.

9. Arend Lijphart, *Patterns of Democracy: Government Forms and Performance in Thirty-six Countries* (New Haven: Yale Univ. Press, 1999).

10. California Constitution, Article XXI, "Reapportionment of Senate, Assembly, Congressional and Board of Equalization Districts," Section 1.

11. Personal interview, Tim Hodson (former senate legislative staff member), September 25, 2008.

12. United Nations Assistance Mission in Afghanistan, "Fact Sheet: Single Non-Transferable Vote (SNTV) System."

13. Woodrow Wilson, *Congressional Government: A Study in American Politics* (Boston: Houghton Mifflin and Company, 1901).

14. Douglas J. Amy, *Real Choices/New Voices: How Proportional Representation Elections Could Revitalize American Democracy* (New York: Columbia Univ. Press, 2002).

15. Mikva quoted in Steven Hill, *10 Steps to Repair American Democracy* (Sausalito, CA: PoliPoint Press, 2006), 65.

16. Gerald C. Lubenow and Bruce E. Cain, *Governing California* (Berkeley: Institute of Governmental Studies, 2006).

17. William H. Riker, "The Two-Party System and Duverger's Law: An Essay on the History of Political Science," *American Political Science Review* 76 (1982), 753–766.

18. Mark Baldassare, Dean Bonner, Jennifer Paluch, and Sonja Petek, "Californians and Their Government," Public Policy Institute of California Statewide Survey, Sept. 2008.

19. California Secretary of State, "Report of Registration."

20. Richard H. Pildes, "The Decline of Legally Mandated Minority Representation," *Ohio State Law Journal* 68 (2007), 1139–1184.

21. Clarence Thomas, Majority Opinion, *Holder vs. Hall* (1994), from "Justice Thomas on Full Representation Voting Systems": http://archive.fairvote.org/index.php/blog/media/brochures/npv_brochure.pdf?page=544, accessed January 2010.

22. Kathleen L. Barber, *Proportional Representation and Electoral Reform in Ohio* (Columbus: Ohio State Univ. Press, 1996), 295.

23. Hans P. Johnson, "A State of Diversity: Demographic Trends in California's Regions," Public Policy Institute of California, *California Counts: Population Trends and Profiles* 3(5): 3 (May 2002).

24. For data on spending by candidates and independent expenditure committees in recent legislative races, see California Fair Political Practices Commission, *Independent Expenditures: The Giant Gorilla in Campaign Finance* (Sacramento, June 2008).

25. Calculated from data on the number of state legislators (National Conference of State Legislators, www.ncsl.org/programs/legismgt/about/numoflegis.htm), population estimates by the U.S. Census Bureau (http://factfinder.census.gov/servlet/SAFFPopulation), and the California Department of Finance (www.dof.ca.gov/Research/Research.php), accessed January 2010.

26. Alexander Hamilton, James Madison, and John Jay, *The Federalist: A Collection of Essays* (New York: Colonial Press, 1901), 305.

27. Ibid., 49.

28. California Constitution, Article IV, "Legislative," Section 7.5.

29. For a skeptical assessment of the effects of redistricting reform, see Eric McGhee, *Redistricting and Legislative Partisanship* (San Francisco: Public Policy Institute of California, 2008); and Mark Paul, "Redistricting Reform Draws a Map of Great Disappointment," *San Francisco Chronicle*, 28 Jan. 2007. The Bay Area Council, a business organization representing major firms in the San Francisco Bay Area, led a drive to call a constitutional convention; and the idea received strong support from members of the Courage Campaign, an online progressive community. See www.repaircalifornia .org; Jim Wunderman, "California Government Has Failed Us," *San Francisco Chronicle*, 21 Aug. 2008; and "Should the Courage Campaign Call for a Constitutional Convention?" at www.couragecampaign.org/page/s/ConstitutionVote.

ELEVEN **A People's Convention for California**

1. League of Women Voters of California, "Briefs on a Long Constitution: A New Look at California's Constitution," pamphlet, San Francisco, 1964, 16.

2. Letter to Samuel Kercheval, July 12, 1816. For Jefferson, Virginia failed this test. He added that he was not one who "look[s] at constitutions with sanctimonious reverence, and deem them like the arc of the covenant, too sacred to be touched." Joyce Appleby and Terence Ball, eds., *Jefferson: Political Writings* (Cambridge: Cambridge Univ. Press, 1999), 212–215.

3. Carl Brent Swisher, *Motivation and Political Technique in the California Constitutional Convention, 1878-79* (Claremont, CA: Pomona College, 1930), 50–52, 67, and Ch. 5, fn. 30. Walton Bean, *California: An Interpretive History*, 2d ed. (San Francisco: McGraw-Hill, 1973), 140.

4. On the 1960s commission, see Joseph R. Grodin, Calvin R. Massey, and Richard B. Cunningham, *The California State Constitution: A Reference Guide* (Westport, CT: Greenwood Press, 1993), 18–21. New York's constitution, by contrast, had 45,000 words, Massachusetts' 11,361. Also see League of Women Voters "Briefs," 8.

5. Constitution of the State of California, originally Section 26 of Article I, "Declaration of Rights."

6. Pat Ooley, "An Overview of the History of Constitutional Provisions Dealing with State Governance," presentation to 1993 California Constitution Revision Commission: http://worldcat.org/arcviewer/1/CAX/2006/06/05/0000020402/viewer/file24.html, p. 3, accessed Aug. 2, 2009.

7. Grodin et al., *California State Constitution*, 19. Bruce E. Cain, "Constitutional Revision in California: The Triumph of Amendment over Revision," in *State Constitutions for the Twenty-First Century*, ed. G. Alan Tarr and Robert F. Williams (Albany: SUNY Press, 2006), 59–61.

8. League of Women Voters, "Briefs," 17.

9. Bay Area Council, "California Constitutional Convention Q&A," 17 Dec. 2008, 2. Vladimir Kogan, "Lessons from Recent State Constitutional Conventions," Bill Lane Center for the American West, Stanford University, 2009, 1.

10. New York convention proponents in 1997 failed at this: a small majority initially in favor of the convention turned at the time of ratification into a three-to-one opposition because of deceptive television ads. Peter Galie, presentation, "Getting to Reform" conference, Sacramento, 14 Oct. 2009.

11. Repair California, 16 Sept. 2009, poll by EMC Research. Field Poll, Oct. 2009, California Opinion Index, "State Constitutional Reform and Related Issues," San Francisco.

12. J. Wunderman, "California Government Has Failed Us," *San Francisco Chronicle*, 21 Aug. 2008.

13. League of Women Voters, "Briefs," 17.

14. Senator Loni Hancock, press release, 4 Sept. 2009. Hancock introduced a constitutional amendment in the senate in 2009 to let the annual budget be passed by a majority vote. Some conservatives in the state also circulated a petition to establish an only part-time legislature.

15. Schwarzenegger in Jennifer Steinhauer, "In Budget Deal, California Shuts $41 Billion Gap," *New York Times*, 20 Feb. 2009. Peter Schrag, "Reforming California," *Sacramento Bee*, 24 Sept. 2006. Dan Walters, "California's Crisis of Governance Undermines Democratic Theory," *Sacramento Bee*, 4 July 2004. See also Jack Rakove, "Roll Over, James Madison, It's the California Recall," *San Francisco Chronicle*, 21 Sept. 2003.

16. Woodrow Wilson, *Constitutional Government in the United States* (New York: Columbia Univ. Press, 1908), 56–57. "It is manifestly a radical defect in our federal system that it parcels out power and confuses responsibility as it does." W. Wilson, *Congressional Government* (1885; reprint, Gloucester, MA, Peter Smith, 1973), 187.

17. C. H. McIlwain, *Constitutionalism, Ancient and Modern* (Ithaca: Cornell Univ. Press, 1947), 142–144. Walters, "California's Crisis...".

18. Madison, "Federalist No. 10," 78.

19. "To Have and To Have Not," Budget Brief, California Budget Project, June 2009, and chapter three, 54–55.

20. "That [capital] cannot defend itself without resorting to all the vices of plutocracy seems inevitable." William Graham Sumner (1888), "Democracy and Plutocracy," in *William Graham Sumner: Social Darwinism*, ed. Stow Persons (Englewood Cliffs, NJ: Prentice-Hall, 1963), 140.

21. Machiavelli, "Discourses on Livy," *The Prince and the Discourses*, ed. Max Lerner (New York: Modern Library, 1950), 161. Tocqueville stressed, e.g., the importance of daily involvement in public affairs. *Democracy in America*, ed. Thomas Bender (New York: Modern Library, 1981), 53–55, 400.

22. Peter Schrag, "The Newtonian Machine," *Sacramento Bee*, 15 Feb. 1995 and "When Government Goes on Autopilot," *Sacramento Bee*, 16 Feb. 1995.

23. "Although the Legislature provides for the convention, it does not in any way control it." League of Women Voters, "Briefs," 16. Thomas Paine, "The Rights of Man," in *Thomas Paine*, ed. H. H. Clark (New York: Hill and Wang, 1961), 92.

24. Swisher, *Motivation and Political Technique*, 24.

25. Constitution of the State of California, Article XVIII, Sect. 2.

26. Steven Hill, "The Big Constitutional Convention Question: Who's Going to Fix California?" *Los Angeles Times,* 22 June 2009.

27. On the important distinctions, see Hanna Pitkin, *The Concept of Representation* (Berkeley: Univ. of California Press, 1972), 73–80. I have not addressed here the possibility that the U.S. Department of Justice might challenge a jury plan under either the Fourteenth Amendment or the Voting Rights Act of 1965 because it arbitrarily changes the method of delegate selection prescribed in the state constitution.

28. Hill predicted great things from "professional staffers and facilitators" and delegates linked by "live webcast, interactive television and keypad devices for instant polling." "Yes, Virginia, 'Average' Californians Can Manage a Constitutional Convention," *Sacramento Bee,* 2 August 2009.

29. British Columbia used a variant of the jury method in 2004 to convene a group of 160 members who met for eleven months to study and prepare a measure to change the province's electoral method from single-member majoritarian to proportional representation. The assembly worked well but addressed only this one issue. The final measure received a vote of 58% and needed 60% to pass. Mark Warren and Hilary Pearse, *Designing Deliberative Democracy: The British Columbia Citizens' Assembly* (Cambridge: Cambridge Univ. Press, 2008).

30. Richard Matthews, *The Radical Politics of Thomas Jefferson* (Lawrence: Univ. of Kansas Press, 1984), 82.

31. This program, again, is the editor's alone.

32. California Constitution Reform Commission Final Report, Executive Summary, 16; Also Mark Baldassare and Ellen Hanak, "California 2025: It's Your Choice" (San Francisco: Public Policy Institute of California, 2005), 35.

33. At 2008's highest price of $130 a barrel, it would bring in $2 billion. Michael Hiltzik, "A California Tax on Oil Drilling? Why Not? *Los Angeles Times,* 15 June 2009.

34. CCRC Final Report, 31–32.

35. Ibid., 25–26.

36. Bayard Still, "California's First Constitution: A Reflection of the Political Philosophy of the Frontier," *Pacific Historical Review* 4(3): 226 (Sept. 1935). Delegate Charles T. Botts added, "To engraft any legislative enactment on the constitution is anti-republican"(224).

37. Barry Keene, "The Dangers of Government Gridlock and the Need for a Constitutional Convention" (Sacramento: Center for California Studies, 1992), 2–3. Cain and Persily, "Creating an Accountable Legislature: The Parliamentary Option for California Government," and Brady and Gaines, "A House Discarded? Evaluating the Case for a Unicameral California Legislature," in *Constitutional Reform in California,* ed. Bruce E. Cain and Roger E. Noll (Berkeley: Univ. of California Institute of Governmental Studies, 1995).

38. The rulings conferring free speech rights over campaign contributions were *Buckley v. Valeo* (1976), *First National Bank of Boston v. Bellotti* (1978), and more recently, *Citizens United v. Federal Election Commission* (2010).

39. Adam Smith, *The Wealth of Nations,* ed. J. C. Bullock (New York: P. F. Collier and Sons, 1909), 129.

40. President Roosevelt in 1933 put it more strongly: "No business which depends for existence on paying less than living wages to workers has any right to continue in this country." Statement on the National Industrial Recovery Act (NIRA), June 16, 1933.

41. CCRC Final Report, 72. Tocqueville's view was that "Without power and independence, a town may contain good subjects, but it can have no active citizens." Tocqueville, *Democracy,* 53.

Index

About the Editor

R. JEFFREY LUSTIG (1943–2012), was a professor of government at California State University, Sacramento. Author of *Corporate Liberalism:
The Origins of Modern American Political Theory,
1890–1920,* he also wrote numerous articles on
American and Californian politics and political theory, the corporatization of the modern university,
and on immigration, race, and class. He was director of the Center for California Studies at California
State University, Sacramento, founding chair of the
California Studies Association, and a trustee of
the California Historical Society.